PARTIES AN

JOHN FREARS

Parties and Voters in France

HURST & COMPANY, LONDON

© John Frears, 1991
All rights reserved
First published in the United Kingdom by
C. Hurst & Co. (Publishers) Ltd.,
38 King Street, London WC2E 8JT
and in the United States of America by
St. Martin's Press, Inc.,
175 Fifth Avenue, New York 10010
Printed in England

ISBNs
Hurst   1–85065–057–8 (cased)
        1–85065–058–6 (pbk.)
St. Martin's   0–312–06028–9 (cased)

Library of Congress Cataloging-in-Publication Data

Frears, J. R., 1936–
    Parties and voters in France / John Frears.
        p.   cm.
    Includes bibliographical references and index.
    ISBN 0–312–06028–9 (long-life paper)
    1. Political parties—France.   2. Elections—France.
    3. Referendum—France.   I. Title.
    JN2997.F73   1991
    324.244—dc20   90–22794
                                                        CIP

In memory of Sheila and Dick Talbot

PREFACE

This is not a new edition, it is a new book. When I wrote *Political Parties and Elections in the French Fifth Republic* in 1976, the central issue of French politics was the one great test to which the Fifth Republic had not been put. Was the peaceful alternation of power from government to opposition, normal in other democracies like Britain, West Germany and the United States, possible? It had never happened. The Fifth Republic had survived other tests: everyone had said that after the departure of de Gaulle there would be chaos, but in fact President Pompidou's peaceful election and assumption of power in 1969 did more than anything else to establish that the Fifth Republic was not just a transitional crisis regime but a set of institutions with that very widespread public support we call legitimacy. However, a change of government in the context of the mid-1970s would have meant the accession to power of the Union of the Left – with Communists sharing power in a major Western country for the first time since 1947 – and the fear of constitutional crisis. There was intense speculation about what would happen with Giscard d'Estaing as President and a Union of the Left majority in Parliament. Would the Socialist leader François Mitterrand have to be appointed Prime Minister? Would he exercise policy leadership and bring to an end twenty years of Presidential supremacy, or would the President refuse to hand over power to the new majority? Would the army and the civil service accept the leadership of a government of the left or would there be some kind of a *coup d'état*? In 1976 I concluded optimistically:

> Some day French democracy has got to submit to the test of the peaceful alternation of power. The Constitution of the Fifth Republic has endowed France with institutions that have permitted effective and democratic government for two decades. It is true that this process has been greatly helped by a party system which has always produced a parliamentary majority in support of the President of the Republic. To assert, however, that the institutions can only function if President and Parliamentary majority are in permanent mutual agreement, that power must never change hands, that no way can be found to make alternative democratic choice work, that no adaptation of political institutions or political attitudes is conceivable, is to pronounce that democracy in France is a house of cards indeed.

Change of government did not come in the expected form. Everyone expected the Union of the Left to win the 1978 Parliamentary election

v

while Giscard d'Estaing was still President. In fact not only did the left not win in 1978, the Union of the Left, as we shall see in chapter 6, broke up. Alternation of power occurred when François Mitterrand, the Socialist Party leader, won the Presidential election in 1981. It was entirely peaceful and the succeeding years of Socialist government maintained absolute continuity of defence and foreign policy and posed no threat whatever to the social, political, or economic order. There were some token Communists in the government from 1981 to 1984 but, with their party a steadily weakening electoral force, no-one talked of a 'Communist takeover'. The last great test of the Fifth Republic's institutions – the 'cohabitation' of a President and a Parliamentary majority composed of his political adversaries – finally arrived in 1986 when a disciplined alliance of Gaullist and centrist parties, the RPR/UDF, won a Parliamentary majority. Jacques Chirac, the leader of the RPR, was appointed Prime Minister and took over policy leadership. There were some battles for influence and control in foreign affairs and defence, the traditional 'Presidential domaines' (see chapter 12), and the President did not merely return to the role of an 'opener of flower shows' in Pompidou's famous phrase, but skilfully prepared the return of Presidential supremacy to himself at the 1988 election. However under 'cohabitation', it was the Prime Minister who ran the country with the support of his Parliamentary majority, just as in a traditional Parliamentary democracy like Great Britain. As with all the previous tests of the Fifth Republic, it was found once again to work perfectly well. Cohabitation did not bring the Republic's institutions crashing down. Why ever did people suppose that it would?

The Nuffield Foundation generously supported the research for this book, and I would like to express my gratitude.

August 1990   JOHN FREARS

CONTENTS

TABLES

KEY TO ABBREVIATIONS

Gaullists and Centre

CD	Centre Démocrate
CDS	Centre des Démocrates Sociaux
CDP	Centre pour la Démocratie et le Progrès
MRP	Mouvement Républicain Populaire
PDM	Progrès et Démocratie Moderne
PSD	Parti Social Démocrate
Rad	Radical Party
RI	Républicains Indépendants
PR	Parti Républicain
UDF	Union pour la Démocratie Française
RPF	Rassemblement du Peuple Français
RPR	Rassemblement pour la République
UDR	Union des Démocrates pour la République
UDT	Union Démocratique du Travail
UDVe	Union des Démocrates pour la Vème République
UNR	Union pour la Nouvelle République
URC	Union du Rassemblement et du Centre (1988 alliance)

Left

CERES	Centre d'Etude de Recherche et d'Education Socialistes (left-wing of PS – renamed S et R: Socialisme et République)
CIR	Convention des Institutions Républicaines
FGDS	Fédération de la Gauche Démocrate et Socialiste
MRG	Mouvement des Radicaux de Gauche
LO	Lutte Ouvrière
MPPT	Mouvement pour un Parti des Travailleurs
PC or PCF	Parti Communiste Français
PS	Parti Socialiste
PSU	Parti Socialiste Unifié
RGR	Rassemblement des Gauches Républicaines
SFIO	Section Française de l'Internationale Ouvrière
UDSR	Union Démocratique et Socialiste de la Résistance
UGSD	Union de la Gauche Socialiste et Démocrate

Right

CNIP	Centre Nationale des Indépendents et Paysans
FN	Front National

UDCA   Union pour la Défense des Commerçants et de l'Artisanat
            (Poujadist)

Other organisations

CFDT   Confédération Française et Démocratique du Travail
CFTC   Confédération Française des Travailleurs Chrétiens
CNPF   Confédération Nationale du Patronat Français
CGC   Confédération Générale des Cadres
CGT   Confédération Générale du Travail
ENA   Ecole Nationale de l'Administration
FEN   Fédération de l'Education Nationale
FNSEA   Fédération Nationale des Syndicats d'Exploitants Agricoles
FO   Force Ouvrière
JAC   Jeunesse Agricole Chrétienne
JOC   Jeunesse Ouvrière Chrétienne
MODEF   Mouvement de Défense de l'Exploitation Familiale
OAS   Organisation de l'Armée Secrète
SNI   Syndicat Nationale des Instituteurs

VAL D'OISE

SEINE S† DENIS

YVELINES Hte PARIS

SEINE VAL DE MARNE

ESSONNE

NORD

Pas-de-Calais

Nord

Somme

HAUTE PICARDIE

Seine-Maritime Oise Aisne Ardennes

NORMANDIE

Manche Calvados Eure Meuse Moselle

BASSE NORMANDIE Seine-et- Marne LORRAINE

Finistère Orne Marne CHAMPAGNE Meurthe-et- Bas- Rhin

Côtes-du-Nord REGION -Moselle

BRETAGNE Ille-et-Vilaine PARISIENNE -ARDENNE Vosges ALSACE

Morbihan Eure-et-Loir Aube Haut- Rhin

Loire- Mayenne Sarthe Loiret Yonne Haute- Haute Territoire-de- Belfort

Atlantique Maine-et-Loire Loir-et-Cher Côte-d'Or Saône

PAYS DE LA LOIRE CENTRE BOURGOGNE Doubs

Indre-et-Loire Cher Nièvre FRANCHE-COMTE

Vendée Deux Vienne Indre Saône-et-Loire Jura

Sèvres

POITOU-CHARENTES Haute- Creuse Allier Ain Hautes- Savoie

Charente- Vienne Rhône

Maritime Puy-de- Loire RHONE-ALPES

Charente LIMOUSIN Dôme Savoie

AUVERGNE Isère

Corrèze Haute

Dordogne Cantal Loire Ardèche Drôme Hautes- Alpes

Gironde Lot Lozère

AQUITAINE Lot-et- Aveyron Alpes-de- Alpes-

Garonne Gard Vaucluse Haute- Maritimes

Landes Tarn-et- Provence

Garonne Tarn Bouches-du- Var

MIDI-PYRENEES Hérault Rhône PROVENCE

Gers Haute COTE D'AZUR

Pyrénées- Garonne LANGUEDOC-

Atlantiques Aude Hte Corse

Hautes- Ariège ROUSSILLON CORSE

Pyrénées Pyrénées-Orientales

Corse du Sud

CARL 1976

REGIONS OF FRANCE

xvi

1

FRENCH POLITICS TODAY

Why, it was asked in the preface, did few expect the Fifth Republic, set up in conditions of severe crisis in 1958, to endure? The answer is that France experienced almost 200 years of discord about what regime to have, and that discord followed several more centuries of struggle to unite the territory under one government. So the image of France as a divided and unstable political society has some historical substance. There have been sixteen constitutions since the French Revolution, and each one, as Jack Hayward has put it,[1] has been 'a treaty, a partisan procedural device . . . not endowed with the sacredness or permanence attributable to a constitution that symbolises fundamental agreement about political values as well as about political procedures'. Change has been abrupt and violent. Since 1789, revolution has disposed of two further monarchs – the last of the Bourbons in 1830 and the last king of all, the 'bourgeois monarch' Louis-Philippe, in 1848. *Coups d'état* have sent three of the five Republics packing – the First was despatched by Napoleon Bonaparte on the 18th Brumaire 1799, the Second by his nephew Napoleon III in 1851, and the Fourth by the army revolt in Algiers as recently as 1958. Four other regimes were finished off by defeat in war: the First Empire at Waterloo in 1815, the Second Empire in the Franco-Prussian war at the battle of Sedan in 1870, the Third Republic by German tanks in the same north-eastern part of France in 1940, and the Vichy regime, which governed the southern half of France by permission of the Nazis who had occupied the northern half, collapsed with the liberation of France in 1944. In this turbulent history, says the American writer Roy Pierce, no regime 'enjoyed unchallenged legitimacy. Each one is threatened by reactionaries or radicals or both. Efforts are made by dissident groups to weaken the existing regime . . . in order to replace it with another political system.'[2] For revolutionaries 1789 was *à refaire* in 1848, in that short-lived revolutionary government of Paris, the Commune of 1871, and in the Popular Front of 1936. Other movements like Boulangism, the cult of the popular but fatuous General who appeared to be organising a *coup d'état* in 1886, the anti-Dreyfusards, who in the 1890s rallied in the name of patriotism to the cause of refusing a pardon to a Jewish officer wrongly convicted of

1

spying, *Action française* in the 1920s and 1930s, or the Vichy state in the 1940s, wanted to wind the clock back to an authoritarian monarchy. In this climate of turbulence and threats, regimes tended not merely to change violently but to oscillate from one extreme to another. Authoritarian regimes were followed by democratic regimes with no provision for firm government at all, in turn to be followed by another authoritarian regime with no provision for liberty. The weak but democratic Third and Fourth Republics respectively succeeded the authoritarian and anti-libertarian First and Second Empires. The authoritarian First and Second Empires respectively succeeded the chaos of the First and Second Republics. Democracy and government were, in David Thompson's phrase, 'two poles too far apart for the vital spark of democratic government to flash between them'.[3]

In all that I have written about France for nearly twenty years my main theme has been that the Fifth Republic is that elusive synthesis of democracy and effective government and that it has acquired legitimacy as well. There are no longer any social groups that want to overthrow the Republic – not Catholics, not workers, not peasants (if there are

Table 1.1.   REGIMES SINCE THE FRENCH REVOLUTION

	Regime	*Ended by*
Up to 1789	Bourbon Monarchy	Revolution
1792–99	First Republic	*Coup d'état* – 18 Brumaire
1799–1814	Consulate of Napoleon and First Empire	Napoleonic Wars
1814–30	Monarchy – Bourbon Restoration	Revolution – the 'July Days'
1830–48	The July Monarchy – Louis-Philippe	Revolution – the 'June Days'
1848–52	Second Republic	*Coup d'état* – 2 December 1851
1852–70	Second Empire – Napoleon III	Franco-Prussian War
1870–1940	Third Republic	Second World War – the Fall of France
1940–4	Vichy – Marshal Pétain	Second World War – the Liberation
1944–6	De Gaulle Provisional Government	Peaceful transition
1946–58	Fourth Republic	*Coup d'état* – 13 May 1958
1958–	Fifth Republic	

still any peasants), not the army, and not the Communist Party. The last-named has supported the institutions of the Fifth Republic, particularly during the Union of the Left period when it was most likely to have won a share of power, and in any case has become a marginal political force.

This political change has been associated with immense economic and social change. France since the end of the 1950s has become the world's fifth industrial power, and the standard of living enjoyed by its workers and farmers is among the highest in the world. There is nothing that eliminates friction and discontent as effectively as sustained economic growth. Even when growth was threatened by the economic difficulties experienced by all Western countries in the 1970s and early 1980s and unemployment in France reached 2.5 million, there was no threat whatsoever to political stability. There have been great changes in social structure: a huge increase in the white-collar service sector, a huge decline in the numbers engaged in agriculture from nearly 40% before the war to around 7% today with all its implications for individualist peasant attitudes and the peasant way of life, and tremendous changes in the role and behaviour of women in society. In short, France has become a modern high-technology post-industrial secular society with a modernised political system.

The historic social cleavages based on religion have virtually disappeared. The Catholic Church had been 'counter-revolutionary' right from 1790 when the clergy were required to swear allegiance to the Revolutionary authorities. Catholic parts of France, notably the Vendée in the west where Catholics were massacred in 1794, resisted the Republic. For more than a century the church, the nobility and the Catholic faithful were seen by Republicans, Radicals and Socialists as upholding superstition against Reason, a hierarchical social order against equality, the authority of a single individual ruling by divine right against the representatives of the people's will. Religion was removed from public education – even today there are no prayers or religious instruction or even Christmas carols in state schools. There is 'no reference to God in any of the Republican constitutions, no prayer at official functions, no "In God we trust" on French coins, no religious oath for office holders' (Henry Ehrmann).[4] Opposition between left and right in France tended to be reduced to that between partisans and adversaries of the Catholic Church, and still today, as we shall see, there is a strong correlation between religious practice and the propensity to vote for parties of the centre and the right. However, modern France has become an increasingly secular society. Since the Second World War, when Catholics as well as Communists played their part in the Resistance, there has never been any question of systematic Catholic opposition to the Republic. In fact Catholic votes, which supported de Gaulle, provided the electoral basis for the Fifth Republic. France's version of a Christian Democrat party – the post-war MRP – has disappeared (see chapter 5). Catholic trade unionism has virtually disappeared: the CFTC (French Confederation of Christian Workers) turned itself into the CFDT (French Democratic Confederation of Labour) in 1964 and became closely associated with the Socialist Party. The latter does just as well nowadays in traditionally Catholic regions such as Brittany as it does in its old industrial strongholds like the North. Catholic education remains important but is entirely financed by the state – although, as was seen in 1984, the French middle class is prepared to take to the streets to stop too much state control.

There have been two genuine, as opposed to imaginary, crises during the Fifth Republic: the Algerian war (1958–62) and the Events of May 1968. It has withstood both. The first was resolved mainly by the leadership of General de Gaulle, who stood firm in the face of an army revolt, and the support given to him by the public as the proper constitutional authority of the state. (The story of this is told in chapter 2.) The Events of May 1968 had all the appearance of a regime-threatening crisis. However, there is a difficulty with countries that have a myth of revolution: they are rather unpredictable. S.E. Finer wrote at the time that 'the tradition, nay the cult, of insurrection, of Michelet's concept of the Revolution as Goddess, is still alive and numbers many worshippers.'[5] What began as a student protest against authoritarian rules in universities spread into a general strike lasting about six weeks and accompanied by all the traditional revolutionary folklore – strike committees authorising essential services, road-blocks and barricades, demonstrations and tear-gas – but nobody turned off water or power, which presumably could have been done quite easily, and above all nobody did any shooting. Blood only flowed in substantial quantities when petrol supplies were resumed for the Whitsun week-end, and this produced 120 deaths in road accidents. The Communist Party, still the largest party of the left in 1968 though, as is argued in chapter 8, no longer having revolution by violence as one of its objectives, tried to limit the whole affair to the question of wages. It opposed 'leftist adventures' and presented itself as 'the great and tranquil party of order', trying to get workers back to work when an offer on pay had been made. It clearly did not consider May 1968 an opportunity for revolution. At one point towards the end of May, it is true, the government appeared to totter and de Gaulle hurriedly left the capital to assure himself of army support if military intervention became necessary. In the end, however, the strike was resolved by the whole country being given a pay increase, and the political difficulties came to an end with a stirring speech from de Gaulle and an election (chapter 13) which gave the Gaullists a landslide majority. I therefore tend to interpret the Events of May as evidence of the solidity rather than the fragility of the Fifth Republic's institutions.

Political parties, which are the subject of this book, have been a part of this transformed political and social order – in particular what has turned out to be the great innovation of the Fifth Republic: the capacity of certain parties to win a majority at elections and to sustain governments in office. Most writers have defined parties either as groups of people with a common objective for government or as organisations with the explicit purpose of seeking to acquire control of government – in liberal democracies through electoral competition. In most modern states, whether democracies or not, the main political party or parties have become permanent institutions of state with very important functions to perform in the recruitment of political leaders (Presidents, Parliamentarians, local and regional political élites, etc.), the formulation of policy alternatives which they intend as government policy, mobilisation of support for their nominees and programmes, and control of government. One thinks of the main parties in Britain, West Germany, South Africa, Japan, Australia or India and many other pluralist states where parties perform these roles – not to mention the Communist parties in Communist-ruled states. France has at last acquired parties of the 'major institution of state' variety – first the Gaullist Party, now the Socialist Party, perhaps always the Communist Party though not in a governmental role at national level.

The last of the functions of parties mentioned above was control of government. This is difficult to pin down but is normally taken to mean that if the nominees of a party fill the principal decision-making offices and lay down policies to be followed, then that party is in control of government. This, of course, begs the question as to whether the party leaders in power are really implementing party choices or are at the mercy of events or merely following the recommendations of the professional administration, but as a framework for analysing the functions of political parties it is indispensable. Competition between parties for the power to govern is central to the democratic process, and if electoral victory does not confer the power to determine policy, then electoral choice has no meaning. Furthermore, if political parties are not providing a country's political leaders, then it is more than likely to be the army or a traditional aristocracy that is.

Indeed one of the weaknesses of the political order in France before the Fifth Republic was the failure of political parties to fulfil these functions. Many political leaders were 'non-party' – General de Gaulle himself being the prime example. Most parties were loose networks of electoral committees for local and regional 'notables' without a national policy or a mass organisation for mobilising national opinion. Voter identification with parties was low. In a well-known study published in 1962, Converse and Dupeux found that only 45% of French people identified with a party in comparison with 75% of Americans, and that only 29% of the French, compared with 95% of Americans, knew how their families voted.[6] Above all, parties failed to govern. In the fragmented multi-party systems of the Third and Fourth Republics elections hardly ever conferred the right to govern on any united majority, no party saw support for the government of the day and the defence of the government's record before the electorate as its role or duty. Government reposed not on the popular will as transmitted by parties but on deals and combinations by groups of individuals and 'independents' and segments of parties in the corridors of the National Assembly. Henry Ehrmann has written that after the Second World War 'there existed a serious chance for a thorough overhauling of the party system'. The Communist, Socialist and MRP parties jointly had 75% of the popular vote, and 'all were intent on governing the country by an effective coalition government. Yet after a few transitional years, and due to the cold war as well as to domestic pressures, the country reverted to the traditional forms of atomistic representation and rule by shifting coalitions of the centre which now included the Socialists.'[7]

General de Gaulle, who despised political parties, described this situation of no responsible government and no responsible opposition as the '*régime des partis*'. However, a *régime des partis* was exactly what it was not, and it was only when a party composed of the General's own supporters started to win parliamentary majorities, ready to see sustaining the government as its main job in Parliament and defending it as its main job outside, that we can talk about a *régime des partis* in France. It is the emergence of such majorities, of such dependable support for government, that has been the most remarkable change of all, and it has greatly contributed to the governmental stability of the

Fifth Republic. The Gaullist UDR party helped to elect and to give disciplined support to President Pompidou after the trauma of the General's departure. The Socialist Party gave President Mitterrand the full backing of its Parliamentary majority and its organisation in the country. It was because a proper disciplined alliance of parties – RPR and UDF – won the election of 1986, and was clearly unavailable for Fourth Republic-type deals with the Socialists that Mitterrand had no hesitation in accepting that he had to appoint its leading figure, Jacques Chirac, as Prime Minister and that Chirac in his turn was able to rely on disciplined support for his government's programme of legislation. The principal political leaders in France today are party leaders: it was as leader of the Socialist Party that Mitterrand became President, it is his grip on the party machine of the RPR that has made Jacques Chirac up till the present the natural Prime Minister and Presidential candidate for his side, it was the lack of a party organisation that was such a handicap to Raymond Barre in his Presidential bid in 1988. The era of the self-declared 'above-party' candidate for the Presidency is over. The candidates for the Mitterrand succession will be determined by the Socialist Party, the RPR, and the UDF. In 1990 there was even talk of these last two selecting a joint candidate at some kind of nominating convention. The main changes in the party system that have come about since my earlier book on parties in France have been the flowering of the Socialist Party into a party with, as the French say, a 'majority vocation'; the break-up of the Union of the Left and the marginalisation of the Communist Party. In almost every part of the country 75–85% of the voters are choosing the big moderate parties of government – Socialist or RPR/UDF.

Since the late 1950s, therefore, an economy that has for most of the time been expanding vigorously and remaining internationally competitive, a decline of traditional social conflicts, and a new acceptance of the country's political institutions have changed almost all the traditional reference-points for observers of French politics and society. Political leaders, on the basis of electoral victory in the country and consistent support in Parliament, give political direction to government policy. Although one can argue, as I have indeed frequently done, that the checks and balances on those in power are seriously inadequate, this is an important part of democratic government, and political parties are at the centre of that new democratic strength – which is where they should be. The next chapter suggests that the transition to this much more healthy state of affairs was the great contribution of Gaullism.

NOTES

1. *The One and Indivisible French Republic*, London: Weidenfeld and Nicolson, 1973, p. 1.
2. *French Politics and Political Institutions*, New York: Harper and Row, 1968, p. 7.
3. *Democracy in Modern France*, Oxford University Press, 1958, p. 14.
4. *Politics in France*, Boston: Little, Brown and Co, 1958, p. 48.
5. *Comparative Government*, London: Allen Lane, 1970, p. 326.
6. 'Politicisation of the electorate in France and the United States', *Public Opinion Quarterly*, Spring 1962, pp. 1–23.
7. *Politics in France*, p. 198.

2

THE IMPACT OF DE GAULLE

'In the sweeping changes which transformed French life in the twenty years after 1945, the political sector lagged behind.'[1] The economic transformation was on the way as the old conservative employers, discredited by collaboration with the Nazis in the war, were replaced by more dynamic managers. Growth and expansion were preached with missionary zeal by Jean Monnet, founder of the French experiment in national economic planning. A more expansionist economic outlook was accompanied by profound social changes. The birth-rate, static for a century, began to rise. The old social divisions based on religion began, as we have seen, to decline in importance. Fewer and fewer small farms meant less and less influence for the small farm mentality and the peasant's defensive individualism.

The political class, however, failed to give expression to these changes in the form of coherent and forward-looking government. No majority could be found to keep any government in office longer than a few months. Ostrich-like and pusillanimous, the regime faced crisis – particularly colonial crisis, first in Indo-China (Vietnam) and then in Algeria – with nothing more vigorous than parliamentary intrigue. On 13 May 1958, the Fourth Republic was threatened by a military *coup d'état* in Algiers. There was no will to resist. 'The Republic was not murdered; it committed suicide.'[2]

France needed to be equipped with a new and more effective political order, and it was. The next few years saw the solution of the colonial crises, the building of a new legitimacy for political institutions which has made the Fifth Republic a more widely accepted regime than any of its predecessors since the Revolution, and the transformation of the party system into one which gives expression to the majority will and to the democratic requirement of accountability. The enormous contribution of one man to this process of change entitles us to explore the notion of charismatic legitimacy and its role in the emergence of a new political order.

Charismatic authority, defined by Max Weber, is a title to rule based on 'devotion to the specific and exceptional sanctity, heroism, or exemplary character of an individual person'.[3] It characteristically

9

appears as a transitory phenomenon in countries going through periods of great turmoil and change, most particularly those that are in transition from traditional society to modern nation-state. As societies turn away from an unresponsive traditional élite or a colonial occupier, often a single leader – such as Gandhi, Nkrumah, Mao Tse-tung or the Ayatollah Khomeini – emerges to embody the legitimacy of the new political order. The word charisma is often used to describe the exceptional capacity to inspire loyalty and devotion that we find in leaders like Winston Churchill or President Kennedy, but this is a misuse: charismatic leadership occurs where a single leader's capacity to inspire creates legitimacy, that is to say acceptance, for a new political order. The examples above are from the developing world, but in post-war Western Europe in nations with special problems of transition to modernity two important leaders stand out as charismatic in the sense that confidence in them as individuals enabled the building of a new political order: Konrad Adenauer in West Germany and General de Gaulle in France.

General de Gaulle clearly regarded himself as being in the mould of a charismatic chieftain. In a famous broadcast on 29 January 1960, at the time of another Algiers uprising, he actually claimed *'une légitimité nationale que j'incarne depuis 20 ans'*. It was a personal claim to represent the legitimacy of the nation, despite the intervening Republics and Constitutions and Parliamentary elections, since the day of his most famous broadcast of all – the London declaration of 18 June 1940 calling for resistance to the surrender of France. The whole life and style of this remarkable man looks like a self-conscious preparation for the role of saviour. The earlier writings like *Le fil de l'épée*, a series of presumptuous but magnificent staff college lectures, set out the qualities of leadership for the 'man of character' – reserve, dignity, mystery and contempt for the rules which bind lesser men. Part of his leadership style lay in his command of heroic symbolism. He chose Bayeux, the first French town to be liberated in 1944, for a speech containing the whole Gaullist constitutional doctrine of a strong state and a strong executive; he chose radio and not television for speeches to the nation at moments of great crisis – in the Algerian war, for example, or in the general strike of May 1968 – because his speech of 18 June 1940 had also, inevitably, been on radio; and at his presidential press conferences he would sit enthroned, like Louis XIV, with all his government in attendance. His memoirs and speeches might have been written by Chateaubriand. The literary style, the richness of historical sweep, the elegance of language, the oracular

subtlety, the egotism, place them among the most remarkable docu-
ments of our time. Some have claimed that the cult of the hero in de
Gaulle makes him a kind of fascist leader. But those who would do so
should compare the speeches of de Gaulle with the demented raving of
Hitler or Mussolini.

There can be little doubt that the legitimacy of the new political
order, the Fifth Republic, was founded to a large extent upon de Gaulle.
In particular this is true of three critical elements of the new order: the
preservation of the state and of national unity during the solution of the
Algerian crisis, the acceptance of new political institutions based on a
directly elected Presidency, and the emergence of a modern party
system. It was the crisis in Algeria, with the army in revolt against the
legal government of France, that destroyed the Fourth Republic. The
French army, after the ignominious defeat which it had suffered in Indo-
China at Dien Bien Phu in 1954, and the million settlers, who had made
Algeria more like an exotic region of France than a colony, were determined to hang on to this jewel of the French empire. More and more
troops, more and more resources, more and more brutal repression were
directed at suppressing the movement of the Arab population to national
independence, and all were failing in that object. When a sell-out to the
FLN (National Liberation Front) was believed to be imminent, the army
itself rebelled. Convinced that the old soldier, with a nationalistic vision
of the greatness of France, would stand by *l'Algérie française*, the army
supported the return to power of General de Gaulle. In fact de Gaulle
was always careful not to commit himself to the maintenance of French
rule in Algeria. He spoke to an associate in 1955 of 'a wave which
sweeps all peoples towards emancipation. There are fools who will not
understand this.' '*L'Algérie de papa*' was dead, colonial rule over a
subject people could not be maintained in the modern world, French
prestige in the world – particularly with the newly emerging nations
– would depend on a solution that respected a population's rightful
desire of autonomy. The problem was to make the French accept the
vision.

On 16 September 1959 he proclaimed the principle of self-determination for Algeria. Algerians were to be offered three choices: complete
independence, integration in France, or self-government in association
with France. He invited them, in one of the best examples of a Gaullian
oracular riddle, to choose '*la solution la plus française*', which could have
been any of the three! On 24 January 1960 began the 'week of the
barricades' in Algiers as the civilian extremists of *Algérie française*

rebelled against the very idea of independence, and the paratroops did nothing to restore order. De Gaulle appeared on television (in full uniform) and ordered the army to do its duty. It did. New units were brought into Algiers to replace the '*Paras*' (parachute troops). The principle of self-determination was massively adopted by the French in a referendum on 8 January 1961 (see chapter 15) with a 75–25 majority for 'Yes'. Preparations were made for a conference at Evian to discuss arrangements for independence with the FLN. Then on 22 April 1961 came the '*putsch des généraux*' when four of the most prominent leaders of the French army, including General Salan who had played a big part in the events of 13 May 1958 in Algiers that brought de Gaulle back to power, supported by some battalions of *Paras*, seized Algiers. The invasion of Paris was hourly expected. Over the radio, in perhaps the most remarkable speech of the post-war era, de Gaulle ordered the soldiers not to obey their officers if the latter joined the rebellion.

Voici l'état bafoué, la nation defiée, notre puissance ébranlée, notre prestige international abaissé, notre place et notre rôle en Afrique compromis. Et par qui? Hélas! hélas! par des hommes dont c'était le devoir, l'honneur, la raison d'être de servir et d'obéir. Au nom de la France, j'ordonne que tous les moyens, je dis tous les moyens, soient employés pour barrer la route à ces hommes-là, en attendant de les réduire. J'interdis à tout français et d'abord à tout soldat d'exécuter aucun de leurs ordres. . . .
   Françaises, Français! Aidez-moi!

[The state is thwarted, our nation defied, our power and our international prestige shaken, our place and role in Africa compromised. And by whom? Alas! By men whose duty, honour and very reason for existence is to serve and to obey. In the name of France, I order that all means, I repeat all means, be deployed to bar their way, until we can crush them I forbid any French person, and in the first place any soldier, from carrying out a single one of their orders. . . .
French people! Give me your help!]

He assumed emergency powers under Article 16 of the Constitution and ordered the total blockade of Algiers. The rebellion collapsed. There is no doubt that de Gaulle's leadership saved the day. Without it, it is not hard to recognise in the situation after the coup the elements of panic and reinsurance with the supposedly stronger side which had brought down the Fourth Republic.

The storm was not over. The generals in hiding continued their struggle in the OAS (Organisation of the Secret Army) which carried out continuous acts of terrorism in France and Algeria for more than a year, including assassination attempts on de Gaulle himself. But when Algeria chose independence, the French people backed it by a huge 91% majority in the referendum of 8 April 1962. The achievement: civil war avoided, excellent relations with former colonies established, French prestige enhanced by the determined way the nation's leadership had dealt with military insubordination and white settler resistance. It was a defeat for France that had all the appearance of victory. 'For a man of my age and background', de Gaulle wrote in his memoirs, 'it was difficult to have to break the spirit of the French army and give up French territory.'[4] It is unlikely that anyone else could successfully have accomplished it. As Raymond Aron put it, 'the Algerian settlement was the final proof of de Gaulle's political genius.'[5]

The political institutions of the Fifth Republic are of course Gaullist ideas given form and substance. The famous speech at Bayeux in 1946 proposed a regime at the centre of which was a Head of State endowed with executive authority. The 1958 Constitution puts four powerful weapons into the hands of the President of the Republic. He can invoke special powers in a situation he considers to be an emergency (Article 16), he can call for a referendum on certain issues (Article 11), he can dissolve Parliament and call new elections (Article 12), and he appoints the Prime Minister (Article 8). These powers are far from absolute: as we saw in 1986 and the period of 'cohabitation', a disciplined Parliamentary majority opposed to the President can impose a choice of Prime Minister to whom policy leadership then passes. Nevertheless Presidential leadership is a strong element in the Constitution. It was made stronger by the personality of de Gaulle and the circumstances of the Algerian crisis, and stronger still by the 1962 amendment, initiated and carried through by de Gaulle, which brought in direct election of the President by universal suffrage. The other theme of constitutional Gaullism is that a strong executive, on which stability and progress depend, can only be strong if it is free from the interference and harrassment traditionally associated with the French Parliament. The 1958 Constitution lays down in minute detail just how an enfeebled Parliament can be kept in its place.

In what sense can the legitimacy that attaches to the institutions of the Fifth Republic be considered charismatic? One should perhaps not overstress this. De Gaulle was endorsed as Prime Minister in 1958 by a Parliamentary vote of confidence. His request to draft and present a new Constitution was voted by Parliament. The Constitution was adopted by the citizens at a properly conducted referendum. Nevertheless it is scarcely conceivable that any other political leader, even in the crisis

situation of 1958, could have gained the agreement of a political class
steeped in Republican fears of Bonapartism for such a fundamental
change of institutions, and won such massive assent from the public (a
79:21 majority – see chapter 15). In 1958 'Frenchmen wanted before all
else the solution of the Algerian problem and only very incidentally the
reform of the state. For de Gaulle the order was the opposite' (Jacques
Chapsal).[6] The General, at the outset and throughout his period in
power, linked his indispensability in a crisis to support for the institutions he considered indispensable if the country was to surmount crisis.
In 1958 the message was 'If you want peace in Algeria adopt my
Constitution.' In 1962 it was 'If you do not want to risk the chaos that
would follow my resignation, adopt my constitutional amendments.'
One may deplore these methods, but it is hard to see how the regime
could have been established in its present form without them. There was
a generalised desire for institutions making possible stronger government. Opinion surveys had revealed since 1945 a preference for a directly
elected Head of State. The Fifth Republic is now firmly accepted, indeed
it has been for many years. Chaos did not occur after the departure of de
Gaulle in 1969. Chaos did not occur after the socialist victory of 1981.
Chaos did not occur during 'cohabitation' (1986–8) when almost thirty
years of Presidential supremacy came to an end (a temporary end,
because it was re-established at the 1988 Presidential election – see
chapter 12). No major social group challenges the institutions of the
Republic. The contribution of de Gaulle's leadership to this new legitimacy has to be recognised. Perhaps we can allow him his last boast. In
the fragment of memoirs he was working on at the time of his death in
1970 he wrote:

> In France has the state ever had the stability it now possesses without
> damaging liberty? When did the world last see such assurance and serenity
> in the exercise of public authority? Have I not served France well by leading
> her people to so miraculous a change?[7]

The third element of the new political order in France that stems from
the presence in power of General de Gaulle is the modernised party
system which is the subject of this book. In the 1960s the appeal of
Gaullism was the federator of almost all the electors that used to vote for
small parties and independent notables in the centre and on the right. It
also had its effect on the left by pushing the parties of the left into
alliance as the only possible means of avoiding defeat. This alliance
– eventually the Union of the Left – was an important feature of

the evolving party system. The contribution of 'the Gaullist phenomenon' (Jean Charlot)[8] to the transformation of the French political
system has been well documented. The phenomenon is the growth of a
large, disciplined and pragmatic party, which came into existence to give
organised support to General de Gaulle, and which saw its role as
making a coherent parliamentary majority system possible in a country
with a long tradition of loose and unstable multi-party coalitions. It is
inconceivable that such a transformation from a weak multi-party
system to a system with a dominant party could have occurred – despite
his well-known dislike for political parties and his view of himself as
above party – but for the electoral appeal of General de Gaulle.

The electoral appeal of de Gaulle gradually waned, but Gaullism as a
majority party continued throughout the Presidency of Georges
Pompidou. The rise of 'party Gaullism' to replace 'personal Gaullism' is
central to any analysis of the 'routinisation of legitimacy'. 'Routinisation' means the transformation of the authority of a charismatic leader
into the kind of authority more readily transferred to his successors. The
stability and development of a new political system require that a
solution be found to the problem of the heroic leader's departure. If
France in the Fifth Republic displays the timely emergence of charismatic leadership in a period of crisis, it is also an excellent example of its
timely disappearance and replacement by something more appropriate
for normal times.

The year 1962 is widely regarded as the watershed of the Fifth
Republic and a critical year in the 'routinisation of legitimacy'. Up to
1962 the country was dominated by the Algerian problem. General de
Gaulle ruled alone and autocratically with no guaranteed parliamentary
majority to support his ministers. There were periods of crisis, and the
five months from April to September 1961 were a period of 'constitutional dictatorship' under the emergency powers of Article 16. After
1962, Algerian independence and a safe Gaullist parliamentary majority
enabled the regime to sail in calmer domestic waters and broaden out
into spectacular international diplomacy. The new regime with its
modern majority party system (François Borella)[9] 'was really born in
1962'.

April 1962 was the apogee of personal Gaullism. The independence of
Algeria was overwhelmingly supported by the French people at the
referendum of 8 April, only 9% voting against. In the same month one
of the generals who played a leading part in the OAS and the 1961
rebellion, Jouhaud, was condemned to death by the supreme military

tribunal and Salan, the leader, was arrested. In the summer of 1962 de Gaulle broached the question of routinising the legitimacy of the Presidency. The 1958 Constitution laid down that an electoral college of some 80,000 local Councillors and other officials should choose the President. Direct election by the people had been talked about; de Gaulle, who had initially opposed it, indicated in a broadcast on 8 June that universal suffrage was the way 'to make certain, when the time comes, though men come and go, that the Republic can remain strong and well-ordered and will endure'. The Presidential car was machine-gunned by OAS extremists at Le Petit Clamart on 22 August 1962 (an incident that provides an introduction to the popular novel by Frederick Forsyth, *The Day of the Jackal*). De Gaulle's miraculous escape from this incident forcefully underlined how men come and go. On 20 September a referendum was announced: the French people would be asked to decide on 28 October whether they wished the President to be elected in future by direct universal suffrage.

> The President must have the direct confidence of the nation. Instead of having that confidence implicitly – as was the case with me for a historic and exceptional reason – it is necessary that henceforth the President be elected by universal suffrage.

According to Article 89, constitutional changes are supposed to be approved by the two assemblies of Parliament before being submitted to popular referendum. General de Gaulle loftily dispensed with this formality, and Parliament was furious. The President of the Senate, Gaston Monnerville, invoked the Constitutional Council and the National Assembly passed, on 4 October by 280 votes out of 480, a motion of censure on the government. This remains the only occasion in the entire Fifth Republic so far that a censure motion has been successful. As the Constitution provides in Article 50, the censured government resigned. General de Gaulle, accepting the resignation tendered by his Prime Minister Georges Pompidou (a former personal assistant of the President, virtually unknown to the public when he was called from the obscurity of Rothschild's bank in April 1962 to head the government), dissolved Parliament and asked the government to remain in office until the referendum and new elections had revealed the popular will. All the old parties campaigned for a 'No' vote: from the Communists to the *Cartel des Non*, which grouped together the old right-wing independents, the Christian-Democratic centre represented by the MRP, the Radicals and the Socialists. On 18 October de Gaulle hinted he might retire if the referendum result was *'faible, médiocre ou aléatoire'* – weak, mediocre or uncertain. The result on 28 October was not a triumph like the earlier referenda of the Fifth Republic. The 'Yes' vote was 62% but, thanks to abstentions, that 62% was only 46% of those eligible to vote. Pompidou declared that the result nevertheless was *'ni faible, ni médiocre, ni aléatoire'*, so there was no question of the President retiring. Nevertheless the October referendum was a first sign that the appeal of General de Gaulle would not accomplish in normal times what it could in times of turmoil.

From the Parliamentary elections of the following month, however, dates the emergence of the cohesive majority party that was to represent the real transformation of French politics. The November 1962 elections were a triumph for the Gaullists (at that time called UNR-UDT – see chapter 4). They increased their first-ballot share of the vote from 17.6% to 31.9%. With their allies the Independent Republicans (led by Valéry Giscard d'Estaing, the 'Yes'-voting pro-government element of the old independents – see chapter 5) they won 270 seats, an overall majority. 'Thus for the first time in history the French electorate had vote to approve a government's record. The election of 1958 had registered no confidence in the Fourth Republic; that of 1962 recorded approval of the Fifth; the referendum was designed to prevent a return to the old system.'[10] No connoisseur of political strategy could fail to admire the perfect timing: 'General de Gaulle engaged the battle with his opponents at the most favourable moment, on the most favourable terrain, and by forcing them to combine against him in a negative coalition which brought back to the electors too many unhappy memories to have the slightest chance of victory.'[11]

In the years that followed, 'personal Gaullism' steadily weakened as an electoral force. In December 1965 General de Gaulle obtained only 43.9% of first ballot votes in the first presidential election to be held under the new universal suffrage (see chapter 12). In April 1969, in a referendum on regionalisation and reform of the senate (see chapter 15), the 'Yes' vote was only 46.9% and the General resigned as Head of State. However the Prime Minister Georges Pompidou emerged, after the first ballot setback for de Gaulle in 1965, as an able leader of a majority party who realised the necessity of organising the majority so that it could maintain its cohesion and its effectiveness when charismatic authority was gone. Pompidou directed the second ballot campaign for de Gaulle in 1965; he directed the parliamentary election campaign of 1967 in which the government just returned with an overall majority, and that of 1968 in which it had a massive majority (see chapter 12). 'Party Gaullism' in the shape of the UDR survived the resignation of General de Gaulle: its candidate, Pompidou, won the Presidential election of 1969 and it retained the leadership of government and Parliament, winning, with its allies, a further election victory in 1973.

France in the period of the Pompidou Presidency (1969–74) was often called *l'état-UDR* – the UDR state. Nominees of the UDR controlled nearly every centre of power and influence – Presidency, government, parliament, top civil service, public bodies like the television networks and the nationalised industries. The power of the President was based not upon his own electoral appeal but upon his command of a party that was universally present at all levels of national decision-making. 'What distinguishes the Fifth Republic from the Fourth', wrote Ezra Suleiman, 'is not so much the altered institutional arrangements in favour of the executive, nor the relative ministerial stability, as the existence of a majority party which dominates the executive, the legislature, and probably the bureaucracy.'[12]

Gaullism not only survived the resignation of General de Gaulle, but it survived the defeat of the Gaullist party. The UDR candidate Jacques Chaban-Delmas was defeated by Giscard d'Estaing in the Presidential election of 1974 – but the UDR, now under the leadership of Prime Minister Jacques Chirac, remained a prominent element in the government and a predominant element in the Parliamentary majority that supported the new President. Relaunched by Chirac as the RPR in 1976, it was still the largest party in the government majority after the elections of 1978. It was the most vigorous and well-organised part of the opposition in the years of Socialist government (1981–6), and, when the RPR and its alliance partners the UDF (*Giscardiens* and centrists – see chapter 5) won the 1986 elections, Chirac became Prime Minister again and the RPR was dominant in the government. Chirac was the leading candidate against François Mitterrand in 1988. In short the Gaullists, two decades after the death of de Gaulle, are still one of the leading political parties.

Gaullism also had its effect upon the opposition. Presidential leadership of the executive and direct election of the President – an important part of the General's legacy – have had the effect of personalising leadership and polarising political life into a contest between champions from two rival camps. Futhermore, the effect of Gaullism as an electoral force in the 1960s capable of grouping together nearly all the electors of the right and the centre, who in the Third and Fourth Republics used to be scattered over many parties and independent notables, forced the parties of the left to work together or be crushed. In addition, the two-ballot electoral system gives a bonus to would-be majority parties which can attract second-ballot votes from a wide spectrum of opinion, and penalises small parties, isolated parties and extremist parties. The Socialists, after various attempts to build a centre-left alternative to Gaullism, realised from 1965 onwards that the only chance for the opposition to win power was if the non-Communist left were to draw the Communist Party out of its isolation and work with it and the 5 million voters whose loyalty it then commanded. Despite setbacks this alliance lasted till 1977 when the Communists broke the Union of the Left and cost the left the victory in 1978 it had hoped for (see chapters on the left and chapter 13). The logic of the party system created by the 'Gaullist phenomenon' is bipolar. Majority Gaullism condemned the parties of the left to live together, despite their profound differences, at least until the Socialist Party itself became a potential majority party – a party like Gaullism of the 1960s – with, as the French say, a 'majority vocation'.

There are many other examples of the permanent imprint of de Gaulle on political life in France: the olympian style expected of Presidents, the expectation of Presidential leadership, the national consensus on defence and France's role in the world ('*l'indépendance nationale*'), the consensus over political institutions. Government in France has continued, throughout the Presidencies that have succeeded de Gaulle's, to be supported by cohesive and disciplined majorities – either of one party (the Socialists in 1981–6) or more usually of alliances which fight elections as partners (Gaullists and *Giscardiens* or RPR and UDF in 1969–81 and 1986–8). The policies, largely based on de Gaulle's national consensus, have been marked by a remarkable continuity. Opportunistic coalition-building in the style of the Fourth Republic has not reappeared – even in 1988 when the re-elected President Mitterrand and his Prime Minister Michel Rocard, with the Socialist Party a few seats short of an overall Parliamentary majority, tried to win over parts of the centre. The historically surprising development in France of a majority system and a majority habit are explored in the next chapter.

NOTES

1. Philip M. Williams and Martin Harrison, *Politics and Society in de Gaulle's Republic*, London: Longman 1971, p. 63.
2. Dorothy Pickles, *The French Fifth Republic*, London: Methuen 1960, p. 17.
3. *Theory of Social and Economic Organisation*, New York: Collier Macmillan, 1964 edn, p. 328.
4. *Mémoires d'espoir*, vol. I: *Le renouveau, 1958-62*, Paris: Plon, 1970, p. 41.
5. Quoted in Williams and Harrison, *Politics and Society*, op. cit., p. 42.
6. Quoted in Anthony Hartley, *Gaullism*, London: Routledge and Kegan Paul, 1972, p. 157.
7. *Mémoires d'espoir*, vol. II: *L'effort, 1962*, Paris: Plon, 1970, p. 104.
8. *The Gaullist Phenomenon*, London: Geo. Allen and Unwin, 1971.
9. *Les partis politiques dans la France d'aujourdhui*, Paris: Eds du Seuil, 1973, p. 9.
10. Philip Williams, *French Politicians and Elections 1951-69*, Cambridge University Press, 1970, pp. 145-6.
11. *Le référendum d'octobre et les élections de novembre 1962*, Cahiers de la FNSP, directed by F. Goguel, Paris: Armand Colin, 1965, pp. 436-7.
12. *Politics, Power and Bureaucracy in France*, Princeton University Press, 1974, p. 164.

3

THE MAJORITY SYSTEM

The last chapter discussed the emergence since 1962 of a bipolar 'government and opposition' party system in France. The impetus, it has been suggested, came from Gaullism: Gaullism as a federator of almost all the electors of the centre and right, Gaullism as creator of majority government and the majority habit, Gaullism as a force compelling its opponents to unite.

Every Parliamentary election since 1962 – with the exception, in part, of 1988 when the Socialists were a few seats short but not seriously threatened – has been won by a single majority party or by an alliance committed to governing together and to sustaining the government in Parliament. Government-opposition polarity has not, however, produced a two-party system. The UDF, a confederation of centrist parties that supported President Giscard d'Estaing (1974–81) and the Chirac government of 1986–8, exists alongside the Gaullists, often in a spirit of considerable rivalry. It is a remarkable fact that in a country where the word 'coalition' has for generations been synonymous with instability, the pro-government coalitions of Gaullists and centrists have, despite their rivalry, been rock-solid in terms of Parliamentary and electoral discipline since the 1960s. On the left, the balance has shifted since the mid-1970s very much towards the Socialist Party, but the Communist Party of course continues to exist, and the 1986 election was the only one since 1958 (except the Presidential election of 1969) when it had no pact at any stage with the Socialists.

Normally the term 'majority' in the Fifth Republic has meant a Presidential majority. Whoever has been elected President has been able to count on a majority in Parliament. When the Socialist leader François Mitterrand was elected in 1981, he dissolved Parliament; and the electors obligingly gave a Parliamentary majority to the Socialist Party. When the President is leader of the Majority, there is Presidential government. Presidential supremacy was the hallmark of French government right up to 1986. The people expected Presidential leadership when de Gaulle returned to power in 1958; the Constitution of the Fifth Republic gives some important powers to the President – notably the power to appoint the Prime Minister and to dissolve Parliament – and the legitimacy of Presidential leadership was greatly increased by the introduction of direct Presidential elections in 1962. However, Presidential leadership is only possible if there is a Parliamentary majority to permit it. From 1986 to 1988 there was not such a Presidential majority. The President's political opponents won the Parliamentary election, the President ceased to be leader of the Majority, and executive supremacy passed to the Prime Minister Jacques Chirac, who commanded the support of a majority in a Parliament.

Why is a Parliamentary majority so important? The 1958 Constitution constrains the role of Parliament in innumerable ways. Quite minute details of procedure are constitutionally laid down and give the executive all kinds of weapons with which to prevent Parliament from being the nuisance it was in the Fourth Republic. However, there is a way in which the National Assembly can still bring down the government (though of course not the President). Under Article 49 a motion of censure can be passed, but it is very difficult, needing the signatures of one-tenth of the deputies. It is not voted on for forty-eight hours – time for crises to cool down and for governments to twist arms. Only votes in favour of the motion are counted – so abstainers and absentees count as supporters of the government. To be passed, the motion must receive the votes of a majority of the total Assembly membership – today 289 votes. A motion of censure has hitherto been successfully carried only once in the entire Fifth Republic – in October 1962 over the issue of the referendum on direct Presidential elections. However, Article 49 does mean that a President has to appoint a government acceptable to a majority in the National Assembly or, given the Parliamentary discipline that has become such a feature of the Fifth Republic, it will fall.

The Majority in the de Gaulle Presidency, 1958–69

Up to 1962 there was no institutionalised Parliamentary Majority. This was the period of charismatic authority when the General ruled virtually alone, living on his direct relationship with the French people. The National Assembly could have overthrown the government of Michel Debré, appointed by de Gaulle, but that would have provoked the General's resignation and a political crisis. De Gaulle was seen by the right and centre as the nation's sole protector against chaos and Communism, and by the non-Communist left (for example, during the Algiers revolts of January 1960 and April 1961) as the sole defence against military dictatorship. After 1962 there was a Majority. The

Gaullist party UNR (Union for the New Republic) did not have a
Parliamentary majority on its own, but it was able to rely on the
Independent Republicans (RI). This group, led by Valéry Giscard
d'Estaing who had been a member of the government since 1959, was
composed essentially of Independents from the 1958 Parliament who
had not campaigned for a 'No' vote in the 1962 referendum on direct
Presidential elections. As we see in chapter 5, they were by no means
unconditional supporters of every Gaullist initiative, but they repeatedly
made clear that they supported the Fifth Republic and the new institutions making stable government possible, and never threatened the
government by supporting motions of censure in Parliament. Gaullists
and *Giscardiens*, as they came to be called, maintained an electoral
concordat after 1962. It was formalised in 1967 when they contested the
election together under the common banner: 'Fifth Republic'. In 1968
they were together under the banner 'Union for the Defence of the
Republic'.

President Pompidou's Majority

Under Georges Pompidou the Majority was widened. The last year of
the General's reign had revealed some cracks in it. Giscard d'Estaing,
dismissed as Finance Minister in 1966, had gone as far as to announce,
with considerable media attention, that he would not support the
April 1969 referendum on institutional reform. Many Gaullists then
blamed Giscard for the defeat of the referendum and for de Gaulle's
resignation which was the immediate consequence, and many still do.

Pompidou, who had been Prime Minister up to June 1968 and who
was the obvious and natural Gaullist successor to the Presidency,
immediately declared his candidature, which received the endorsement
of the UDR (Union of Democrats for the Republic – the Gaullist
Party's latest label). It looked initially, however, as if he might have
some difficulty in getting elected (see chapter 12). Pompidou also
regarded the overwhelming UDR majority of the 1968 election as
excessively conservative and resistant to progress. Consequently he felt
the need to attract a wider spectrum of support to his candidature.
Above all, he felt he needed the endorsement of Giscard d'Estaing and
the Independent Republicans, who in urgent meetings had been
considering a number of alternative possibilities including a Giscard
candidature. After some uncharacteristic hesitation, Giscard decided that
his hour had not yet come and he declared for Pompidou, who therefore

proclaimed his candidature as expressing *'continuité et ouverture'*: continuity of the achievements of Gaullism and an opening towards more liberal policies in certain fields, notably enlargement of the European Community. His campaign obtained the support not only of Giscard d'Estaing and his friends but also of part of the centre. The various groups of the old centre and right, like the Independents or the MRP (Popular Republican Movement), had long seen their electoral edifice and their leadership crumble away under the appeal of Gaullism. A number of MRP leaders like Maurice Schumann had over the years taken themselves and their electorates off to join the Gaullists. Pompidou now attracted to his campaign, and into the government he subsequently appointed, a number of important centrist figures like Jacques Duhamel, René Pleven and Joseph Fontanet, who had remained in the opposition while de Gaulle was President. Twenty-five out of thirty-six centrist députés joined the new Majority. They formed the CDP (Centre for Democracy and Progress) and fought the 1973 elections alongside Gaullists and *Giscardiens* under the common banner of the government Majority.

The Majority in the Giscard Presidency

The Presidency of Valéry Giscard d'Estaing widened the Majority still further until it included all that remained of the opposition centre. This, as in the case of his predecessor, is explained by the need to build as wide a base of support as possible during the Presidential election campaign. Giscard, who had to oppose the Gaullist Party's candidate Jacques Chaban-Delmas in the first round, was able to attract to his campaign, and into the government he appointed after the election, those centrists who had remained in opposition to President Pompidou. The leading figure in this group was Jean Lecanuet, who had been a Presidential candidate against de Gaulle in 1965 and the leader of CD (Democratic Centre – successor to the MRP). In 1971 these opposition centrists, whose MRP origins go back to a Christian Democrat tradition, had joined forces with the Radical Party, which belongs to the tradition of the old anti-clerical left, to form the Reform Movement. The Radicals split over this alliance, which essentially embraced those who rejected both Gaullism and any pact with the Communists. The leading 'Reformers' brought some valuable support to the Giscard candidature. After the first-ballot collapse of the Chaban-Delmas candidature, which had foolishly restricted its appeal to the epic of the Resistance and to 'heroic' Gaullism, the UDR gave its support to Giscard d'Estaing. In consequence the new Majority extended from the Gaullists to parts of a Radical Party which for most of the 1960s had been linked to the Socialists and the left.

Giscard's Presidential Majority was less cohesive than the Majority of his predecessors, since Gaullism can never be entirely happy with national leadership in non-Gaullist hands. The first government appointed by Giscard was led by Jacques Chirac (leader of the UDR and of its subsequent metamorphosis, the RPR), but the government of Raymond Barre, appointed after the resignation of Chirac in 1976, had Gaullist support of a much less unconditional kind than that which the UDR gave to Chirac's government, and that support was less unconditional than it had given to the governments which served under Presidents Pompidou and de Gaulle. Nevertheless the RPR remained the largest element of the Barre government's Parliamentary majority and continued to sustain it.

The Majority in the Mitterrand Presidency

When François Mitterrand won the Presidency in 1981, the parties that had formed the opposition under Giscard now became the Majority. No significant part of Giscard's Majority changed sides. The only minuscule exception was the individual defection of Pompidou's Foreign Minister and former staff member Michel Jobert, who had a tiny party of his own. The 1974 boundary between government and opposition, between right and left, stayed exactly where it was.

The Socialist Party had a Parliamentary majority on its own after the June 1981 election. Nevertheless, Mitterrand's government and Presidential majority included, alongside the PS, the MRG (Radicals that had not wanted to join Giscard's Majority in 1974), the PSU and the Communist Party.

In 1986 the Majority beaten in 1981 became the Majority again. No-one from the left changed sides. The boundaries between government and opposition were once again the same as in 1974 – except for the presence of an opposition party of the extreme right, the Front National. The Chirac government of 1986–8 governed with a Majority of exactly the same contours as had existed from 1974 to 1981: Gaullists and the UDF, the confederation of parties – *Giscardiens*, Centrists and Radicals – that had supported Giscard. This was the period of 'cohabitation'. France was governed not by the President, as had been the case from 1958 to 1986, because there was no longer a 'Presidential Majority'. Executive power was firmly in the hands of the Prime Minister, who was supported by a stable 'government Majority' in Parliament. The Majority habit and the Majority system continued.

'*Cohabitation*' was an aberration in the Fifth Republic (though likely to occur again), and the supremacy of the President was restored at the Presidential election of 1988 (chapter 12). It was not, however, quite the same sort of supremacy as before 1986. The President did not have the support of a Parliamentary majority. The Socialists emerged from the 1988 Parliamentary election as by far the largest party (chapter 13), but were a few seats short of an overall Assembly majority. Presidential supremacy was therefore based, rather like de Gaulle's in the period 1958–62 though of course in very different circumstances, on the absence of a coherent and disciplined opposition willing to bring down the government. The Centrists (basically the CDS plus Raymond Barre – chapter 5), though remaining part of the UDF, formed their own Parliamentary group. In the Parliamentary session of 1988 Prime Minister Michel Rocard was sometimes able to obtain their abstention or even support. If, on the other hand, the Centrists signalled their intention to vote against the Socialist government, the Communists, though vigorously supporting anti-government industrial action outside in the street, would abstain rather than contaminate themselves by voting with the right.

To summarise, 1974 is in retrospect the high point of bipolarisation between government and opposition, right and left, with all the centre and the right supporting Giscard and all the left supporting the Union of the Left. There was no independent centre or opposition centre

Table 3.1. THE MAJORITY UNDER SUCCESSIVE PRESIDENTS

President	Communists	Socialists	Radicals	Centre	Giscardiens	Gaullists	Extreme right
De Gaulle				——————————————		
Pompidou				——————————————		
Giscard				———————————————————————		
Mitterrand (1981–6)	****	———————————————				
Mitterrand (1986–8)				———————————————————————		
Mitterrand (1988–)		—————————				

**** Communists left the government Majority in 1984.

remaining. That, despite speculation about the rebirth of an independent centre, is how the party system has remained ever since. The only exceptions are the small vote for the Greens, whose 3% in the Presidential elections of 1981 held the balance between left and right and who remain capable of mobilising 3–4% (10% in the 1989 Euro-elections), the appearance in the 1980s of a significant vote for the Front National on the extreme right (chapter 10), and the departure of the Communists in the mid-1980s from any alliance of the left at national level.

4

THE GAULLISTS

Charles de Gaulle died in 1970, and yet there is still a large party which everyone calls the Gaullist party. I was even told by one of the younger Gaullist ministers in the 1986–8 Chirac government that tensions within that government (a coalition of Gaullists and the centrist UDF) were between those ministers who had supported de Gaulle and those who had not. A significant number of respondents in opinion polls still give support for de Gaulle as the factor which determines their vote. The party that came into existence to support de Gaulle was the catalyst of the modernised party system we examined in the last chapter. It was the first political party in French history to win a parliamentary majority and to see its role as giving disciplined electoral and parliamentary support to the government. It has been the main government party in the Fifth Republic. Between 1958 and 1988, leaving out the five years when the Socialist Party was in power (1981–6), six out of the seven Prime Ministers have been members of the Gaullist party (Debré 1958–62, Pompidou 1962–8, Couve de Murville 1968–9, Chaban-Delmas 1969–72, Messmer 1972–4, Chirac 1974–6 and 1986–8). Gaullism can therefore claim to be the most important political force in the Fifth Republic.

The RPF

The first Gaullist party dates from the Fourth Republic, not the Fifth. De Gaulle, who had been the leader of the provisional government that restored democracy in France after the Liberation in 1944, resigned from office in 1946 because Parliament was preparing a new parliamentary-type constitution for the Fourth Republic – weak and ineffective as he would consider it. A small party called *Union Gaulliste* was formed, but in April 1947 at Strasbourg the first seriously organised political expression of Gaullism was launched. This was the RPF (*Rassemblement du peuple français*), which quickly became a mass movement with a million members. De Gaulle was its President and at vast rallies used to make, for the only time in his life, demagogic and inflammatory speeches. The message was nationalism, anti-Communism, ferocious opposition to the Parliamentary system of the Fourth Republic, and the call for a strong leader.

In other contexts such a party would have been called fascist – particularly as it attracted a violent, thuggish fringe which continued to be available to Gaullism as a *service d'action civique* right through to the 1970s and possibly beyond. De Gaulle's record, though, is so obviously one of restoring democracy and freedom, and not one of crushing it, that the term is wholly inappropriate. A better description might be 'Bonapartist'. Bonapartism is an important strand of the French political tradition in which public opinion turns from time to time to a 'man of providence' who promises strong leadership, a strong state, national self-assertion and popular sovereignty, not in the sense of Parliamentary government but of a direct plebiscitary relationship between the leader and the people.

The RPF was one of those short-lived political movements of the Fourth Republic which have been called 'flash' parties. (Another was Poujadism – a small traders' protest movement that came from nowhere to get 2.5 million votes and fifty Parliamentary seats in 1956, only to disappear again in 1958.) The RPR won almost 40% of the votes in the municipal elections of 1947; it won 22% and 120 seats in the Parliamentary elections of 1951. In Parliament it was divided between those who wanted to demonstrate outright opposition to the Fourth Republic (which meant voting with the Communists) and those in favour of joining the system. In 1952, twenty-eight members supported the conservative Pinay for Prime Minister. De Gaulle felt this was a typical reappearance of Parliamentarians wanting ministerial jobs for themselves. In 1953 he withdrew to Colombey-les-deux-Eglises for his five-year 'crossing of the desert', and the RPF was at an end. With its demagogic style and its authoritarian character, the RPF was Gaullism's least creditable phase.

RPF members in Parliament participated in many of the governments of the period 1953–8, usually under the label Social-Republicans. The most prominent of these was Jacques Chaban-Delmas, a Resistance hero (Chaban was his underground pseudonym), Mayor of Bordeaux, subsequently President of the National Assembly, Prime Minister, and Gaullist Presidential candidate in 1974.

The UNR

Gaullism, Philip Williams remarked, 'was the movement of a generation. . . Twenty years later the core of the party was still formed by men who had answered the call (in 1940) as resisters or Free Frenchmen. Very many original followers became devotees for life who willingly subordinated their own views (and careers) to the General's successive policies and appeals.'[1] 'Ten telephone calls,' observed Jean Charlot, 'and the little team of faithful supporters from the 1945–47 period, even those who had been disillusioned by the RPF, were reassembled in 1958.'[2] These included Chaban-Delmas, Pompidou, the Fifth Republic's first Prime Minister Michel Debré, the famous writer and adventurer André Malraux, Jacques Foccart who ran Africa for Presidents de Gaulle and Pompidou and was symbolically called back by Prime Minister Jacques Chirac in 1986, and Roger Frey, later to become President of the Constitutional Council. The Union for the New Republic (UNR) was formed straight after the 1958 referendum had brought the Fifth Republic into existence. It included, as well as the old guard of Resistance and RPF militants, some of the activists of the Algiers Committee of Public Safety – the formation of which in Algeria, with the support of the French Army, on 13 May 1958 had brought about the collapse of the Fourth Republic. One of them was Léon Delbeque, the man who got General Salan to shout '*Vive de Gaulle!*' from the Algiers town hall balcony at the end of his speech on the 14th.

The new party fought the Parliamentary election of October 1958 with great success almost before it had time to organise. As Jean Charlot has said, it was 'first and foremost a ministerial team, then a central committee for candidate endorsement, thirdly the largest Parliamentary group in the National Assembly, and only lastly a party'.[3] The whole ethos of General de Gaulle and his followers was that political parties were sordid and petty. So the General could not possibly be the UNR's President, and he made it clear at his press conference in October 1958 that his name could not be used 'even as an adjective' to describe any group or candidate. Nevertheless the UNR managed to use the famous name in the party's statement of aims and ten times in the model election leaflet suggested to candidates – the general message being: support de Gaulle's government, the new constitution presented by de Gaulle, and the renewal of France inspired by de Gaulle, by voting for those who had always backed de Gaulle.

It is a remarkable testament to political flexibility and the power of leadership that the party, formed to support a man brought back to power by those determined to keep Algeria French, held together when Algerian independence became the leader's policy. General de Gaulle's speech on radio and television, announcing the principle of self-determination, was in September 1959 and the first conference of the party – or movement as it prefers to be called – in November centred round the issue of whether fidelity to Gaullism meant fidelity to French Algeria, the commitment which had inspired the 13th May and the restoration to power of de Gaulle, or simply fidelity to whatever the General's policy was at any time. Jacques Soustelle, one of the original Gaullists and one of the French Algeria activists who played a part in bringing the General back to power, and the other *Algérie française* partisans were soundly beaten. The party line was summarised in a letter written by its Secretary-General Albin Chalandon to the rebellious Soustelle – 'we have no other role than that of demonstrating in discipline and unity our total confidence in the Head of State and his Prime Minister. It is a historic role that we are playing.'[4] It was also firmly underlined in the conference motion defining the movement's 'mission' as 'seeing itself as a party of government, closely associated, in initiation and in responsibility, to government action'. This is what makes the UNR such a new and remarkable phenomenon in French political history.

With the extremists of *Algérie française* eliminated – by resignation (Delbeque) or expulsion (Soustelle) – the UNR was able to attract groups of 'Gaullists of the Left' who had never supported keeping Algeria French. This group known as UDT merged with the UNR, victoriously fought the 1962 elections, and faced the calmer years of majority government from 1962 to 1967.

The UDR state

Georges Pompidou, appointed Prime Minister in April 1962, is the principal figure in the second act of Gaullism in power. After de Gaulle failed to win an overall majority at the first ballot of the presidential election in 1965, it was clear that simple reliance on the General's capacity to inspire would be insufficient to maintain Gaullism in power. The Prime Minister became party leader and organiser. Pompidou and de Gaulle had 'complementary attitudes towards party affairs'.[5] The

General was above party, Pompidou – from the second ballot in 1965 on – was the party organiser. The 1967 and 1968 elections saw the Prime Minister in the role of party leader, directing the campaign, addressing the big meetings, making the election broadcasts.

After the narrow win of March 1967 and the party conference at Lille in June, the party was reorganised. A new Secretary-General, too young to have been in the Resistance (Robert Poujade – no relation of the celebrated shopkeeper who founded Poujadism), and a new emphasis on recruiting a mass membership and constituency organisation were the main hallmarks. There were organisations for women and for young Gaullists (UJP). The 1968 elections, held after the great disorders of May, were heralded by a vast and extremely well-organised rally of Gaullists who filled the entire Champs Elysées on 30 May immediately after the General's broadcast in which he called for civic action to counter the threat to constitutional government. The local party organisations became the nuclei of Committees for the Defence of the Republic – rather thuggishly reminiscent of the RPF. The party and its allies contested the June election in this combative spirit under the label 'Union for the Defence of the Republic'. With these initials 'UDR', Gaullism had its greatest electoral victory and the initials were retained as the party's new title: Union of Democrats for the Republic. The dismissal of Georges Pompidou as Prime Minister in July 1968 and the resignation of the General after the unsuccessful referendum of 1969 (chapters 2 and 15) had surprisingly little impact on the effectiveness or cohesion of the UDR as an electoral force.[6] Although Presidential candidates like to present themselves as men of union, above party and never, as in the United States, the candidates of a single party, in fact the backing of a well-organised political party was an indispensable part of Pompidou's victory at the 1969 Presidential election.

In the Pompidou years the party was so dominant that the expression '*l'état-UDR*' (the UDR state) came to be used. In the Elysée (seat of the Presidency), the government, Parliament, public service bodies like television or the banks, and in the higher ranks of the civil service, UDR men were in charge – perhaps the most effective example in the West of what Richard Rose calls 'party government'.[7] There was some friction within the party between fundamentalists (the 'barons' or 'historic' Gaullists) and pragmatists (younger, rather technocratic supporters of President Pompidou like Jacques Chirac). The 'barons' carried the party conference of 1973 at Nantes for a fundamentalist vision of Gaullism (national grandeur, a new social order) but the government machine stayed in the hands of the Pompidou pragmatists.

The UDR in the Giscard Presidency

The presidential elections of May 1974, which followed the death of Georges Pompidou, were uncomfortable and distressing for the UDR. Chaban-Delmas, the candidate endorsed by the movement, was beaten into third place (see chapter 12). Moreover it was clear that many leading UDR figures, notably the Pompidou men in the government, backed Giscard d'Estaing as the candidate most likely to defeat the left. The principal Pompidou protégé Jacques Chirac – Minister of the Interior when the President died – became Prime Minister. Chirac, an ambitious and bold tactician, saw the need for the UDR to recover its morale and to resume its place as the principal element of the presidential majority. He therefore organised in December 1974 a sort of *coup d'état* in which the party's Secretary-General resigned and Chirac imposed himself as the replacement. In 1958 those who thought 'fidelity' meant fidelity to *Algérie française* were beaten by those in the party who defined it as support for whatever policy de Gaulle as Head of State saw fit to pursue. In 1974 those who thought fidelity meant support for the policies of de Gaulle were beaten by those who defined it as support for the government. The 'barons' of the era of 'heroic Gaullism' were out. The unchallenged leader was the Prime Minister Jacques Chirac.

In August 1976 Chirac resigned as Prime Minister. The reason he gave was that the President would not allow him to do his job as leader of the government Majority. Looking ahead to a parliamentary election which might bring a victory for the left, Chirac wanted a more aggressive approach, while Giscard insisted that liberal and humane social reform would win over the uncommitted. Announcing his determination to revive and enlarge the popular audience of Gaullism, Chirac made a triumphant return to Parliament with a by-election victory in the Corrèze. He called a special UDR party conference at which, with 50,000 present, the UDR transformed itself into a new organisation, the RPR (*Rassemblement pour la République*). The vacuum created in the leadership of the movement by Chirac's departure from government, and the disorientation of a party out of power and craving for a strong leader, was ended by the acclamation of Chirac as President of the new party.

The RPR

Rassemblement: the very word takes us back to the days of the RPF. The UNR and the UDR had no President. The RPR does have one. In the

RPR, like the RPF, the President appoints the Secretary-General and the members of the Executive committee. Also like the RPF, the RPR began life with a vast rally where all had come to worship the leader and to hear the call to arms against Communism and national decadence. The President and leader of the RPF was of course General de Gaulle. At the Porte de Versailles rally in December 1976 the badges said 'Chirac, I believe in him'. In 1989, despite two Presidential election defeats and some stirrings of challenge from the *rénovateurs* on the more progressive wing of the movement (see below), the RPR was still the creature of Jacques Chirac.

As befits a party which considers itself the prime defender of the de Gaulle legacy, it has modelled its internal (organisation on the institutions of the Fifth Republic. It has a President, a 'Prime Minister' (the Secretary General), a 'government' (Executive Committee), and a 'Parliament' (National Council) before which the Secretary General in an annual report 'engages his responsibility' (like the Prime Minister before the National Assembly) and which even has six permanent committees just as laid down for Parliament in the Constitution of the Fifth Republic. Like the Socialist and Communist parties it is a highly structured and well-financed organisation with a mass membership – 850,000, so it claims in the French tradition of obvious exaggeration.

The basic unit of organisation is the Parliamentary constituency, which elects a Committee, composed of local Councillors and ordinary members, and a secretary. As in other parties the constituencies are grouped into Federations at *département* (county) level. The Federal Secretaries, in the RPR as in the Communist Party, are appointed by the Secretary General (like the government appointing *Préfets* to continue the parallel with the state favoured by Gaullists), but the Federal Committee elects its own President and its representatives on the National Council. At national level every three years are held the *Assises nationales*, a great rally open to all members, which elects the President (Chirac ever since 1976) and 100 members of the National Council, which could be, like the organised 'tendencies' that are such a feature of Socialist Party organisation (see chapter 7), elected from rival lists of '*rénovateurs*' and Chirac loyalists. The National Council also has members elected by the Federations, Members of Parliament, former Prime Ministers, and National and Federal Secretaries as *ex-officio* members, and members representing professional sections (for example, there are RPR groups in banking and medicine), women and youth organisations. The National Council elects the Bureau Politique which also includes some *ex-officio* members like the Presidents of the RPR Parliamentary groups (National Assembly and Senate). The President appoints the Executive Committee, each of whose members is responsible for a sector of activity, a sector either of policy or of organisation (such as elections or training). The main publication of the RPR is *La lettre de la nation*, which is really a daily press briefing issued so that RPR reactions to topical issues can be relayed to the mass media. *La lettre de la nation* also has a well-produced weekly magazine which gives news, extensively reports the party leadership and its views, and presents the party line on everything from the budget to foreign policy issues for RPR activists. The RPR always seems to have plenty of money although, as usual with French political parties, it is impossible to say how much or where it comes from. Like all governmental parties in France it has been able to use staff seconded from ministerial, municipal and parliamentary sources. It has occasionally been alleged to receive substantial election contributions from France's client-states in Africa. The Secretary-General in 1990 was Alain Juppé, a close associate of Chirac at Paris City Hall and as a minister in the 1986–8 government.

Gaullist beliefs

Nationalism, as country after country has shown, is a very potent political force, and Gaullism is perhaps the purest expression of nationalism in the contemporary Western world. The central core of Gaullism is the concept of *l'indépendence nationale*. De Gaulle's view was that the nation-state is the one significant political unit in the modern world. The French nation must be independent in everything: militarily independent with its own nuclear weapons maintained in a state of credibility, industrially independent with French firms internationally competitive in all important sectors, politically independent (of East and West, of supranational entities like a politically integrated European Community). Furthermore it must claim a great power role in the world – diplomatically, economically and, through the French language and the existence of so many French-speaking states, especially in Africa, culturally.

'*L'indépendence nationale*' and the claim to a world role was a natural response to the humiliations of the Second World War: the surrender to the Germans in 1940, the occupation, and the Liberation by the Americans, British and Canadians in 1944. Philip Cerny[8] has shown how the notion of *grandeur* (greatness) was for General de Gaulle the indispensable basis of national cohesion and unity. The French needed to be proud of their country if they were to support effective political institutions and produce a dynamic economy. This equation appears to be true for the recovery of many nations with a proud past – certainly Britain and the United States. De Gaulle was triumphantly successful in achieving it, and the formula '*indépendence nationale/grandeur*' has become not merely the central reference for the Gaullist party but the basis of a national consensus including centrists, Socialists, and even to some extent Communists.

Other parts of the Gaullist faith are connected to nationalism. Gaullists believe in a strong state led by a strong President as the best way to achieve the nation's objectives. In the Gaullist view, France was weak in the Third and Fourth Republics because Parliament's powers constantly to harrass and overthrow governments made effective decision-making impossible. The Fifth Republic was set up to change all that, and it was Gaullists who formed the Union for the New Republic (UNR) to defend its principles. The basic principles of the Gaullist state are a strong executive in which the President is pre-eminent, a legislature with very limited powers to interfere with the executive, popular sovereignty expressed through referenda as well as through elections, and a strong state which resists regional autonomy: a set of ideas both distinctive and bold. The particular devotion to presidential power was put slightly in abeyance during the period of 'cohabitation' (1986–8). In fact 'cohabitation' was not a big problem for Gaullists because there were no fundamental differences between President Mitterrand and Prime Minister Chirac over defence or foreign policy, the particularly sensitive 'Gaullist' domains, and because Chirac, with a Parliamentary majority behind him, was effectively the head of the executive anyway. Like Gaullist doctrine on 'national independence', Gaullist support for the institutions of the Fifth Republic has become part of the national consensus.

Another aspect of the strong state, characteristic of Gaullism and based on nationalism, is a philosophy of the interventionist state. In the interest of national prestige and power, the state must promote industrial modernisation and development. This has been the policy consistently followed by all French governments in the Fifth Republic. When the Socialists were in power (1981–6), there developed among the opposition, including the RPR, a vogue for 'liberalism'. Liberalism has two senses: economic liberalism, meaning a reduction of state intervention, and social liberalism, meaning more decentralisation and more freedom and civil liberties for the individual. Gaullism has never been a form of liberalism but is concerned in the social sphere to uphold the unity of the state, law and order, and the values of the family, and in the economic sphere to promote 'grandeur'. My own view is that the extensive privatisations carried out in the name of liberalism by the Chirac government (1986–8) do not reflect a change in this basic interventionist philosophy. It has been argued (for example, in a book called *Droite, année zéro* by Jean-Louis Bourlanges[9]) that one of the reasons for the defeat of Chirac in the 1988 Presidential election was the apparent departure by his government from the old Gaullist norms of a strong welfare state and an economy in which sectional interest groups were kept in their place. Other writers like Jean Charlot take the view that Gaullist attitudes to the state's social and economic policies have pragmatically varied according to the situation at the time.

This section was entitled 'beliefs' rather than 'policies' because French political parties do not on the whole have policies in the sense of a detailed programme. The parties present themes or broad options to the public – much more sensible than being locked into excessively detailed plans or driven to explain minute proposed changes to taxation before they are even in government as British political parties have to do. The basic theme of Gaullism in the 1990s is what it was in the 1960s: 'In joining us you will participate in a vital political action which, in the footsteps of General de Gaulle and Georges Pompidou, is that of defending the idea of a France built on national greatness, dignity, and social progress.'

The Gaullist electorate

It is very doubtful whether there really is a Gaullist electorate. General de Gaulle achieved support from all sections of society including manual workers. So did the UDR when de Gaulle was in power. In the early 1970s, however, with Pompidou as President, there began the big shift of industrial workers back to the left – though this time to the Socialist Party not the Communists – and the new classes of the tertiary sector (white-collar, public services) went to the Socialists as well. Consequently the people voting for the RPR today are much more like a traditional right-wing electorate than a true Gaullist one: farmers, professional people, practising Catholics, the retired. In addition the appeal of Jacques Chirac, while no doubt stirring some of the same authoritarian and nationalist impulses as the General, is not of the same quality at all. One could have been a good Gaullist in the sense of identifying strongly with the achievements of de Gaulle and wanting his heritage to continue, and voted since his death for all kinds of parties and candidates – for instance, Giscard d'Estaing, de Gaulle's Finance Minister, in 1974, or Raymond Barre in 1988. Finally the RPR/UDF alliance, as has been pointed out elsewhere in this volume, presents analytical problems. In most elections in the Fifth Republic there has been a single candidate of the alliance to vote for in each constituency – so how much of the RPR/UDF electorate is 'Gaullist'? Obviously not just those who vote RPR, because many would have voted UDF if they could. Equally obviously the UDF vote contains those who would have voted RPR if they could. Even in elections where the RPR and UDF have had candidates standing against one another (1978 for example) it was noticeable that there was a tendency to vote for the best-known local personality. Subject to these important reservations, the accompanying table shows the electoral fate of 'Gaullism' since its inception. The Parliamentary elections of 1981, 1986 and 1988, and the Euro-elections of 1984 and 1989 are excluded because in all these cases the RPR was in alliance with the UDF and was not the dominant partner, as the UNR/UDR had been in the 1960s and early '70s. Also excluded is Chirac's 2nd ballot score in the 1988 Presidential election in which he remained as the sole representative of the anti-Mitterrand opposition (see chapter 12).

Renewal?

After the defeat of Chirac in the Presidential elections in 1988, a movement for the renewal of the centre-right began to be organised. The leading figures were younger (in their forties) and on the progressive wing of the party: Philippe Séguin, a successful and prominent Minister for Social Affairs and Employment in the 1986–8 Chirac government, and Michel Noir, who in 1989 defeated the old guard (of the UDF) to become Mayor of Lyon, a great political prize. These have been the most outspoken opponents of any pact with the Front National – indeed Séguin only just held his Parliamentary seat in 1988 because the FN called on its first ballot voters to vote against him. In 1989 the *rénovateurs*, as they came to be called, having considered and then rejected the idea of a separate list at the Euro-elections, organised a 'Convention of the reunited opposition' and called for the formation of 'a single, pluralist, and decentralised political movement uniting the

Table 4.1.   GAULLISM IN ELECTIONS SINCE 1945

		million votes	%
4th Republic			
1946	Union Gaulliste	.3	1.6
1951	RPF	4.1	21.2
1956	Social Republicans	.5	3.9
5th Republic			
1958	UNR	4.0	19.5
1962	UNR and allies	7.0	37.8
1965 (Pres.)	General de Gaulle		
1st ballot		10.4	43.7
2nd ballot		12.6	54.5
1967	UNR and allies	8.5	37.7
1968	UDR and allies	9.9	44.7
1969 (Pres.)	Pompidou		
1st ballot		9.8	44.0
2nd ballot		10.7	57.6
1973	UDR and allies	8.5	36.0
1974 (Pres.)	Chaban-Delmas	3.6	14.6
1978	RPR*	6.3	22.5
1979 (Euro)	Chirac list	3.3	16.2
1981 (Pres.)	Chirac + Debré + Garaud**		
1st ballot		6.0	20.9
1988 (Pres.)	Chirac		
1st ballot		6.1	19.9

*RPR and UDF, though allies, had separate candidates in most constituencies.
**Dissident Gaullists have been included.
(For exclusions, see commentary in accompanying text.)

whole opposition'. This idea arises out of the perception that the division and rivalry of the opposition parties and their leaders had led to a continuing series of defeats at the hands of Mitterrand and the Socialists, and that defeated and somewhat discredited leaders, such as Giscard and especially Chirac, were still sufficiently in command of the present machinery to be difficult to replace as Presidential candidates. The proposition for a new force, the Convention proposed, should be put to a referendum of the opposition's electors (not party activists), there should be united organisations at regional level, a joint conference of all opposition parties should be held to organise a merger, and a single Parliamentary group should take the place of the existing three (RPR, UDF and Centre Union). Another idea is that there should be some proper means of selecting a joint Presidential candidate for the next election (due in 1995), either something like the British Conservative Party's method of a vote by all the party's members of Parliament or even by the American method of primaries, in which the general public votes, and a nominating Convention.

NOTES

1. *Crisis and compromise*, London: Longmans, Green, 3rd edn 1964, p. 133.
2. *L'UNR: étude du pouvoir au sein d'un parti politique*, Cahiers de la FNSP, Paris: Colin 1967, p. 303.
3. Ibid., p. 23.
4. See Jean Charlot, *Le Gaullisme*, Paris, Colin, 1970, p. 102.
5. F.L. Wilson, 'Gaullism without de Gaulle', *Western Political Quarterly*, 1973, p. 106.
6. See R.G. Schwartzenberg, *La guerre de succession*, Paris: PUF 1969.
7. 'The variability of party government', *Political Studies*, December 1969, pp. 413–45.
8. *The Politics of Grandeur*, Cambridge University Press 1980.
9. Paris: Flammarion, 1988.

5

LIBERALS AND CENTRISTS

France has never had a great Liberal Party in the way experienced by Canada or the United Kingdom. Furthermore, the word 'liberal' in France does not mean the same as it does in English. In France its principal meaning is opposition to state intervention or control. Liberalism is therefore mainly economic free-market liberalism although President Giscard d'Estaing, who always hoped to see the emergence of a French Liberal Party, tried to give the word a more social significance: a society based on tolerance, responsibility and freedom for the individual, and a less authoritarian style in government.

The UDF

The small parties that supported Giscard, either before he was President or during his 1974 presidential campaign, united in 1978 to form a *Giscardien* confederation. Called the UDF (Union for French Democracy), it in fact took its name from the book *Démocratie Française*[1] in which the President had set out his liberal political philosophy. Giscard's star has waned since his defeat in 1981, so the UDF is no longer referred to with its old *Giscardien* label, but it still exists. It was an ally (and rival) of the RPR in opposition (1981–6) and in the election victory of 1986. It was a coalition partner (and rival) in the Chirac government of 1986–8. Following the re-election of François Mitterrand and despite presidential talk of *ouverture* (coalition between Socialists and centrists), the UDF fought the 1988 Parliamentary election as an ally of the RPR. After the election, part of the UDF (the CDS plus Raymond Barre) formed a separate Parliamentary group called the Union of the Centre (UDC) and even fought the 1989 Euro-elections with a separate list led by Giscard's former Minister of Health Simone Veil against the RPR/UDF list led by Giscard himself, but they remained part of the UDF, and the UDF continued to exist and form part of the opposition.

There are two important features about the UDF. The first is that it is a very loose confederation of small parties.[2] Maurice Duverger in his famous book on political parties in 1951 said there were two kinds of party: mass parties with a mass membership, ideology and discipline, and the 'cadre' parties which were electoral committees for a few notables without much in the way of strong policy commitments or party discipline.[2] The UDF proves the longevity of Duverger's second category. Each of the parties that make up the UDF has its own organisation, headquarters, leadership, local branches and national congresses. However, they are all small parties in which a Parliamentary élite and regional or municipal notables play a predominant part. The second important feature of the UDF is that the parties forming it are very diverse in origin and tradition. This makes cohesion difficult, especially since each is so determined to preserve its own separate existence. The three main ones are the Republican Party (the original *Giscardiens*) which is liberal-conservative, the CDS which belongs in the Christian Democrat tradition and the Radical Party which was the old anti-clerical left and scourge of the Catholic Church in the Third Republic.

The UDF itself scarcely has a structure. Its first Secretary-General, Michel Pinton, who had been one of the organisers of Giscard's successful Presidential election campaign of 1974, wanted the UDF and its leadership to have a high profile, to make policies and to be a *Giscardien* Liberal Party. However, the component parties were not prepared, after the defeat of Giscard in 1981, to support anything like this. Its next Secretary-General saw himself as a coordinator and administrator, not as a political leader. The UDF has a Paris headquarters, but with a small staff, and is directed by the *Bureau de l'UDF* on which the component elements are represented – the three parties mentioned above, a group of dissident ex-socialists (the PSD) and the *adhérents directs* (a group of direct members, of whom the best known is Raymond Barre, who do not belong to any of the affiliated parties and exist as a separate entity). Also represented on the Bureau are the *Perspectives et Réalités* clubs. *Perspectives et Réalités* is the most authentically *Giscardien* of all the components of the UDF. The clubs were set up by Giscard in 1966 as think-tanks for new liberal ideas and political discussion, and as nurseries of pro-Giscard political talent. They grew rapidly and, by the mid-1970s there were over 200 clubs and a total of 20,000 members, mainly professional, business and administrative people. They have their own elegant headquarters in Paris and an organiser who was a civil servant on Giscard's Presidential staff. Finally there are seats on the UDF Bureau for certain prominent individuals like Giscard himself (indeed Giscard became President of the UDF in 1988, replacing Jean

Lecanuet) and Simone Veil, former minister and President of the European Parliament, leader of the joint UDF-RPR list at the 1984 European elections and, as mentioned above, of the rival centrist list in 1989; there are also seats for leaders of the UDF group in the National Assembly and the UDF *'intergroupe'* in the Senate – so-called because UDF supporters are scattered across three groups in the Senate.

The functions of the UDF as an organisation are imprecise. There is no joint organisation for communications, joint party conference, joint training for candidates, joint network for local councillors or joint finance. However, there is joint preparation of major campaigns, and some coordination of public statements and, above all, of *investitures* – i.e. the arrangements for designating and endorsing election candidates with the UDF label and for conducting negotiations with the RPR. The *investiture* function is by far the most important of the UDF's organisational activities. The proportional representation system used in the 1986 elections involved the presentation of lists of candidates in each *département*. A UDF commission, chaired by the President of the UDF group in the National Assembly and representing all the elements of the UDF, first had to arbitrate between the competing bids from UDF component parties for good places on lists, then negotiate with the RPR on whether to have joint lists or separate lists, and finally seek as many list leaderships and 'electable' places for the UDF on joint lists as possible. Membership figures are always hard to arrive at for French political parties. The total for all the components of the UDF together is probably between 60,000 and 100,000.

The UDF lacks a leader, which in 1990 is its greatest problem. Its component parties have a strong network of regional élites and *notables*. There is a substantial electorate willing to vote for a 'centrist' candidate in Presidential elections, although allowance has to be made for the special circumstances in each election (see chapter 12). It has played a prominent part in government, providing a President, a Prime Minister and shoals of ministers. The only people connected to the UDF who appeared in 1989 to be of *envergure nationale* were the UDF President Giscard d'Estaing, who seemed unlikely ever again to be a successful Presidential candidate despite his good performance as head of the RPR/UDF list in the 1989 Euro-elections (27% – see chapter 13); Simone Veil, whose popularity and prominence in the public eye date from her abortion law reform as Health Minister in the mid-1970s, but who was damaged by a bad performance as head of the separate Centre list in the 1989 Euro-elections (8%); and Raymond Barre, whose

Table 5.1.   UDF 'NOTABLES'

	PR	CDS	Radical	UDF	Other	Total
Ministers (1986)	6	6	2		2	16/38
Députés (1988)						128/577
Centre Union Group		37		2	1	
UDF Group	57	13	3	14	2	
Senators (1989)	47	51	6	27	2	133/321
Centrist Union group						68
Republicans and						
Independents group						52
Democratic Left group*						23
European Parliament (1989)						20/81
Christian Democrat group		4		1	1	
Liberal group	7		2	2	2	
Independent					1	
Presidents of Regional	6	4	1	2	1	14/22
Councils (1986)						
Presidents of *Conseils*	14	17	3	10	1	45/95
Généraux (1988)						
Mayors of large towns	22	25	8	16	3	74/394
(over 20,000 pop.) (1989)[†]						

*Includes some 'Presidential Majority' – see chapter 13.
[†]Including Toulouse, Rouen and Versailles (CDS), Nancy (Rad.), Amiens, Toulon and Caen (PR), Nîmes (UDF) and Perpignan (other).

Table 5.2.   THE CENTRE IN PRESIDENTIAL ELECTIONS

		1st ballot %	2nd ballot %
1965	Lecanuet	15.8	
1969	Poher	23.4	42.4
1974	Giscard d'Estaing	32.9	50.7
1981	Giscard d'Estaing	27.8	47.8
1988	Barre	16.5	

political star is in decline. Raymond Barre, Prime Minister under Giscard in 1976–81, has also a rather Gaullian contempt for political parties. He runs his own show – pompously entitled CLES (Liberal European and Social Convention). It is not a party, of course – more a kind of forum. To stress his independence of political parties, Barre has regular meetings with President Mitterrand, occasionally says good things about the actions of the Socialist government, and keeps himself – unlike most important politicians in France – somewhat aloof from city government in his constituency (Lyon – although he did unfortunately endorse the losing list of the outgoing centrist Mayor, Francisque Collomb). He also greatly annoyed his UDF associates by not voting for Parliamentary motions of censure in 1988 and 1989. None of the leading figures in the UDF (except in the CDS) gave him proper backing as Presidential candidate in 1988. It has repeatedly been emphasised that a party in the Fifth Republic needs a credible Presidential candidate. The UDF, in 1989, had not got one.

The UDF's other serious problem is that it is locked into an inescapable alliance with the RPR – like hell in Sartre's *Huis clos*. This disciplined, long-lasting alliance is, as we have seen, one of the novel features of the Fifth Republic's party system. It has lasted in government, in opposition, in Parliament and in elections for more than a quarter of a century. Even for the late joiners (CDS and Radicals) it has lasted since 1974. Yet the alliance has been characterised by skulduggery of a truly Shakespearean character: in 1969 Giscard killed the king (de Gaulle) by calling for a vote for 'No' in the 1969 referendum; in 1974 Chirac made Giscard king by backing him in the Presidential election; in the 1981 Presidential election Chirac killed King Giscard. In the years up to the 1988 election, as Jean-Louis Bourlanges in *Droite, année zéro*[3] has pointed out, the Chirac camp was much more concerned to stop Raymond Barre than to stop Mitterrand, so great was its confidence that the Socialists were bound to be defeated. Although moderate, liberally-inclined, voters, especially from the new salaried middle class, are now voting socialist because the selfishness and authoritarianism of what passes for liberalism in the RPR/UDF does not appeal, the UDF is locked into its alliance with the RPR. The reason is that every UDF *député* was elected by the combined anti-socialist electorate in each constituency. One hears from the more progressive people in the UDF expressions of hope that a party of 'new men' will emerge, based on anti-authoritarians in the RPR, social democrats in the PS, and the moderate centrists in the UDF. This could happen – under the impetus, perhaps, of the Presidential candidature of someone like Philippe Séguin from the moderate anti-Chirac wing of the RPR, and Presidential candidatures do restructure the centre and right, as we saw in chapter 3.

The Republican Party (PR)

The largest component of the UDF is the Republican Party. Until 1977 its members were called the *Républicains Indépendents* (RI), and they had been the original supporters of Giscard d'Estaing when, in 1962, he

called on the electorate to support General de Gaulle in the referendum
on direct presidential elections. The other conservatives, independents
and moderates, not to mention Radicals, the Christian-Democratic
MRP and the whole of the left, opposed this constitutional innovation
in the name of hallowed Parliamentary tradition, and went down to
heavy defeat in both the referendum and the election that immediately
followed (see chapters 2, 13, and 15). Giscard's little group survived and
became a distinctive part of the Gaullist-dominated government
coalition.

The most influential historians of the right and centre parties in
France are René Rémond and François Goguel. The former[4] classified
three historic strands in the French right: the straight 'legitimist'
monarchists, the 'Bonapartists' who are more democratic but favour
authoritarian leadership in the hands of one man, and thirdly the
'*Orléanistes*' – the moderate, bourgeois and liberal right. It was the
'*Orléanistes*' who, according to this classification, are the ancestors of
today's Republican Party – against absolutism, against crude or doctri-
naire anti-clericalism in the early days of this century, in favour of bal-
anced budgets and sound money – the kind of government represented
by Poincaré in the 1920s or Pinay in the 1950s. François Goguel, in his
famous book on the Third Republic,[5] makes the historic distinction
between what he calls the 'party of established order' and the 'party of
movement', preferring these terms to 'right' and 'left'. The conservatives and *modérés*, who were never organised into political parties until
after the Second World War, he classifies as belonging to the 'party of
established order'. They were important in the Third and Fourth
Republics with their electoral strongholds in the regions of rural
Catholicism.

Descendants of the '*Orléaniste*' part of the 'party of established order',
or, if you will, the *Giscardiens*, the Independent Republicans at all events
found themselves in 1962 grouped round the brilliantly rising star of the
young Minister of Finance, who was the grandson of a Third Republic
minister and inheritor of his Parliamentary seat in the Puy de Dôme.
They adapted themselves very skilfully to what was in 1962 the new
politics of stable majority government. They were a reliable part of the
new Parliamentary majority that supported the Presidential leadership of
de Gaulle. However, particularly after Giscard himself left the government in 1966, they proved themselves to be effective critics whenever de
Gaulle or the government appeared to act in an authoritarian manner or
to abuse their powers. The RI's role as a Parliamentary ginger group in

the 1960s was, as Philip Williams put it, 'rather like that of France within the Atlantic Alliance'.[6] 'A few – or even many – RI abstentions would not bring the government down but they acted as a useful alarm signal. UNR members might resent the greater independence of their allies . . . but they were sometimes glad of an indirect channel of protest to the government.'

When Giscard left the government in 1966 and began to launch himself as a serious political leader with an alternative style and policies to de Gaulle, he formed the RI into a political party, not just a Parliamentary group, with a regional structure in the country, and also launched the *Perspectives et Réalités* clubs referred to above. This was the period in which Giscard used his famous phrase '*oui . . . mais*' – support for stable government but not unconditional support for everything de Gaulle did and particularly not for the 'solitary exercise of power'. He was particularly critical of de Gaulle's European policy and his nationalistic outbursts like '*Vive le Québec libre!*' in 1967. Giscard played a big part in the eventual defeat of de Gaulle when he announced that he would not be voting 'Yes' in the 1969 referendum, de Gaulle's last appeal for the confidence of the French people, and for this act of parricide most Gaullists have never forgiven him. However, after some hesitation Giscard and the Independent Republicans supported Georges Pompidou at the Presidential elections that followed the resignation of de Gaulle, while most other elements of today's UDF remained in the opposition. It was not until Giscard himself was a candidate for the Presidency, after the death of Pompidou in 1974, that he was joined by the Centre Democrats and the Radicals and offered to bring them into his Presidential majority. It was from then on that the whole of the non-Gaullist part of the majority were collectively known as the *Giscardiens*.

One curious feature of the Independent Republicans and subsequently the Republican Party is that, although it appeared for a long time to be a one-man band, wholly dedicated to the liberal image and progressive themes of Giscard d'Estaing, the party often looks more like a traditional conservative party than a centrist one. Many of its leading members have always been right-wing and authoritarian. Some of its prominent Parliamentarians in the early days were ex-RPF. President Pompidou's favourite Independent Republican was Raymond Marcellin, a conspicuously illiberal Minister of the Interior and the one who was alleged to have had the offices of the satirical weekly *Canard Enchaîné* 'bugged'. Even Giscard's closest associate Michel Poniatowski, when he was Minister of the Interior in the Giscard Presidency, had a very illiberal record of suspected executive interference in judicial proceedings. There was also an absence of unanimity between the ideas of Giscard and the opinions of his electors and party members. While Giscard himself was pressing 'liberal' reforms like legal abortion, they would have found maintaining law and order and fighting communism more to their taste. Even today it is the PR which is much more prepared to contemplate pacts with the Front National than the other components of the UDF.

The current leader of the PR is its Secretary-General François Léotard. He launched himself as a national leader with some successful appearances on television, and then in the Chirac government in 1986 he became Minister of Culture and Communication, which included responsibility for radio and television. He has youthful good looks and enunciates progressive liberal themes in a style that is still called 'Kennedy-like'. Publicity photos show him jogging in Manhattan – a powerful combination of symbols. He has strong Presidential ambitions. However, in the 1988 Presidential election, the UDF, including the PR, were supposed to support Raymond Barre. Léotard, who had been persuaded not to stand, could scarcely conceal his personal preference for Chirac. This has made him deeply distrusted by many in the UDF, especially Raymond Barre and his associates, some of whom, like Charles Millon and Emmanuel d'Aubert, are leading PR Parliamentarians. In 1989 his Parliamentary colleagues even declined to elect him as President of the National Assembly's UDF Group. In fact he was beaten by the more progressive *rénovateur* Millon.

The CDS

The second most important component of the UDF is the descendant of the Christian-Democratic MRP. It took a long time for Catholics to accept a democratic Republic, and they were regarded by their political opponents right up to the Second World War as reactionaries whose real desire was the restoration of the monarchy and a 'hierarchical authoritarian state modelled on their Church'.[7] There was, however, a progressive Catholic tradition in France in the liberal Catholicism of Sangnier's 'Sillon', and the short-lived political party *Action Libérale Populaire* in the early years of the twentieth century, and the small *Parti Démocrate Populaire* (of which the founder of the European Community and France's most famous Christian Democrat, Robert Schuman, was a leading member) in the 1920s and '30s. It was the Catholic leaders of the

Resistance in the Second World War, who had demonstrated their commitment to democracy and the Republic, who at the Liberation formed the MRP (*Mouvement Républicain Populaire*).

In the three elections of 1945–6 the MRP's score averaged 25% of the votes cast. For a brief moment it was the largest party in France. The MRP participated in almost every government of the Fourth Republic and provided three Prime Ministers including the almost permanent Foreign Minister of France and father of Europe, Robert Schuman. When General de Gaulle left the government in 1946 and set up the RPF, vast numbers of MRP voters deserted the MRP for Gaullism. Gradually the MRP dwindled almost to a regional party, with residual strength in the most strongly Catholic regions of the West and Alsace-Lorraine. The MRP backed General de Gaulle when he returned to power in 1958, and various MRP leaders served in early Fifth Republic governments – notably Maurice Schumann as Foreign Minister. The MRP supported de Gaulle over Algerian independence, but MRP ministers resigned over the issue of European integration on the occasion of de Gaulle's disparaging remarks on the subject in May 1962. The MRP went into opposition but some leading figures, such as Maurice Schumann, rejoined Gaullism, received the investiture of the UDR at elections and eventually re-entered the government.

In the 1960s, as French society became more secular under the impact of rapid industrial modernisation, the MRP transformed itself into the *Centre Démocrate* and the old Catholic trade union CFTC (French Confederation of Christian Workers) into the CFDT (French Democratic Confederation of Labour). The leader of the Centre Democrats was Jean Lecanuet, who had made a favourable impact on the public as a Presidential candidate against General de Gaulle in 1965. Under his leadership most of the Centre Democrats remained in the opposition under Pompidou as well as under de Gaulle. In 1973 they formed an alliance with the Radical Party called the Reform Movement. The 1973 election (see chapter 13) was one which might have been won by the Socialist-Communist alliance, the Union of the Left. To help prevent this the Reformers, though part of the opposition, made a second ballot pact with the government coalition so that the 'Stop Communism' vote would not be split. In 1974 they backed Giscard d'Estaing for President and entered the government coalition. In 1976 they became the *Centre des Démocrates Sociaux* (CDS) so that some of the pro-Pompidou centrists who had departed in 1969 could rejoin the centrist ranks. Since 1978 the CDS has been a central element in the UDF, ideologically slightly less

favourable to economic liberalism than its partners, and the most firmly
Barriste.

The CDS remains predominantly Christian-Democrat. Most of its
élites descend from the MRP. Pierre Méhaignerie, the current President
and a minister in the Chirac and Barre governments, and other leaders
like Jacques Barrot had fathers who were MRP *députés*. Other leading
figures like Lecanuet or Bernard Stasi were MRP. Their European
Parliament members sit with the Christian-Democrat group. In the
Senate they have their own group, *Union Centriste*, which had seventy
members in 1988, and they decided after the Parliamentary election in
June 1988 also to have their own National Assembly group, separate
from the UDF – the UDC (Union of the Centre) with thirty-four
members in 1989. In other words they consider themselves to be ideologically distinct from what the PR calls 'liberalism' – the unregulated
market economy and what one leading CDS figure described as
'l'égoisme social'. They also claim to be socially distinct in that their
grassroots members are often families with a background of Catholic
trade-unionism while the PR members are Parisian top civil servants. In
the 1989 Euro-elections there was a Centre list, separate from the
RPR/UDF, loosely based on the CDS and led by Simone Veil, but it
scored only 8% (see chapter 13). Despite this apparent separatism, the
leadership of the CDS is the closest to the *'rénovateur'* movement,
discussed in the last chapter, for a completely reorganised and united
centre-right to replace the old RPR/UDF alliance.

The Radicals

The third party of the UDF is the Radical Party or *Parti républicain radical
et radical-socialiste*, to give its full historic title. Formed in 1901, it is the
oldest party in France. Historically it has always been regarded as a party
of the left, as belonging to Goguel's 'party of movement'. Radicalism in
the Third Republic was the inheritor of the traditions of the French
Revolution: for the Republic, for the enlightenment, for science, for
reason, for individualism, for private property, for patriotism, for Parliament, above all for the separation of church and state. It was against
aristocracy, the Church, absolutism, excessive state power. Most of the
great names of the Third Republic are associated with radicalism:
Gambetta, Clemenceau, Herriot. Never socialist, it sometimes joined
forces with the Socialists as in 1924 or the 1936 Popular Front. Never
Catholic, it or parts of it were frequently to be found in alliance with

'the party of established order' – in coalitions between the World Wars, for example in 1919, 1926, 1934.

Since the Second World War the Radical Party has experienced a number of disastrous splits, so that what remains is a tiny fragment. It was always diverse. One celebrated member, Pierre Cot, was a fellow-traveller of the Communist Party, some were quite far to the right and quit the party over the issue of keeping Algeria French, and some, like Michel Debré or Jacques Chaban-Delmas, Radicals in the 1940s, were ardent Gaullists. The first big split came in 1955 between the supporters of Edgar Faure, who wanted the Radical Party to continue as an adroit and pragmatic government party with no particular ideological constraints, and the supporters of Pierre Mendès-France, who wanted the party to be a dynamic and progressive force for social reform. Mendès-France was a vigorous reforming Prime Minister in 1954–5 who successfully extricated France from its disastrous colonial war in Indo-China. Many people who were to become prominent in the Socialist Party of the 1970s like François Mitterrand and Charles Hernu would have liked to see a great *rassemblement* of the democratic left under Mendès-France. However Mendès lost control of the party in 1957 and he and his friends left it in 1959. He remained a man of the left, and eventually, with Michel Rocard, became a leading figure in a small and rather revolutionary fragment of French socialism called the PSU.

The Radicals, except for Mendès-France, did not oppose the return to power of General de Gaulle in 1958. However, although ex-Radicals like Edgar Faure found their way into government from 1966 on, the party was part of the opposition from the end of the Algerian war in 1962 to the death of Pompidou in 1974. In the late 1960s they joined François Mitterrand's FGDS (Federation of the Democratic and Socialist Left) in electoral alliance with the Communist Party. After the electoral debacle of 1968 (chapter 13) and the Soviet invasion of Prague had re-awakened anti-Communist instincts, the FGDS broke up. Under the leadership of a modernising newspaper publisher Jean-Jacques Servan-Schreiber the party formed an alliance – called, as we have seen, the Reform Movement – with the other opposition party not aligned with the left, the *Centre Démocrate*. This caused yet another split. Those Radicals whose electoral strongholds were in the traditional bastions of the republican left, basically in the southern half of the country and particularly the South-West, preferred to ally themselves for electoral or ideological reasons to the Socialists and Communists. In 1972 they formed their own separate party the MRG (*Mouvement des Radicaux de*

Gauche) which is closely allied to, indeed dependent upon, the Socialist Party and, as part of the Union of the Left, signed the *Programme commun* with the Socialists and Communists.

The official Radical Party (sometimes known as the *Valoisiens* because their office has always been in the Place de Valois since the Radical golden age of the Third Republic) became part of Giscard's Presidential majority in 1974. Its leader Servan-Schreiber was even a minister for about ten days (until he criticised French nuclear tests). It participated in the creation of the UDF in 1978 and was, with the rest of the UDF, part of the RPR/UDF opposition in 1981–6. Despite its anti-clerical tradition it even joined the other opposition parties in the big protest in 1984 against the Socialist government's proposals to reform Church schools: 'We have always been against monopolistic power. It used to be the Church. Now it is the state.' In 1986 its leading members, notably André Rossinot, Mayor of Nancy and party President until 1988, joined the Chirac government, and in 1988 it returned with the rest of the UDF and RPR to the opposition and refused '*ouverture*' (coalition with the Socialists).

Votes for the Centre

The table below shows how votes for the centre in France are still strongest in the most traditionally Catholic regions of the country in the north-west (Loire, Brittany, Normandy) and the east (Alsace-Lorraine). The regions in the southern half of France that have begun to figure as strong regions for the centre reflect another traditional aspect of support: support for *notables*. The Auvergne is the home region of Giscard d'Estaing (indeed, in 1988 he was President of its Regional Council) and the Rhône-Alps is the electoral base of Raymond Barre, who is a *député* for Lyon.

Since the mid-1970s there have been, as we saw in the chapter on Gaullism, no sociologically distinct electorates for RPR and UDF. Practising Catholics, farmers, professional people, the retired – a classic conservative electorate. In the European Parliament elections of 1989, however, where there was a separate Centre list, led by Simone Veil, as well as the RPR/UDF list led by Giscard d'Estaing, it was noticeable that the 8% who voted for Veil contained a high proportion of young voters, of people who classified themselves as Centre, of people who had voted for Raymond Barre in 1988, and hardly any manual workers. Simone Veil's vote also conformed to the classic geography of Christian

Table 5.3. VOTES FOR THE CENTRE

	Lecanuet, 1965 %	UDF, 1978 %	Barre, 1988 %
Paris Region (Île de France)	14.4	18.1	14.9
North	10.6	16.5	15.0*
Picardy	13.6	20.1	14.1
Upper Normandy	19.6(4)	20.1	16.1
Lower Normandy	22.9(2)	38.0(1)	19.4(3)
Brittany	18.6(5)	24.6(6)	19.3(4)
Loire	23.2(1)	24.6(6)	21.7(1)*
Champagne	16.0	21.1	16.4
Lorraine	15.2	27.2(3)	17.3*
Alsace	22.8(3)	25.4(5)	18.4(5)
Franche-Comté	16.1	24.5	15.8
Burgundy	18.5	16.3	16.1
Centre	16.3	23.5	17.6
Poitou	16.8	24.1	17.7
Limousin	8.5	4.5	8.7
Auvergne	16.5	28.1(2)	16.6
Rhône-Alps	11.8	27.0(4)	19.5(2)*
Aquitaine	15.4	13.6	15.5
Midi-Pyrenées	15.1	15.6	14.7
Languedoc	12.6	23.5	13.7
Provence – Côte d'Azur	11.7	21.9	15.0
Corsica	7.7	18.1	13.0
France	15.8	21.4	16.6

* Leading candidate of the Right and Centre 1988

Democracy in France – the Catholic regions of the West, Alsace-Lorraine, and the Rhône.

There are a few other small elements in the UDF – a few ex-Socialists called the PSD (*Parti social-démocrate*), a few independents, and a few notables who just use the appellation UDF – but the PR, CDS and Radical Party are the main organised parts of the liberal centre in France today. They have in common an antipathy to the authoritarian style of Gaullism with its cult of the leader, and to the 'collectivist' policies of socialism. They also share a recent past in which they supported the liberal reformism of President Giscard d'Estaing, and they also support the 1980s liberal rallying cry of '*moins d'état*'. However, the UDF is still too diverse and too divided to be a great French Liberal Party. That is something which has never existed.

NOTES

1. Paris: Fayard, 1976.
2. *Les partis politiques*, Paris: Armand Colin, 7th edn, 1951.
3. Paris: Flammarion, 1988.
4. *The Right Wing in France from 1815 to de Gaulle*, Philadelphia: University of Pennsylvania Press, 2nd edn, 1966.
5. *La politique des partis sous la IIIème République*, Paris: Eds du Seuil, 1948.
6. *The French Parliament, 1958-1967*, London: Geo. Allen and Unwin, 1968, pp. 107–8.
7. R.E.M. Irving, *Christian Democracy in France*, London: Geo. Allen and Unwin, 1973, p. 12.

6

THE LEFT

We saw in chapter 2 how the sustained success of Gaullism – as an electoral force, as a disciplined majority, as the source of legitimacy for the Fifth Republic's political institutions – also brought about the birth of an opposition. In the 1960s it became obvious that the only way Gaullism could be defeated was by the formation of an alliance of opposition parties – in the form, at the very least, of a second ballot pact. In a two-ballot electoral system, a divided opposition pitted against a cohesive government party capable of winning 35–40% at the first ballot is doomed.

The left in France is traditionally divided, often bitterly so, and it is not easy to establish what are its components. In the nineteenth century to be on the left meant being in favour of the Republic, democracy, reason and liberty, and against authoritarian rule (Bonaparte or the monarchy) and the Catholic Church. In the twentieth century the term has come to mean, among other things, opposition to capitalism, sympathy for the oppressed, and socialism. In France today, these notions are not very helpful: everybody is in favour of the Republic and the Socialists are not in favour of socialism. Lee Wilson offers the most practical approach: 'The French left is defined to include those parties that by tradition, if not doctrine, have been placed on the left.'[1] Essentially this means the Communist Party, the Socialist Party and, up till the early 1970s when they allied themselves with Christian democracy and joined the Presidential majority of Giscard d'Estaing (see chapter 5) leaving behind them the *Mouvement des Radicaux de gauche* (MRG), the Radical Party.

Until the recovery heralded by the 1973 Parliamentary elections, the picture of the left in the Fourth and Fifth Republics had been one of decline and failure to adapt to social and political change. The French economy was expanding, especially in the industrial and dynamic north and east. The traditional bastions of the left were in the backward south. The institutions of the Fifth Republic brought the voters what they wanted – stability and strong government. Opinion polls since the war had revealed a majority of electors, including those on the left, in favour of a strong, directly-elected Presidency. However, the parties of the left

Table 6.1.　THE LEFT IN PARLIAMENTARY ELECTIONS SINCE 1945

	Communist %	Socialist %	Radical etc. %	Total Left %
Fourth Republic				
1945	26.2	23.4	10.5	60.1
1946 (June)	25.9	21.1	11.6	58.6
1946 (Nov.)	28.2	17.8	11.1	57.1
1951	26.9	14.6	10.0	51.5
1956	25.9	15.2	11.3	52.4
Fifth Republic				
1958	19.2	15.7	8.3	43.2
1962	21.7	12.6	7.8	44.5
		Socialists and allies	*Other Left*	
1967	22.5	19.0	2.1	43.6
1968	22.0	16.5	4.0	41.2
1973	21.4	20.8	3.3	45.8
1978	20.7	25.5	3.6	49.3
1981	16.7	37.8	1.9	55.8
1986	9.7	32.1	2.2	44.0
1988	11.3	37.5	.4	49.2

Table 6.2.　THE LEFT IN PRESIDENTIAL ELECTIONS

	Communist %	Socialist %	Other Left %	Total Left %
1965	–	32.2	–	32.2
2nd ballot	–	45.5	–	45.5
1969	21.5	5.1	4.8	31.4
2nd ballot	–	–	–	–
1974	–	43.4	3.5	46.9
2nd ballot	–	49.3	–	49.3
1981	15.4	25.9	5.6	46.9
2nd ballot	–	51.8	–	51.8
1988	6.8	34.1	4.5	45.4
2nd ballot	–	54.0	–	54.0

fought to resist these innovations. The growing number of young voters, the decline of religion as a determinant of political attitudes, the industrialisation of the country were factors that might have been expected to favour the left, but they failed to do so, at least till the 1970s. In contrast it was the Gaullists who were able 'to portray themselves as the innovators in French politics' (F.L. Wilson),[2] and it was the Gaullists and not the Socialists whom the bright young reforming technocrats in the 1960's joined. In 1946 12 million people – 57% – voted for the left. The 12 million level was not recovered till 1974, nor a percentage score in the mid-fifties till 1981.

The first attempt to revitalise the non-Communist left in the Fifth Republic came from outside the party system. A number of political clubs, in the best tradition of the Jacobins of the French Revolution, began to be formed for the purpose of generating political ideas and changing the political order. There were socialist clubs like CERES (Centre for Socialist Study, Research and Education), which still exists as a left-wing tendency (now renamed *Socialisme et République*) in the Socialist Party; progressive Catholic clubs like the Club Jean Moulin, named after the wartime Resistance hero; and labour union clubs. As the 1965 Presidential elections, the first by universal suffrage, began to appear on the horizon, the clubs played an active part in the left's preparation for that event. No longer interested only in research and discussion but ready for full participation, many of the important clubs, whose members included prominent political figures such as François Mitterrand and Charles Hernu (later Defence Minister at the time of the notorious Greenpeace affair in 1985), got together and formed in 1964 the CIR (Convention of Republican Institutions). The CIR had an organisational structure and became, with the Socialist and Radical parties, one of the three components of the FGDS (Federation of the Democratic and Socialist Left – see chapter 7), formed in 1965. 'The club movement went into politics with the explicit goal of creating a new, simplified party system by uniting the forces of the left and centre-left into a single powerful party.'[3] Wilson considers that the clubs' greatest achievement was the integration of Catholics into the political life of the left – 'truly an innovation in French politics'.[4] They were also a source of new ideas and new leaders, although they often tended to be the personal followings of and vehicles for prominent individuals.

A Presidential election, like an impending execution, concentrates the mind. In addition to focussing the intellectual and political activity of the clubs, the approaching 1965 election brought about another attempt to create an alliance of the democratic left with a realistic chance of defeating Gaullism. This was the launch by a small group of journalists and politicians of 'Mr X' as a Presidential candidate who would recreate a modernising union of all moderates – Socialists, MRP, Radicals. 'Mr X' turned out to be Gaston Defferre, the powerful Socialist Mayor of Marseille (a very unsuccessful Socialist Presidential candidate in 1969 –

see chapter 11 – and Minister of the Interior after 1981). The strategy adopted by Defferre is known as the 'third force' strategy, and was familiar throughout the Fourth Republic when most governments were coalitions of all moderates against the extremes of left (Communists) and right (essentially Gaullists). It did not work in the Fifth Republic. MRP and Socialists were not willing to work together and Gaullism was no longer an extremism but the pillar of the Republic's political institutions.

The third attempt to reinvigorate the non-Communist left was also related to the 1965 Presidential election. This was the creation of the FGDS, a structured merger of the Socialists, Radicals and CIR, which was an inseparable part of François Mitterrand's first Presidential campaign. The aim when the FGDS was founded in September 1965 was the eventual creation of a single party, but in fact that never happened. Individuals could not join the Federation, but had to be members of one of the affiliated organisations. It operated very effectively in the 1967 Parliamentary elections – every constituency had a candidate bearing the FGDS label. François Mitterrand became leader of the Federation on 9 December 1965 – between the two ballots of the Presidential election.

The principal aim of the FGDS was to constitute an effective electoral force against Gaullism. It was neither long-lived nor successful: the electoral decline of the left was not halted either in 1965, 1967 or 1968, and the Federation collapsed after the resignation of Mitterrand as leader in 1968. It was nevertheless important for two reasons. First, the left was able to present itself at the 1965 Presidential election and the 1967 Parliamentary elections, thanks to Mitterrand and the FGDS, in a much more united and effective way although it could not stop the victory of Gaullism. Secondly, the strategy on which the FGDS was based, was the one to which the non-Communist left under the same leadership, returned in the 1970s with much greater success. That strategy was alliance with the Communists. In the 1960s and 1970s the PCF had a numerous and apparently stable body of 4–5 million electors (around 20%). There was no possibility of defeating Gaullism without their support. Alliance with the Communists is not a new idea. Léon Blum, the Socialist leader of the Popular Front (a governmental alliance of Communists, Socialists and Radicals in 1936), said: 'One cannot carry out a socialist policy in France without the support of those popular forces which look to the Communist Party.'

One difficulty with such a strategy was that Communist support could be a poisoned chalice. The PCF, for so many years the leading party of the left, had a somewhat Stalinist aspect that moderate voters found intimidating. Sometimes (see chapter 8) the Party would exert itself to combat this negative image – in the mid-1960s and mid-1970s, for example. Yet at other times, as in 1968–9 or 1977–81, it would positively exult in being a hard-line Communist Party, giving enthusiastic support to the Soviet Union, dealing ruthlessly with dissidents in its own ranks, aggressive and hostile to all non-Communist groups in France. Whatever the PCF did, however, its opponents always sought to foster the Stalinist image and the fears of totalitarian dictatorship it appeared to inspire. Another difficulty of the strategy of alliance with the Communists was that the Party expected to be something more than a reservoir of votes for the threadbare Socialist and Radical parties: a full partner in policy formulation and eventual government power.

The Mitterrand strategy followed a twofold pattern. First, it was an effort to build up the non-Communist left to be a single united and electorally-attractive force able to be the senior partner in any alliance with the PC – especially any eventual government coalition. Secondly, it was an effort to bring the PC out of its isolation and encourage it to move in a more liberal direction. Mitterrand repeatedly asserted that the millions of Communist voters were not to be regarded as untouchables but *français à part entière* – full members of French political society. He repeatedly sought and obtained Communist signatures on joint Socialist/Communist statements guaranteeing respect for democratic freedoms if the left came to power. The FGDS and the Communists supported Mitterrand's Presidential campaign in 1965. The vote for the left was still much lower than in the days of the Fourth Republic but it was the launch of Mitterrand as a credible Presidential figure and of hopes for a united left. In 1965 the FGDS published its charter for a 'new society'. In May 1966 Mitterrand and the FGDS formed a *contre-gouvernement* ('shadow cabinet') to demonstrate to public opinion that the FGDS was a source of responsible and dynamic national leadership capable of forming an effective government. For the 1967 Parliamentary elections it presented FGDS candidates and established a second ballot pact with the Communists for mutual *désistement*. The FGDS and the Communists would each present candidates at the first ballot, but in every constituency all candidates of the left would withdraw in favour of the one 'best placed to win'. It worked well: the left's total share of the vote was slightly down on 1962, but Parliamentary representation was increased by more than forty seats. The government majority almost lost its overall control of Parliament, and there was an encouraging readiness among Socialist, Radical and Communist voters to play their part in the alliance at the second ballot.

In February 1968, the FGDS and the Communists published a joint declaration listing their points of agreement and their points of divergence on a programme of government. This, says Borella, 'was a text of prime importance, the first of its kind in France, which seemed to open at last the way to the winning of power by the united left.'[5] It was a false dawn. Almost at once, the pressure of singular events reopened the old fissures between the Communist and non-Communist left, and by the end of the year the FGDS was dead. First there was disagreement over the Events of May – the student revolt that turned into a general strike. The PC did not consider May 1968 to be a revolutionary situation, but was at the same time very unhappy about other groups appearing to outstrip it in revolutionary fervour. It employed its organisational skills on the side of order: to resist 'adventures' and prevent demonstrations and strikes from getting out of hand. Some Socialists, on the other hand, allowed themselves to be more affected by the extraordinary mood of revolutionary romanticism. On 29 May, believing that his hour had come, François Mitterrand announced, without consulting the PC, that he was ready to be a candidate for the Presidency and suggested the formation of a caretaker government under the prestigious former Prime Minister Pierre Mendès-France who, to the fury of the Communists, had just taken part in a huge left-wing student rally at Charléty stadium denouncing the Communists for their rigidity and treachery! The climate of mutual suspicion and resentment left by the Events of May, and by the very serious electoral defeat which followed it (chapter 13), was made worse by the Warsaw Pact invasion of Czechoslovakia in August 1968. Quite apart from the stresses and strains which this created inside the PC between those who felt that the Soviet Union must always be supported and those who favoured a measure of self-determination, the invasion aroused all the old fears of totalitarian Communism imposed by Soviet tanks.

The initial reaction of the PCF leaders to the invasion was to express 'surprise and reprobation' on the rather nationalistic grounds that Czech national territory was sovereign. However, it became clear as time went on that the Party did not approve of the 'Prague Spring' and its liberalising reforms, and it endorsed 'normalisation' – the reimposition of Stalinism in Czechoslovakia under Husak, the leader installed to replace the reformer Dubček. This was exactly the kind of crisis to make people uneasy about the PCF's attachment to democratic values. It harmed the Party's appeal in France and undermined those who felt that a Socialist/Communist alliance was the only way to defeat Gaullism. Roger Garaudy, a leading Communist intellectual and member of the PCF's *Bureau politique*, asked (and was expelled from the Party for pursuing the point): 'Does it weaken the French Communist Party or, on the contrary, does it not remove an obstacle to its wider appeal, if I ask that the party should say clearly: "The socialism we want to bring in in France is not the socialism imposed by Brezhnev on Czechoslovakia"?'[6] The PCF was back in one of its intransigent and non-unitary phases. In the Presidential elections of 1969 there were four candidates of the left, including Gaston Defferre for the Socialists (campaigning with Mendès-France at his side – a ticket calculated to arouse little enthusiasm from the Communists) and Jacques Duclos for the PCF. Duclos achieved a respectable score, mainly because the credibility of the Socialist challenge was low (see chapter 12), but the left as a whole recorded its worst ever post-war score of 31.4%.

Once again it was an electoral rendez-vous which gave the first sign that the climate might be thawing. In the important local elections of March 1971, Union of the Left lists which included Communists and Socialists were presented in several important cities and were successful in quite a number (Le Havre and Calais for example). The approach was pragmatic: where the Socialists thought they could get on better locally without the Communists (Lille, Marseille, Nantes), they did so. In June 1971, the new PS was launched at the famous Epinay-sur-Seine Congress of Unification (see chapter 7) with François Mitterrand as First Secretary. The strategy was that of the old FGDS – unity of the left and agreement on a common programme with the Communists, and, as before, an effort to build up the strength and prestige of the Socialists so that they could be seen as the equal if not the senior partner. There were difficulties: the two parties could not agree, for instance, over the line to take in the 1972 referendum (see chapter 15) over the enlargement of the European Community. However, on 27 June 1972, there was finally agreement over a joint manifesto or platform, the *Programme commun de la gauche*, and a nationally binding second-ballot electoral pact for the 1973 elections. This alliance went 'much further in linking the two sister parties than either the 1934 Popular Front agreement, or the electoral pacts of 1967–8'.[7] In July the 'Left-Radicals' (those members of the Radical Party who did not wish to follow the rest of their party into an alliance with the *Centre Démocrate* (chapter 5) signed the *Programme commun*, and formed a first-ballot coalition with the PS (rather like the old FGDS but without its structure, and called for the 1973 elections the UGSD – Union of the Socialist and Democratic Left).

From the 1930s to the 1980s the left only ever had electoral success when it went into battle stressing what united it and not what divided it. This in turn depended very often on whether world events authorised the PC to coexist amicably with non-Communist parties. These conditions were fulfilled in 1973, and the elections that year at last saw a reversal of the long decline of the left. With 46% and 11 million votes at the first ballot, the left was somewhere near its immediate post-war level of support. It did not win the election, but its election was the first in which the possibility of a win by the left was an issue (and the beginning of all those interminable debates about the constitutional options for a President faced with a hostile Parliamentary majority which eventually ended with 'cohabitation' in 1986).

The new PS, which was much more dynamic, much better organised, much better led by François Mitterrand, and had much more appeal to the voters, had achieved a new position of strength from which to conduct its dealings with the Communists. The Mitterrand strategy – the 'rebalancing' of the left to build an alliance which the PCF could not dominate – seemed to be succeeding. The PS attracted new adherents like Michel Rocard (later – in 1988 – to become Prime Minister) and most of his small left-wing revolutionary party, the PSU; the alliance with the Left-Radicals, now called MRG, flourished; and the 1974 Presidential election – 'the occasion for a massive display of left-wing unity' – was, with the support of 13 million votes and 49.3% at the second ballot, all but a famous victory.

The mid-1970s turned out to be the high point of the Union of the Left. It was possible at that time to make the error of supposing it to be a permanent alliance on the grounds that the PCF really had no alternative. It could never win power on its own. It could never win in a democratic country by proposing something profoundly unacceptable to voters like the Soviet model of socialism. The mid-1970s, furthermore, were the period when 'Euro-Communism' was in vogue, a liberal version of Communism more suitable for democracies and the subject of endless discussion at the time. As we shall see in chapter 8, the PCF at this time showed evidence of profound change. Its twenty-second Congress in 1976 declared that Lenin's notion of Dictatorship of the Proletariat had become outdated, and the existence of Soviet labour camps and repressive measures against people for their opinions were for the first time acknowledged and denounced. The change was summarised thus by Georges Mamy in *Nouvel Observateur* (12 January 1976):

> For fifty years the PCF lived in its minority shell, scarcely believing it could succeed. Since 1974 its militants have known that the attainment of power – not alone certainly, and only with a limited programme – is no longer impossible. Gradually outlooks and attitudes have been modified by this new factor, which imposes new behaviour and a different approach to problems that they might actually have to deal with tomorrow or the day after.

A strong influence at that time was the Italian Communist Party and its leader Enrico Berlinguer. The PCI is the largest Communist party of the non-Communist world and always led the way in distancing itself from the Soviet Union and such Soviet actions as the invasion of Czechoslovakia. It was seen in Italy as the best defender of the under-privileged, and the most effective and least corrupt provider, in cities like Bologna, of municipal government. It had been gaining ground in local and regional elections, and was considered to have a good chance of winning the Italian Parliamentary elections of 1976. It declared itself in favour of the European Community, the Atlantic Treaty and democratic liberties. The PCI made strenuous efforts to convince the PCF what an albatross it was for Western Communist parties to appear too closely identified with Soviet attitudes, and that the credibility of all of them would be damaged if any of the important ones conveyed the impression of a Stalinist outlook on Western democratic liberties.

In 1977 Socialists and Communists fought the Municipal elections, which decide control of all the town halls in France, on joint Union of the Left lists (see chapter 14). This was the united Left's most impressive performance – wins in 156 out of the 221 large towns and cities, and an equal readiness by voters to vote for the left whether the list leader and potential Mayor was Communist or Socialist. Then it all started to go wrong. The Communists took the decision later that year to put into reverse the whole Union of the Left process. The first indication was the publication of a wildy unrealistic economic plan on the eve of François Mitterrand's television debate with Prime Minister Raymond Barre. Then there was the demand for an update of the *Programme commun* and insistence on two points: that the programme of nationalisation it contained be enlarged to include companies in which firms to be nationalised held minority holdings, and commitment to a higher figure for the statutory minimum wage. There were meetings all through the spring and summer. On 14 September the MRG walked out in protest at the inflexibility of the PC, and on 22 September 1977 the negotiations broke down completely. Six months before the crucial 1978 Parliamentary elections, in which the left, well ahead in the opinion polls, were expected to win their first chance of power, six months after the left's best-ever electoral performance in the local elections, the Union of the Left was in ruins.

During the six months up to the elections, the PCF turned all its guns on the Socialist Party. In previous periods of left-wing unity (the mid-1930s, 1945–6, 1967), the PC had made electoral gains. In the mid-1970s it had not done so. All the electoral gains had gone to the PS, which had rapidly become, for the first time in history, not merely the leading party on the left but the 'first party of France' as well. Furthermore the electoral gains of the PS were being made at Communist expense. Had not Mitterrand declared in a speech to the Socialist International – making a prophecy that was to be exactly fulfilled in 1988 – his aim of building a Socialist Party in France that could attract 'three of the five million electors who vote communist'? The greater electoral attraction of the PS meant that, with a two-ballot electoral system, PS candidates were likely in more and more constituencies to run ahead of Communists in the first ballot and, by virtue of the PS-PC electoral pact, to eliminate them. This fear was to come true in the 1980s: at the 1981 election half of the Communist seats in Parliament (42 out of 86) were lost not to the right but to the Socialists – because incumbent Communist *députés* had to stand down for Socialist candidates who ran ahead of them in the first ballot. Finally, the PC feared that the PS would certainly dominate any government of the left and that pledges would have to be secured from the Socialist leadership now rather than after an electoral victory. From September to the elections in March the PS was accused of 'veering to the right'. The PC did all it could to reassert its identity as a Communist Party. There would be Communist ministers, its posters insisted. A government of the Left would 'make the rich pay'. There might be a second ballot-pact with the Socialists, or there might not. In other words the PC did everything it could to recover its own distinctively Communist electorate which it had been losing to the PS, even if the price was the undermining of the left's great electoral opportunity by frightening away moderate votes – the inevitable consequence of the PC taking a high and aggressive profile. The destruction of the Union of the Left and the chance of a long-awaited and long-prepared electoral victory is one of the most extraordinary episodes in post-war political history.

Since 1977 there has been no strategic alliance of Socialists and Communists at national level, although many local Union of the Left municipal governments have continued. In 1981, paradoxically, it was the collapse of the Communist vote that made it possible for François Mitterrand, the man who had always believed that a Socialist-Communist alliance was the only way for the opposition to come to power in France, to win the Presidency. With only 15% for Georges Marchais at the first ballot, it was no longer possible for the right to scare the electorate by suggesting that a Socialist President would be dominated and manipulated by the Communists. The PCF invited its voters to support Mitterrand in the second ballot, and the new President appointed four Communist ministers in the government, the most senior only being Minister of Transport, and this only after the PC had signed a statement on foreign and domestic policy agreeing, among other things, to respect France's alliances and to support Soviet withdrawal from Afghanistan. Participation in government did not reverse the decline in the electoral fortunes of the PC, and indeed may well have accentuated it by causing it to be involved in unpopular government measures. Indeed with hindsight one could argue that to join the government was a fatal mistake from the Communist Party's point of view. At all events it withdrew from government in 1984 (see chapter 8).

The only pacts since have been tactical pacts at the second ballot – except for the maintenance of Union of the Left Councils and lists at the 1989 local elections in a number of cities (chapter 14). This survival is at first sight curious, given the state of relations between the parties. How do they manage the partnership necessary to govern a town? The answer, according to various Socialist mayors, is that they do not. The pact is necessary to both parties for electoral reasons in a very large number of towns. In addition, according to Socialist Mayors, the Communists need paid jobs for their full-time party workers. French local councils are generous payers of allowances and providers of office accommodation and staff to mayors and *maires-adjoints* (comparable to committee chairmen in Britain). The price of these perquisites in a Socialist-led town is to refrain from criticism of Socialist policy and to vote for the budget. Communists have a slightly different view: 'Our line is simple: we respect the undertakings we have made.'

In the elections of 1988 the PC called on its voters to stop the right from winning by voting for Mitterrand at the second ballot of the Presidential election, and there was a second-ballot pact for the Parliamentary elections. The voters in France understand very well the tradition of 'republican discipline': there should only be one candidate of the left at the second ballot in any constituency, and if you basically identify with the left you should vote at the second ballot for that candidate.

At the end of the 1980s, what had seemed about to become a permanent feature of French political life in the 1970s – Union of the Left – has still not reappeared despite *perestroika* and a conciliatory mood in the Soviet Union, which always used to be reflected by conciliatory behaviour from Communists in France as well. The big change on the left has been the emergence of the PS as a majority party in the country, like Gaullism in the 1960's, and the electoral marginalisation of the PC.

NOTES

1. F.L. Wilson, *The French Democratic Left, 1963–1969*, Stanford University Press 1971, p. 24.
2. Ibid., p. 61.
3. Ibid., p. 106.
4. Ibid., p. 104.
5. *Les partis politiques dans la France d'aujourd'hui*, Paris: Eds du Seuil 1973, p. 155.
6. See R. Garaudy, *Toute la vérité*, Paris: Grasset 1970, p. 111.
7. V. Wright and H. Machin, 'The French Socialist Party in 1973', *Government and Opposition*, Spring 1974, p. 143.

7

SOCIALISTS

'Pre-Marxist Socialism, place of birth – France': thus Claude Willard entitled the first chapter of his book on French socialism and communism.[1] Gracchus Babeuf, in *Manifesto of the Equals* (1796), declared 'We are all equal, are we not? Let there be no difference between human beings but in age and sex! Since all have the same needs and faculties, let there be for all one education and one standard of life!' Saint-Simon, through his review *L'Industrie* (founded 1816), promoted a technocratic utopia in which the wasteful anarchy of a market economy would be eliminated. Fourier proposed in 1808 a social order based on harmonious communes or coöperatives. There was a socialism of Christian and messianic inspiration associated with Lammenais. There was revolutionary socialism (Auguste Blanqui). There was anarchist socialism represented by Proudhon, who uttered the famous phrase 'property is theft'. There was the libertarian and humanist socialism of Jean Jaurès, the great pacifist orator murdered on 31 July 1914. Resolute Marxists and those who identify with the class struggle have had outlets in the form of the French Communist Party since 1920 or the unions, especially the CGT (General Confederation of Labour, formed in 1895).

One would have thought, therefore, that this rich tradition of pre-Marxist and non-Marxist socialism would have led, as in other West European countries, to a social-democratic party in which the influence of Marxism was slight. Yet while the action of French Socialists in power at national or local level has been reformist and moderate, its doctrine remained anchored for generations in Marxist and revolutionary ideology. Revolution in France, in particular the Revolution of 1789, is a powerful myth, in the sociological sense of myth – an inspiring story that moulds behaviour. Even at its most opportunistic and anti-Communist moments, as under the leadership of Guy Mollet in the 1950s, Socialist rhetoric always returned to the theme of revolution. It was not till towards the end of the Socialists' first prolonged experience of being a party of national government in 1984–5 that one could say that they had become a social-democratic party purged of Marxism.

The SFIO

There were a number of competing socialist movements in France in the last years of the nineteenth century. Some were revolutionary – the *Guesdistes* (the Marxist *Parti ouvrier* led by Jules Guesde) and *Blanquistes*. Some were reformists – especially the 'possibilists', as Paul Brousse's Federation of Socialist Workers was called. The Second Workers' International, at its Amsterdam congress in 1904, urged them all to unite. In 1905, in response to this appeal, the SFIO (French Section of the Workers' International) was founded. The 1905 programme defined it as a 'class party whose goal is to transform capitalist society into a collectivist or communist society'. That subtle word 'transform', as George Lichtheim noted, 'struck the requisite balance between the reformist and the anarcho-syndicalist tendencies.'[2] From the start, however, they were divided – over whether to enter 'bourgeois' governments or not, over whether to oppose war or fight in it, over whether to join Lenin's Communist International or not.

The Bolshevik revolution of 1917 had caused great excitement and hope among socialist movements in all countries. The SFIO sent two delegates, Cachin and Frossard, to make contact with Russian Bolshevik leaders and discuss membership of the Third International created by Lenin in 1919. They brought back the famous '21 conditions' for membership: purge of reformists, clandestine organisation, rejection of 'bourgeois legality', agitation in the army, rejection of patriotism, acceptance of instructions from the Comintern – these were some of them. This was debated at the Congress of Tours in December 1920 and delegates voted by a 3–1 majority to accept and join. Consequently the party, with all its assets, offices, and newspapers – notably *L'Humanité* of Jean Jaurès – became the French Communist Party. However Léon Blum, proclaiming that 'someone must stay and look after the old firm [*la vieille maison*]', led the minority away to continue the SFIO. It gradually gained membership and in 1924, as part of the *Cartel des gauches* with the Radical Party, it won 101 Parliamentary seats.

More than a decade of intense hostility between the SFIO and the Communist Party began to thaw in the mid-1930s as the rise of Fascism in Europe became more threatening. After the riots of the extreme right in Paris in February 1934, Socialists and Communists joined forces in an anti-fascist rally. In 1936 the Popular Front, composed of Socialists, Communists, and Radicals, won its famous electoral victory. With Léon Blum as Prime Minister, this was the period of celebrated social reforms like the forty-hour week and holidays with pay. It was also the period in which France, like the other democracies, greatly encouraged Hitler by refusing aid to the Republican forces fighting Franco in the Spanish Civil War, and by embracing the policy of Appeasement at the Munich meeting in September 1938.

Although a large part of the SFIO, in Parliament and outside, accepted Marshal Pétain and the Vichy regime (1940–4), its leaders emerged with honour from the Resistance. Supporters and members of the Provisional Government of General de Gaulle after the Liberation, the Socialists obtained more than 23% of the votes at the October 1945 election – a performance they never equalled until 1978 – and claimed a membership of 350,000, the highest ever. Four Socialists served as Prime Minister in the Fourth Republic: Blum, Gouin, Ramadier (who expelled the Communists from Government in 1947) and Mollet. Blum tried to seize the opportunity after the Liberation to persuade Socialists to drop much of their ideological baggage (after all, the revolutionaries had supposedly formed their own Communist Party back in 1920), to 'emancipate them from a Marxist creed they had long ceased to take seriously, and to open it to new blood from the Resistance organisations'. However Guy Mollet, Secretary-General from 1946 right to the end in 1969, whose name was to become the synonym for opportunism, managed to persuade the party to condemn 'all attempts at revisionism, especially those inspired by a false humanism, the real intention of which is to mask that fundamental reality – the class struggle'. The party's doctrinal effort was 'to enrich Marxism . . . not to dilute it'. No phrase could more graphically illustrate the stupendous and persistent self-deception of the SFIO.

The SFIO in the Fourth Republic dwindled into what the Radicals had been in the Third – deeply conservative defenders of the old republican and anti-clerical faith. Comfortably installed on local councils (over half the members of the party in 1965 were councillors) or in Parliament, functioning in big towns as a 'mutual aid society for municipal employees' (Philip Williams),[3] the party, in the name of a fearless refusal to compromise its doctrine, rejected all progressive policies and initiatives. As Prime Minister in 1956–7, Guy Mollet supported keeping Algeria French and the disastrous Anglo-French attempt to recover the Suez Canal. He opposed all attempts to build effective alliances either with the Communist left or the Catholic centre. It was on the long-dead issue of state aid to church schools that he torpedoed the attempt to build a centre-left alliance of Socialists, Radicals and the MRP round progressive policies and the possible presidential candidature of Gaston Deferre in 1965 (see chapter 6). The rejuvenation of the left and electoral recovery were initiated outside the SFIO (chapter 6), especially by the initiatives of François Mitterrand (never a member of the SFIO) and the creation of a new Socialist Party in 1971.

The Parti Socialiste (PS)

The metamorphosis of socialism was marked in the best tradition of the French left by the names of four congresses: Alfortville, Bagneux, Issy and Epinay. The FGDS, the Federation of Socialists and Radicals created by François Mitterrand after his first Presidential campaign in 1965, which had negotiated an effective electoral pact with the Communists, was disbanded in 1968 – the victim of a new outbreak of Stalinist intransigence in the Communist Party and of doubts by Radicals about an alliance with the left. At Alfortville (May 1969) the SFIO made the bad decision to present a candidate (Gaston Defferre) at the Presidential election in that year (he got 5%) and the better decision to wind up the SFIO and form a new Socialist Party. At Bagneux (June 1969) 'a basis of agreement for all Socialists' was worked out – no centrist alliances, the will to build an alliance with the Communists, the regrouping of 'all currents of democratic socialism'. At Issy (July 1969) the new party was established with Alain Savary (later to be Minister of Education under Mitterrand) as General Secretary. It did not have 'all currents of democratic socialism' – in particular it lacked François Mitterrand and his federation of 'clubs' (the Convention of Republican Institutions – see chapter 6) – but it did start the indispensable process of rejuvenating the party. Some 70% of secretaries of *département* (county) federations were replaced over the next two years, and their average age fell by twenty years. In 1970 Mitterrand and his organisation decided to join the new party, and so a 'congress of unification' was held at Epinay in June 1971 – regarded as the historic moment when the revival of French socialism began. The new party, by a very narrow majority, elected François Mitterrand its leader (or First Secretary) and decided upon a strategy of left-wing unity (an alliance and joint programme of government with the Communist Party). By 1973 most of the Radicals had been retrieved from their centrist alliance (see chapter 5) and were included, for the elections that year, in the UGSD (Union of the Socialist and Democratic Left – when the Socialists had been weaker in the mid-1960s the S and the D had been the other way round in the FGDS). In 1974 the PS gained new forces. Michel Rocard, a future Prime Minister, and the majority of his party the PSU – an increasingly revolutionary group that had split from the SFIO in 1958, strongly supported the student movement in 1968, and included among its members the prestigious former Prime Minister Pierre Mendès-France – joined the PS. So did the leaders of the CFDT, France's second largest trade union organisation, and its leading activists. So did some prominent individuals like Jacques Delors, formerly on the staff of Gaullist Prime Minister Jacques Chaban-Delmas, later to become Mitterrand's Finance Minister and the decisive influence for economic 'realism' against Socialist dreams in 1983–4, and later still President of the European Commission and the *bête noire* of Margaret Thatcher. Mitterrand declared at the 1975 congress: 'We

Table 7.1. SOCIALISTS IN ELECTIONS SINCE 1945

		m. votes	%
1945	SFIO	4.5	23.4
1946 (June)	SFIO	4.2	21.1
1946 (Nov.)	SFIO	3.4	17.8
1951	SFIO	2.7	14.6
1956	SFIO	3.2	15.2
1958	SFIO	3.2	15.7
1962	SFIO	2.3	12.6
1967	FGDS	4.2	19.0
	(Soc. + Radicals)		
1968	FDGS	3.7	16.5
1973	PS + allies	4.9	20.7
1978	PS + allies	7.0	25.0
1979 (Euro)	PS + allies	4.8	23.4
1981 (Pres.)	Mitterrand		
1st ballot		7.4	26.1
1981	PS + allies	9.4	37.8
1984 (Euro)	PS + allies	4.1	20.8
1986	PS + allies	8.7	31.9
1988 (Pres.)	Mitterrand		
1st ballot		10.4	34.1
1988	PS + allies	9.2	37.5
1989 (Euro)	PS + allies		23.6

(Elections are Parliamentary – first ballot – unless stated otherwise. Exclusions: 1965 and 1974 Presidential elections where Mitterrand was the candidate of the left as a whole, and the second ballot of 1981 and 1988 for the same reason.)

must make the Socialist Party the first party of France.' In the 1980s that is exactly what the PS became.

The 1970s were a period of considerable electoral success for the new Socialist Party. There was an effective alliance with the Communists and big gains were made at the 1973 Parliamentary elections. Mitterrand, at the head of a united left, very nearly won the Presidency in 1974. The left did exceptionally well at local elections, winning control of 156 of the 221 large towns in 1977. Most of the electoral gains were made by the PS, which explains, as we saw in chapter 6, the growing Communist disenchantment with the Union of the Left. Despite the break-up of the Union of the Left in 1977–8 and the disappointment of hopes of winning the 1978 elections (chapters 6 and 13), the PS achieved a higher share of the vote in 1978 than any other party. In 1981 Mitterrand won the Presidency and the Party a Parliamentary majority for the first time in its history. Even in 1986 and election defeat for the Socialist government, the party still scored 32% – a figure undreamed of in the 1960s. Then in 1988 came the remarkable re-election of François Mitterrand as President, in a campaign from which, admittedly, both the Socialist Party and Socialism were notable by their absence, followed by 37.5% and a near Parliamentary majority for the PS in June to support a Socialist government under Michel Rocard. Like Gaullism in the 1960s, the Socialist Party has become a party with, as the French say, a 'majority vocation'.

The PS as a party of government

The Socialist Party, throughout its revival in the 1970s, was a distinctly socialist party; as David Bell and Byron Criddle[4] have pointed out, it had to be. François Mitterrand, who by background is not a Socialist and took a party card only on the day he became leader of the relaunched PS at Epinay in June 1971, had always pursued, from his first Presidential campaign in 1965, the strategy of alliance with the Communists to defeat Gaullism, seen by him as authoritarian and anti-Republican. Gaullism was such a dominant force in the 1960s that if the left was divided it would have no hope of winning. This was all the more true with a two-ballot electoral system which required at the very least a second-ballot pact between opponents of Gaullism. To be an ally of the Communists you must at least be a socialist party. The pre-1981 PS was committed to a 'break with capitalism' and to a substantial programme of nationalisation.

The Socialists in government made a radical start. There were significant increases in welfare benefits, legislation on shorter hours, civil liberties legislation in the field of crime and punishment, a Keynesian 'dash for growth' in the form of increased public spending, and nationalisation of the banks (those that had not already been nationalised in 1945) and certain large industries. This was the period in which Nicole Questiaux, a socialist intellectual and author of books about class, declared she was 'Minister for National Solidarity [social security and health] not Minister for Accounts' and was therefore not going to worry about the social security and health service deficits. The Minister for Industry and Research, another leading figure from the left of the party, proposed measures for an even more technocratic and interventionist state. By 1983, however, difficulties with France's balance of payments, and the decline in the competitiveness of French industry, partly but by no means wholly caused by the Socialist government's policies like shorter working hours for all with no reduction in pay, forced an about-turn. Economic policy was now based on words like 'rigour' and 'realism' and directed by the moderate Finance Minister Jacques Delors. Pierre Bérégovoy, one of Mitterrand's closest associates, replaced Nicole Questiaux and set about reducing those social security and health service deficits. In 1984 some mild reforms proposed for the relationship between the state and Roman Catholic schools (an old socialist issue) provoked massive middle-class protests and were dropped. In 1985 the Socialist government sent the French secret service to sink a pacifist vessel, the Greenpeace *Rainbow Warrior*, in the port of a friendly country (Auckland, New Zealand), an act which resulted in the death of a crew member, because it threatened to inconvenience French nuclear tests in the Pacific.

There are two points to note about this transformation from radical to increasingly moderate government party. One is that socialist parties which do this normally find themselves, as did the Wilson and Callaghan governments in Britain and the Schmidt government in West Germany, the object of increasing criticism from their own party. In France this did not happen to any significant extent. The PS, and its First Secretary Lionel Jospin (successor to François Mitterrand in that role), saw their primary role as being to support the President and proclaim the achievements of the government. Jospin and other leading party figures were regularly briefed at the Elysée Palace. Successive party congresses saw none of that 'We want socialism now' rhetoric or accusations of betrayal so familiar to observers of British Labour Party conferences. At the 1985 Socialist Congress in Toulouse, Charles Hernu, the Defence Minister who had to resign over his handling of the Greenpeace affair (the bungled sinking in New Zealand referred to above), received a standing ovation as he entered the hall!

The second point is that events confirmed what Jean-Louis Quermonne has predicted: 'Presidential power will progressively detach itself from its party origins to base itself more and more on the state.'[5] Socialists in government followed the pattern set by their predecessors. The first Prime Minister appointed by a new President is usually a prominent political leader. After a few years the President appoints a 'technician' Prime Minister. De Gaulle started with Debré and four years later appointed Georges Pompidou, an unknown former member of his private staff. President Pompidou started with the leading Gaullist Jacques Chaban-Delmas and three years later chose a former civil servant Pierre Messmer. Giscard d'Estaing started with Jacques Chirac and two years later appointed 'the best economist in France', the technocrat Raymond Barre. Mitterrand followed this path. His first Prime Minister was his number-two in the Socialist Party, Pierre Mauroy, Mayor of the northern socialist city of Lille. In 1984 he appointed Laurent Fabius, an ENA-educated technocrat who had served on Mitterrand's staff when the President was First Secretary of the Socialist Party. The themes of the Fabius government, later to be put before the public in the 1984 election, were modernisation, efficiency and competent management of the state. By the 1988 Presidential election the PS was almost absent. The President ran his own campaign, with his own policies and his own slogans – notably 'national unity' – at rallies where he spoke alone on a stage decorated only with the colours of the national flag. The Prime Minister appointed after the election, Michel Rocard, was throughout the 1970s known as a heretic insofar as traditional socialism is concerned.

Party policy today has a distinctly governmental look about it. Even the 1988 manifesto 'Propositions for France', prepared during the Chirac 'cohabitation' government when the party was in opposition (though not in opposition to the President), contains much that would be objectionable to more orthodox Socialist parties like the British Labour Party: a tax system designed to stimulate investment, top priority for the fight against inflation, a generous scheme for a minimum national income but accompanied by a requirement to undertake community work or training, and of course 'nuclear deterrence – guarantor of peace'. Overall the tone is both generous and technocratically modernising. There is one extremely cautious gesture in the direction of traditional socialism: 'None of the privatisations [of the Chirac government] must be considered irreversible.' Shareholders, tremble!

Mitterrand as a political leader

Socialist Party leaders, on their rare appearances during the 1988 campaign, tended to cite the name of Mitterrand along with the other great heroes of the left: Jaurès, Blum, Mendès-France. He may not have quite their inspirational quality but he has done more than any of them to build a national majority for the left and give it in an extended period of power.

The French in the Fifth Republic have so far invariably chosen as President men of great intellect and culture. François Mitterrand is entirely characteristic in this respect, so is he in developing a rather lofty view of his office, but he differs from de Gaulle, Pompidou, and Giscard d'Estaing in that his background is a very long period in politics, national and local. He was *député* and *conseiller général* of the Nièvre and mayor of the small town of Château-Chinon virtually from the start of the Fourth Republic in 1946 to his election as President in 1981. He had been a prominent figure in the Resistance as organiser of the National Movement for Prisoners of War and *déportés* (workers requisitioned for German factories). During the Fourth Republic he was eleven times a minister and as Minister of the Interior under Mendès-France had to deal with the first incidents of what was to become the Algerian War. Although Mitterrand started his political life with no particular identification with the left, nor with any significant political party like the Socialists or Radicals – indeed, as we have seen, never joined the Socialist Party until he became its leader in 1971 – he had by the mid-1950s become one of the leading figures of the moderate left. He was profoundly opposed to the 'anti-Republican' way the leadership of the country was handed over to one man in 1958 and he continued to oppose de Gaulle's regime of 'personal power'. He was rather unfairly discredited by what was generally believed to be a fake attempt on his life in 1959 (the '*observatoire* affair') and from 1959 to 1965, as de Gaulle did in the 1950s, Mitterrand experienced a period in the wilderness, a 'crossing of the desert'. As we have seen he emerged as sole Presidential candidate of the left in 1965 (chapters 6, 12, and above) and so began the period of the Mitterrand strategy to rebuild the moderate left into a viable political force and to build a Union of the Left, uniting Socialists and Communists, capable of defeating Gaullism at the polls.

He has three great achievements as a political leader. The first was the creation of a Socialist Party with a 'majority vocation'. It took a long time – from his first Presidential election in 1965. In power under Mitterrand the Socialist Party, freed from the necessity of an alliance with an increasingly marginal Communist Party and exposed after twenty-five years of opposition to the realities of governing, became less and less socialist. By 1986 one never heard any more about nationalisation, the class struggle or of course nuclear disarmament, a policy dropped by the left years ago. The Socialist Party today is a mainstream consensus party with national unity and solidarity – that is to say social justice – as its principal themes: the irresistible appeal of non-socialist socialism.

The second achievement was in proving that alternation of power without upheaval was perfectly possible in France. Mitterrand was the first opposition leader to win power in the twenty-three years of the Fifth Republic. Everyone said there would be chaos or worse if the Left ever won an election, but in fact there was just the same calm transfer as happens in other democracies. The national consensus on the political institutions of the Fifth Republic, on defence, and on France's role in the world, all were scrupulously respected by the new President. Democratic liberties such as the freedom of information, the independence of the judiciary, or the rights of accused persons have been strengthened. Indeed one can say that since the beginning of the Mitterrand Presidency there has been no challenge to the economic, social or political order of the Republic, and the President's Socialist Party has become the leading defender of national consensus values.

Mitterrand's third achievement as a political leader was his democratic acceptance and tenacious performance of the role of 'cohabitation' President. As with the alternation of power, everyone said that 'cohabitation' would never work. There were some problems, particularly over the maintenance of Presidential authority in defence and foreign policy (see chapter 12 – section on 1988), but the stability of the Republic, constitutional government and the broad outlines of the national consensus were triumphantly upheld. These are great services to democracy and to the Republic.

Party organisation

With ministerial power, enlarged municipal power and Parliamentary majorities has come larger organisation. An earlier book by this author referred to the smart new offices of the PS being rather like those of a fast-growing advertising agency. The building in the rue de Solférino, occupied by the PS since its conquest of power in 1981, has the air of a large and successful merchant bank. Most of its leading figures are prominent in government and the regions, its membership is predominantly middle-class and professional, its publications are mainly designed to promote support for government policies: it has travelled a long way since the Epinay congress of 1971.

Organisation, however, is still based on the same structure and with the same peculiarities as in the old days. The basic unit of organisation is the local *section* (town, village or *quartier*). There are some workplace *sections* too, as in the Communist Party, but these have not developed very well – and in any case offend against the humanitarian principle, defended by the current party leader Pierre Mauroy, that an individual's concerns go far wider than his work. The *section* has a bureau and an executive and is represented at *département* level by a delegation in proportion to its membership. The *fédération* (*département* level) is the sovereign unit as far as the local application of party policy is concerned, and its secretariat and bureau are the important regional party leaders. It sends delegates (one each) to the National Convention and to National Congress. For National Congress the *fédération* is represented in proportion to the size of its membership. It has two delegates for the first 250 members, one for each subsequent 250 and one congress vote for every twenty-five members plus one for the '*fédé*'. Thus a *fédé* with 900 members would send five delegates and get 37 congress votes, and one with 12,000 – like Bouches du Rhône (for years the personal fief of the late Gaston Defferre, Mayor of Marseille) – 49 delegates and 481 votes. It holds conferences before National Congresses at which it is decided, on the basis of the strength of voting for different motions, how the *fédé*'s delegates will spread its votes at Congress. The National Convention meets twice a year to provide a contact between the rank and file membership and the leadership of the party. Much more interesting is the National Congress, which meets once every two years and where the great battles between currents of opinion are fought out.

The PS must be one of the only political parties in the world where different tendencies or currents of opinion have a recognised, indeed institutionalised, place – and this despite a rule which actually forbids organised tendencies! New members are asked what *courant* they wish to attach themselves to. The *courants* tend to be organised around leading personalities in the party – *Mitterrandistes, Rocardiens* and so on – but they have a related ideological or political content too: backing for the party leadership, a 'social-democratic' critique of old-fashioned socialism (Rocard), moderation and attachment to working-class traditions and roots (Mauroy), and a more radical Marxist approach (notably *Socialisme et République*, which used to be called CERES – Centre for Socialist Study, Education and Research – and is the most left-wing and organised of the *courants* with its own offices and journal). David Bell and Byron Criddle produced an excellent account of how the *courant* system works in their book on the PS published in 1984.[6] Each *courant* circulates a lengthy motion usually setting out some vast perspective like the future of socialism in which keen-eyed delegates will spot coded messages indicating whether its authors are sympathetic to the market economy ('being ·realistic') or espouse a traditional class orientation. These and various *textes de synthèse* (compromise motions) are discussed, as noted above, at Federal congresses where the *section* representatives vote and determine the composition and political orientation of the *fédération*'s delegation to National Congress. Further attempts at compromise motions and alliances between *courants* are made at Congress – often in lengthy and stormy meetings between leading figures and their lieutenants. Deals are struck and the final vote on the different motions (or compromise motions) determines the proportion of seats on the governing bodies of the party allocated to each *courant*. The 1979 Congress was a particularly animated one with the Mitterrand motion getting 40% of the vote, Rocard's 21% and CERES 15%. Mitterrand formed an alliance with CERES to form the party's ruling majority. In 1990 the feuding between tendencies and the leading personalities in the Party at its Congress at Rennes had so negative an effect on its standing with public opinion that it called forth a rebuke from President Mitterrand. In the end a tortuous compromise was arrived at back in Paris: it linked a 'synthesis' text, saying that the Party would fight against inequalities but at the same time pursue a policy of a strong franc and a 'great national ambition' (a Gaullist phrase) for the country, with a distribution of seats and roles in proportion to the strength of each *courant* at the Congress.

Congress elects the *comité directeur* (its membership of 131 reflecting the proportion of votes cast for each *courant*) which controls the party and determines policy between congresses, meets the Parliamentary group and secures its compliance with party policy, and elects the party's Executive Bureau (twenty-seven members and thirteen substitutes proportional to *courants*). The Executive Bureau is responsible for day-to-day direction of the party and assigns responsibility in specific areas to National Secretaries. In 1988 all forty Executive members and substitutes had an area of responsibility: internal such as finance, organisation or elections, or public such as cultural policy, the environment or women's rights. After the Presidential elections in 1988 the *comité directeur* voted for Pierre Mauroy, the party leader from its traditional bastion in the North, Prime Minister in 1981-4 and Mayor of Lille, as the party's First Secretary over President Mitterrand's preferred candidate Laurent Fabius (ENA graduate and Prime Minister 1984-6). After the Rennes Congress in 1990 a deal was agreed whereby the *comité directeur* would have 34 from the Mauroy/Jospin (Minister of Education in 1990)/Mermaz faction, 30 Fabius supporters, 26 Rocardians, 7 left-wing Socialisme et République – the *courant* of the Minister of Defence Chévènement), 3 for the ever-present Poperen. In the Secretariat Mauroy would remain party leader and his *courant* would have four portfolios and the role of party treasurer, the Fabius group 4 including the title of 'No. 2' as well as the local government and overseas portfolios, the Rocard group 3 including elections and Europe, Socialisme et République[1] (international relations), and Poperen 1. In the days when the PS was in opposition the leading figures in the party were those who held the roles of National Secretaries. However ministerial office is obviously not compatible with full-time party work so, with the PS in government, most of the National Secretaries are secondary figures.

There were, according to Bell and Criddle,[7] some 250,000 party members in 1982, many of whom pay a subscription related to their income. It is difficult to say anything about finance of political parties in France because it is particularly occult, although in 1989, partly as a result of a series of scandals not long before involving alleged local campaign contributions by firms in return for services rendered, the Socialist government proposed to introduce state finance for political parties as in West Germany. The party has a large staff at its Paris headquarters, but it also has the services of hundreds of Parliamentary assistants and personnel on the staff of Socialist town halls, particularly in the *cabinet* of the Mayor. This writer once attended a 'Republican dinner' organised by the local PS in a small town in Brittany, and attended by more than 1,000 people. The event had been organised, including the sale and distribution of tickets (always the biggest task), by the town hall.

The PS is far more democratic in its selection of candidates than other French political parties, where candidates tend to be designated by the leadership in Paris (taking account of local factors of course). Parliamentary candidates are chosen by the members living in the constituency, and a similar rule applies for local elections. This does not stop the Elysée Palace using its influence to find good seats for associates of the President (like Ségolène Royal or Fréderique Bredin). Sometimes the local party objects, but political power usually prevails – over the party if not over the electors, who sometimes prefer the local Socialist dissident who refuses to step down (e.g. Glavany – President's choice – beaten in Hautes Pyrenées in 1988).

There is a safeguard against candidate selection by small local cliques: if membership is less than 1/500th of the electorate, the *Fédération* or national organisation makes the final decision. A special National Congress decides on any Socialist candidature for the Presidency. Since there has never yet been a contest for the Presidential nomination (although there surely will be for 1995), this has not been employed other than for a pre-campaign rally, and not even for that in 1988 because Mitterrand was not the Socialist candidate but the President of all the people!

The Socialist electorate

The most remarkable aspect of Socialist electoral performance since the rise of the PS started in the early 1970s has been the party's success in traditionally Catholic regions, which were virtually 'closed' to the left before then. The accompanying table shows how weak the party used to be in Normandy, Brittany and Alsace-Lorraine and how today it is at or near its national average there. Analyses of electoral behaviour still show practising Catholics voting predominantly for the centre and right, so what is the explanation for this Socialist breakthrough? The answer is that although the party has made gains among both churchgoers and non-churchgoers, the real change has been in the fact that non-churchgoing or nominal Catholics, a sector in which support for the left is strongest, have now become a majority of the entire population. Non-practising Catholics and people with no religion at all represent two-thirds of the French population today.

Table 7.2. CATHOLIC RELIGION AND VOTING SOCIALIST (%)

	1967	1986
Religion in the electorate		
Regular churchgoers	25	14
Occasional churchgoers	22	15
Non-churchgoers (nominal Catholics)	} 53	52
No religion		14
Other religions		5
% of each group voting Socialist		
Regular churchgoers	8	16
Occasional churchgoers	23	30
Non-churchgoers (nominal Catholics)	29	35
No religion	34	47
Other religions		41

The other sociological factor in Socialist success has been related to class. The PS is the strongest party among white-collar employees (42% even in 1986, a not particularly good year for the PS). One of the features of a modern high-technology society is the growth of the tertiary sector (services) and the decline of numbers in agriculture and manual occupations in industry. The PS is sometimes called the 'party of the tertiary sector' because of its massive support among this 'new class' of office workers, technicians and employees in the public services such as health and education, which have expanded so tremendously since the late 1950s. As with trends in religious practice, the PS seems to be in tune with the times. As far as manual workers are concerned, their numbers may be declining (a real problem for the Communist Party, traditionally the working-class party in France), but they are voting Socialist too (an even bigger problem for the PC). In 1978, 36% of workers voted Communist and 27% Socialist. By 1986 the figures were reversed: 20% and 34%.

If one takes the performance of Mitterrand at the second ballot in 1988 – not really a 'socialist vote', admittedly, but more the contemporary limit of a general vote for the left – one finds 74% of manual workers, 65% of younger age groups (25–34), 70% of teachers and health workers, and 74% of non-churchgoing nominal Catholics voting for him.

Table 7.3.   SOCIALIST ELECTORAL SUPPORT BY
REGION – TWO
DECADES OF GROWTH
(Parliamentary elections – 1st ballot)

	1967	*1978*	*1988*
Paris Region (Île de France)	12.4	21.0	32.4
North	28.0	28.2	41.2
Picardy	19.4	21.7	37.3
Upper Normandy	15.2	22.4	40.2
Lower Normandy	12.1	22.7	36.3
Brittany	9.3	24.8	41.0
Loire	13.6	24.2	38.5
Champagne	18.7	23.0	39.1
Lorraine	10.2	26.1	37.6
Alsace	8.7	19.8	30.0
Franche-Comté	26.8	30.7	39.7
Burgundy	30.0	29.6	40.8
Centre	21.5	23.9	36.8
Poitou	18.5	27.9	43.3
Limousin	31.4	24.4	37.9
Auvergne	28.6	26.9	33.8
Rhône-Alps	16.6	25.2	35.0
Aquitaine	27.2	30.7	44.0
Midi-Pyrenées	30.2	34.2	47.7
Languedoc	24.8	25.8	37.6
Provence – Côte d'Azur	22.1	22.0	29.4
Corsica	29.3	29.0	32.0
France	19.0	25.0	37.5

Table 7.4. shows how different social groups voted Socialist in 1978 before the PS was a government party, in 1986 after five years of socialist government, and for Mitterrand in 1988 when he stood for re-election as President. In the 1979 European Parliament election (the analytical value of which is greatly reduced by the vast number of abstentions and their perceived lack of importance in people's lives) there was a marked loss of younger voters by the Socialists to the Greens.

The MRG (Left-Radicals)

The different forms of Radicalism and their history figured in chapter 5 because the Radical Party is an element of the UDF. However, when it

Table 7.4.   VOTE BY SOCIAL GROUP – PS 1978 AND
             1986; MITTERRAND 1988

Total vote	1978 (25%)	1986 (32%)	1988 (34%)
Men	25	30	32
Women	25	34	36
Under 25	25	40	35
25–34	24	41	38
35–64	25	33	29
50–49	24	25	33
65 and over	24	23	33
Farmers	17	21	19
Self-employed	23	21	19
Professions/top management	15	32	19
Junior management/clerical	29	42	39
Manual workers	27	34	42
Not working (retired *et al.*)	26	29	34
Women at home		26	
Students		41	
Private sector employees		31	35
Public sector employees		46	41
Catholic (regular)	13	16	18
Catholic (occasional)	20	30	26
Catholic (nominal)	30	36	39
Other religions		41	
No religion	29	47	41
Primary education only			37
Secondary			33
Higher			29

allied itself with the Christian-Democratic centre in 1972 and went on
to become part of President Giscard's majority, some Radicals preferred
to stay in an alliance of the left. These Radicals, no doubt remembering
that the Radical Party is historically part of the left, the Republican
left that upheld the traditions of the French Revolution, the anti-clerical
left that regarded the Catholic Church as the enemy of reason and the
upholder of an archaic order based on the divine right of monarchs,
remembering also that their seats in the traditional south-western

strongholds of the republican left depend on socialist and communist votes at the second ballot, preferred to form their own separate party, the MRG (*Mouvement des Radicaux de Gauche*). It is closely allied to, indeed dependent upon, the Socialist Party and, as part of the Union of the Left, it signed the *Programme commun* with the Socialists and Communists. It was also the first to leave the *Programme commun* when the PCF demanded that it be updated and presented a list of outrageous demands (see chapter 6).

The MRG is a very small party – mainly local notables. Its Parliamentary seats derive from arrangements with the PS who allow the MRG a clear run in certain constituencies. It is therefore permissible to count its votes into the socialist total expressed as 'Socialists and allies'. Just like the official Radical Party, it sees itself as the true representative of radicalism and as the defender of progressive, republican and libertarian values inside its alliance. The two wings of radicalism show no signs of merging although they do sit in the same group in the Senate, the home of traditionalism, and the European Parliament, the home of unconvincing alliances.

The extreme Left

Since this chapter is entitled 'Socialists', it is permissible to find a little space in it to mention at least some of the parties and groups of the extreme left in France, which consider themselves to be the 'true' socialists. There are various Trotskyist sects – notably *Lutte ouvrière*, led by Arlette Laguiller, veteran of three Presidential elections where she scores around 2% and addresses the nation in her election broadcasts as '*Travailleuses, travailleurs*' ('working women, working men'), and the *Ligue Communiste Révolutionnaire* led by Alain Krivine, also twice a Presidential candidate including when he was on national service in the army in 1969 but was nevertheless allowed to advocate revolution on television. There is also a very extreme Trotskyist sect called MPPT (Movement for a Workers' Party) which produced a sixty-seven-year-old retired family allowance official with a long record as a Trotskyist activist (even meriting the pseudonym Lambert) as Presidential candidate in 1988 (0.4%). The best-known party of the extreme left, however, is the PSU (Unified Socialist Party).

The heyday of the PSU was the late 1960s when it was the only party supporting the students in the Events of May and its leaders included Michel Rocard, then a revolutionary firebrand but by 1988 a notably social-democratic and moderate Prime Minister, and Pierre Mendès-France, the brightest star in the Radical firmament, a former Prime Minister who had extricated France from its Vietnam war in 1954. The PSU was formed in 1958 by a merger of various discontented groups: Socialists discontented with the Mollet government's colonialist policy in Algeria (these were called the PSA – the Autonomous Socialist Party), discontented Radicals who supported Mendès, and some Communists and ex-Communists who found the PCF too sectarian. There were also some Christian Socialists from the *Jociste* (Young Christian Workers) movement. In 1968 the PSU enthusiastically supported the students in revolt; it was willing, unlike the Communists, the unions and the Socialists, to embrace a revolutionary alternative and, to the intense and enduring annoyance of the Communist Party, it led a great revolutionary rally at Charléty stadium with the distinguished figure of Mendès-France present. Their candidates got 4% of the vote in the 1968 election and Rocard, as a revolutionary candidate for the Presidency, got 3.8% in 1969. Still arguing for revolution, he also won an extraordinary by-election against the Gaullist ex-Prime Minister Couve de Murville in 1969. The PSU has no pretensions to being a reformist Parliamentary party. Its finest hour after 1968 was the famous work-in at the Lip watch factory in 1973. PSU activists in the CFDT (formerly Catholic but now socialist union), supporting workers' control (*autogestion*) were the leading figures in the prolonged but eventually unsuccessful attempt to keep the factory going after bankruptcy.

In 1974 the PSU split. Michel Rocard persuaded the party to support Mitterrand in the Presidential election, and to attend the Socialist conference in 1974 and argue the case for *autogestion*; he decided that 'the Socialist revolution is not felt in France by the workers to be their great hope', and led some 3,000 PSU members off to join the PS. The influence of *autogestionnaires* and Christians in the PS has been considerable. Since then Rocard has become the leader of the moderate, pragmatic wing of the PS, popular with the general public; while not regarded as a 'true socialist' by the majority in the PS, he is nevertheless a leading candidate to succeed Mitterrand. In the 1980s another leader of the PSU was lured away to join Mitterrand: this time it was Huguette Bouchardeau, PSU candidate in the Presidential elections of 1981 (1%), who subsequently became Minister for the Environment. The majority of the PSU was opposed to this move, and so she left the party. (If the Environment Ministry had been able to control nuclear power it might have been different – like the Greens, the PSU is anti-nuclear.)

The PSU today is a sad little party with hardly any members and no staff except for one part-time assistant ('We don't like bureaucracy'). They continue to support 'social struggles' (mainly strikes like the big one at Peugeot in 1989). They supported the Communist dissident Pierre Juquin in the 1988 Presidential election. In the Euro elections of 1989, they supported the Greens with whom they share many ideas, especially outright opposition to nuclear weapons. They consider the Trotskyist left to range from the sectarian (LO) to the dangerously deranged (MPPT), though they work with Alain Krivine in strikes and demonstrations.

The current debate on the extreme left concerns the 'New Left' and relations with the Greens. The New Left is a federation of the PSU and Pierre Juquin's organisation, with its international supporters like the Italian Democrazia Proletaria and some elements of the German Grünen. The objection to outright support for or even merger with the Greens is the latter's 'neither right nor left' position (see chapter 9). The Greens are preoccupied by the contradiction man/nature rather than the contradiction capital/labour, which inevitably interests Marxists as well. What the New Left would like is a political force to promote a socialist, green, *autogestionnaire*, feminist and anti-racist programme. The Greens, notably absent from 'social struggles', would be valuable partners for much of this programme but not for socialism.

NOTES

1. *Socialisme et communisme français*, Paris: Armand Colin, 1962.
2. *Marxism in Modern France*, New York: Columbia University Press, 1966, p. 33.
3. *Crisis and compromise*, London, Longmans, Green, 1964, p. 99.
4. *The French Socialist Party: Resurgence and Victory*, Oxford University Press, 1984, p. 2.
5. Jean-Louis Quermonne, 'Un gouvernement présidentiel ou un gouvernement partisan', *Pouvoirs* 20 (1982), p. 97.
6. *The French Socialist Party*, op. cit., ch. 10.
7. *The French Socialist Party*, op. cit., p. 198.

8

COMMUNISM

It is difficult to write about Communism with objective neutrality; if you are not a Communist, you are almost certain to be anti-Communist. Waldeck Rochet, leader of the French Communist Party in the late 1960s, said: 'Communists are not members of a mysterious sect or secret society.' Yet to Western non-Communists that is exactly what they seem to be. To the inheritors of an intellectual tradition which stresses tolerance and the freedom to criticise and oppose, the total unanimity of a Communist congress (at any rate of the pre-Gorbachev variety), the five-hour speeches couched in alien jargon, the constant self-congratulation that the party is always right, are quite literally incomprehensible. In a country where there is no systematic persecution or deprivation inflicted on the working class, what is the relevance of a disciplined revolutionary party anyway? In a country where revolution is no longer even on the Communist agenda, why have such a party at all?

It appears that some of these thoughts may have been in the minds of the French electors because the Communist Party, having won 26–28% of the vote after the Liberation in 1945–6, stuck at around 20% for the first twenty years of the Fifth Republic, then dropped in the 1980s to 15% in 1981, plunging below 7% in the Presidential election of 1988 – the lowest share of the popular vote in the entire history of the Party since its foundation in 1920.

The PC has nevertheless been an extremely important strand in the politics of a country in which revolution is a powerful historical myth. It stands apart from other French political parties in its capacity to organise, the training and discipline of its cadres, the commitment of its activists, and its distinctive policies, notably its loyalty to and admiration for the Soviet Union – especially in its pre-Gorbachev form.

History of the Parti communiste français (PCF)

The history of the PCF is often presented as a series of abrupt changes of line. Like a weathercock on a steeple, the Party would suddenly be observed pointing in exactly the opposite direction from a moment before. Abrupt switches of line occur and are implemented with remarkable discipline. In 1977-8 when the Communists decided to break off the Union of the Left alliance with the Socialists which had been their central policy for the whole of the 1970s, an American observer expressed to me his grudging admiration for the tough way they took a decision that was extremely unpopular with a lot of active members, and imposed it without a backward glance. When a switch of line occurs, the Party is always right – and always has been. The history of the party, as we shall see in a moment, can be seen in a similar way: a series of alternating phases, hard-line and uncompromising phases followed by conciliatory phases.

The Party was formed, as the last chapter related, when the Socialist Party decided at the Congress of Tours in December 1920 to accept the invitation to join Lenin's Communist International by subscribing to the famous '21 conditions' – a list that includes clandestine organisation, rejection of 'bourgeois legality' and patriotism, a purge of reformist elements, agitation in the army, and compliance with all decisions of the International. French Communism is therefore, in Annie Kriegel's phrase, 'the grafting of Russian Bolshevism on the body of French Socialism'.[1] Although many Socialists refused, like Léon Blum, to join the new party, it inherited most of the big working-class socialist *fédérations* of the Paris region, all Socialist assets such as the newspaper *L'Humanité*, and much of rural Socialism too, that is to say peasant anti-establishment and anti-clerical hostility. 'In the South', wrote André Siegfried many years ago, 'the Communist is often no more than the reddest of Republicans.' The Mediterranean farmer who shot dead an entire family of British tourists, the Drummonds, in 1952 because they were on his land was a Party member. The first few years are known as the period of 'Bolshevisation' in which it adopted, under control from Moscow, the ideology and organisation of the Lenin model, as modified by Stalin after Lenin's death. The appropriate leadership for this type of organisation was achieved in the person of Maurice Thorez, a miner from the north elected Secretary-General in 1930, schooled and supported by a team of advisers from the Executive Committee of Comintern (the Communist International). The degree of control by Comintern during the 1920s and 1930s was total. Edward Mortimer reports that the 1934 united front with the Socialists was agreed upon cabled instructions from Moscow.[2]

From 1920 to the mid-1930s the Party was at its most extreme. It purged, it expelled, it denounced. It was also considered subversive by the French state and many leading Communists, including Thorez, were rounded up and imprisoned. The strategy of 'class against class' was followed. Everyone was an enemy – the Socialists were 'social-fascists'. The bourgeois state would be 'smashed in all its parts because each part serves only the task of crushing the workers'.

The riots of the extreme right in Paris in February 1934, the rise of Fascism all over Europe and the change of attitude by the Communist International at its seventh Congress in 1935 brought about a change of line. A united front against Fascism was formed in France by Communists, Socialists and Radicals. Known as the Popular Front, this alliance won a famous victory at the 1936 election. The Communist vote doubled to 15%, Parliamentary representation increased from twelve seats to seventy-two, and membership, down in the Bolshevisation period, recovered. As in other countries, many leading intellectuals rallied to Communism during this period because it seemed the only effective and disciplined force against Fascism in Europe. These were the days of the Spanish Civil War and the International Brigade. Hitler and Mussolini sent arms to Franco, the democracies (including France under the Popular Front government) did nothing, and only Russia sent assistance to Republican Spain. The Nazi-Soviet pact in 1939 unleashed a tidal wave of dismay among anti-Fascists, but the PCF loyally accepted the new Moscow line and called on the French people not to fight in an 'imperialist war'.

What happened in the early days of the Second World War and the Occupation is much contested. Communist publications advocated neutrality, and Mortimer gives the Party a reasonably clean record on the charge of collaboration with the Nazis.[3] In June 1941, repudiating the Nazi-Soviet pact, Hitler invaded Russia. Communists say they joined the Resistance before this but, whether that is true or not, there is no doubt that their qualities of organisation and discipline enabled them to play a heroic part in the Resistance and in the battle to liberate Paris in 1944. Many activists were deported, imprisoned, executed or killed in action.

After the Liberation, Thorez returned to Paris from Moscow where he had spent the war years and entered de Gaulle's provisional government. Communist resistance fighters were ordered to disarm, and the Communist ministers were loyal government colleagues, urging workers to increase output and not to strike. Party membership (800,000) and electoral support (28.6%) reached an all-time peak in 1946. There was no question of revolution. Edward Mortimer points out that although the history of the PCF is a history of alternating hard-line and conciliatory phases, there are certain fixed points, which date from the Liberation period.[4] One is that the Party, to some extent in the Popular Front period and to a greater extent during the war, became a national party, attached to values such as patriotism. It has never ceased to be a national party and it is incorrect since the Liberation simply to regard the PCF as the agent of the Soviet Union. The second fixed point is the abandonment of revolution by violence as a method or a goal. There would appear to have been an opportunity for such action in 1944–5; France was in chaos, Communist activists were armed and well-organised, and the Party was at the height of its prestige and popularity. Why was there no attempt at a revolutionary seizure of power? One answer of course is that the American army was present. Another more fundamental reason was that it was already apparent that Communism could not be imposed by force on any nation with any tradition of individual liberty and democracy without the support of the Red Army – support which was not available in Western Europe. At all events, the PCF did not make in 1945, and has not made since, any attempt at violent or revolutionary overthrow of the state.

Just as the honeymoon between the wartime allies of East and West did not last, neither did that between French Communists and their government partners. Prime Minister Ramadier dismissed the Communist ministers on 4 May 1947, and the PCF did not participate in government again until 1981. It remains the only Communist Party in a major Western country to play a part in government.

The Cold War in international affairs which began in 1947 was matched by a cold war in France between the PCF and the rest of the French political system. Another period of intransigence and isolation had begun. As always in these periods, there were signals of exaggerated loyalty to the Soviet Union. For example the Party supported the Soviet repression of the Hungarian uprising in 1956. Like its support for the Nazi-Soviet pact in 1939, this line lost it many members and supporters. The PCF opposed the Fourth Republic, the return to power of General de Gaulle, the Fifth Republic, the constitutional amendment of 1962 on direct Presidential elections: 'Since 1948', wrote Herbert Lüthy, 'the Communist Party has counted only as a dead weight . . . and has sterilised the votes, wishes and demands of five million Frenchmen.'[5]

In November 1962 the second-ballot electoral pact between the parties of the left against all-conquering Gaullism marked the beginning of a long new conciliatory phase which culminated in the 1970s Union of the Left – but the PCF never really stopped being a traditional

'Stalinist' party. Thorez died in 1964. A teacher of revolution, a devoted Leninist, an organiser, a disciplinarian, utterly dedicated to Soviet Communism – the Party was his whole life. The PCF is still in a very real sense the party of Maurice Thorez. Unlike other European Communist parties – in Italy or Spain, for example – it never caught the mood of 'destalinisation' which Khrushchev tried unsuccessfully to inaugurate with his secret speech to the Twentieth Congress of the Soviet Communist Party in 1956. Other parties in China, Cuba, Italy and, with tragic consequences in 1968, Czechoslovakia were claiming the right to choose their own road to socialism. The Soviet Union, under the long 'Stalinist' reign of Brezhnev (1965–82), did not change very much either until the amazing Gorbachev reforms introduced in the late 1980s. However, there has been no *perestroika* in the PCF.

Thorez' successor, Waldeck-Rochet, despite his solid training at the Lenin school in Moscow and his use of standard Stalinist forms of speech and jargon, was incontestably a moderate. He wanted to end the PCF's isolation. The Party under his leadership supported the Mitterrand Presidential candidature of 1965 (chapter 12), made a harmonious and effective electoral pact with the FGDS (Socialists and Radicals) in 1967 (chapter 13), and in February 1968 signed a common declaration with the Socialists setting out points of agreement for a programme of government and points of difference – a process which, renewed in the 1970s, produced the *Programme commun* and the Union of the Left. The emergence of the Union of the Left is related in chapter 6 – as well as the setbacks and vicissitudes that beset that enterprise, particularly in the periods 1968–9 and 1977–81. The Events of May 1968, which appeared to be revolutionary but which were neither started by the PCF nor controlled by it, brought out the Stalinist reflexes of the Party as it reacted to criticism of its role as 'vanguard of the proletariat'. Support for 'normalisation' (the suppression of liberal tendencies) in Czechoslovakia after the Soviet invasion of 1968 revived old fears about the true nature of French Communism. The disunity of the left in the 1969 Presidential elections revealed the collapse of the spirit of cooperation that had existed between Communists and Socialists in the mid-1960s.

Waldeck-Rochet, physically and spiritually broken, it was said, by the invasion of Czechoslovakia and its damaging effect on the image of Communism, was incapacitated by illness and replaced as secretary-general by Georges Marchais. The long reign of Marchais has encompassed both the Union of the Left and its abandonment. It has seen the decline of the electoral audience of the PCF to the point of marginality. It has been a period both of profound change and of profound resistance to change. Marchais, with his aggressive and sarcastic manner, never admitting a mistake and in his heyday not unappealing, strangely enough, on television, is absolutely in the traditional Stalinist mould of Communist Party leader. He was born in 1920 in a Norman working-class family, joined the party at the beginning of the cold war phase of isolation in 1947, was a protégé of Jeanette Thorez, and a member of the Central Committee of the Party from the Thorez days in 1956 onwards. The change has been the acceptance at the 1976 Congress of the Party that the Leninist concept of 'dictatorship of the proletariat' (the phase that is supposed to follow the revolutionary overthrow of capitalism) was no longer an essential step on the road to socialism, and that the Soviet Union was no longer the model for the kind of socialism the Party wished to establish in France. The resistance to change lies in the continuing failure to 'destalinise' – to open up the party to internal debate and acceptance of democratic values as the West's most important Communist Party, in Italy, did in the 1970s trend to 'Eurocommunism'.

Under the leadership of Marchais, the Party continued with the Union of the Left approach. In the period 1972–7 it seemed that it had finally accepted that to win power in a democratic country it had to stop advocating what was unacceptable to the electors – hence the statement, backed by periodic measured criticisms of persecution in the Soviet Union, that the Soviet model was no longer its objective in France. However, as we saw in chapter 6, it became apparent that, unlike in previous periods of conciliatory behaviour, the Party was not making any electoral gains. Gains for the left in the 1970s went to the rejuvenated Socialist Party. The only election in the late 1970s to bring any benefit to the PCF was the 1977 municipal elections. These were fought on united lists in virtually every important town (see chapter 14), so gains for the left brought Communist councillors and mayors in places where they had never been known before.

After the municipal elections of 1977 were over, there came the extraordinary decision to break off the Union of the Left (see chapter 6). For the next four years the PCF was just as hostile to the Socialists as in the previous 'cold war' phase. The achievements of the Soviet Union were described, in a famous Marchais phrase, as 'globally positive'. Marchais on Moscow TV approved the Soviet invasion of Afghanistan in 1979–80. However, after the disastrous first ballot in 1981, when the

Party's Presidential candidate, Marchais, got only 15% of the vote, the decision was taken to support Mitterrand at the second ballot, to seek a second-ballot pact at the subsequent Parliamentary elections, and to enter the government. Charles Fiterman, Marchais' deputy, became Minister of Transport and there were three other Communist Ministers: Jack Ralite (Health – later Employment), Marcel Rigout (Training) and Anicet Le Pors (Civil Service and Administrative Reform). To join the government, the Party had to agree to a joint statement with the Socialists covering respect for France's alliances, disarmament negotiations to include the Soviet SS20s (subsequently of course eliminated by the Reagan-Gorbachev agreement) and the withdrawal of Soviet troops from Afghanistan. They further declared that they would work 'in government with unflinching solidarity'.

In 1983 the Government abandoned its policy of a 'dash for growth' in the face of rising inflation, international pressure on the balance of payments, and rising costs in industry, and a policy of austerity, including a wage-freeze, was imposed. The PCF was opposed to this change. By a cruel irony, however, it became identified with a government becoming increasingly unpopular. When Mitterrand appointed a new Prime Minister, Laurent Fabius, in 1984, the PC left the government and became an opposition party again.

'A period in French political life has ended,' said the motion put to the Party's twenty-fifth Congress in 1985: 'not just the three years of government since 1981 but a much longer period – almost a quarter of a century – in which, upon the idea of a Common Programme of Government, were progressively built the plan and then the victory of a government of the left'. Fiterman described the Congress as witnessing 'the final liberation of the PC', which was at last, as other speakers put it, 'out of the Union of the Left rut'. This change of direction was not accepted by all. In 1978 a significant number of leading Communists expressed their bitter disappointment at the breaking of the Union of the Left. Important Communists have been forced off the Central Committee or out of the Party: Jean Elleinstein, a leading intellectual; Henri Fiszbin, Communist leader in Paris but, after a period as a dissident, elected to Parliament on the Socialist list in 1986; ex-Minister Marcel Rigout; and Pierre Juquin, a leading member of the Central Committee, who had been expressing his disapproval of the party line for some years and became in 1988 a dissident Presidential candidate. In 1985 Juquin told the journal *Nouvel Observateur*: 'There was a period in the history of my party which for me was full of hope: the

Eurocommunist period. At that time, after a long preparation which
went back to Waldeck Rochet, the PCF tried to modify its strategy, to
change itself, to be better adapted to French society, to detach itself from
the soviet model. . . . After 1981, participation in government made me
hope the Party would again find the strength to change. It didn't
happen.'

Party organisation and style

All Communist Parties since the Russian Revolution have been
organised on the basis of 'Democratic Centralism'. The lower echelons

Table 8.1. COMMUNIST ELECTORAL PERFORMANCE, 1920–89
(1st ballot – Parliamentary elections unless indicated)

	Million votes	%
Third Republic		
1924	0.8	9.5
1928	1.1	11.3
1932	0.8	8.4
1936	1.5	15.3
Fourth Republic		
1945	5.0	26.0
1946 (June)	5.1	25.9
1946 (Nov.)	5.4	28.2
1951	4.9	25.6
1956	5.5	25.7
Fifth Republic		
1958	3.9	19.0
1962	4.0	21.8
1967	5.0	22.5
1968	4.4	20.0
1969 (Presidential) Duclos	4.8	21.5
1973	5.1	21.4
1978	5.8	20.6
1979 (Euro)	4.2	20.4
1981 (Presidential) Marchais	4.4	15.5
1981	4.0	16.1
1984 (Euro)	2.2	11.2
1986	2.7	9.7
1988 (Presidential) Lajoinie	2.1	6.8
1988	2.8	11.3
1989 (Euro)	1.4	7.7

of the Party elect the higher ones (in the form of a list of candidates approved at the higher level), and decisions made at a higher level are binding on all the lower ones.

To become a member of the PCF you join a cell (*cellule*; note the evocation of the party's clandestine revolutionary past) – at your place of work if possible. There are workshop cells, production-line cells, office cells. The party rules state that a member's 'first duty' is to join a workplace cell. Other parties organise themselves primarily at the level of local communities, with members of diverse interests and occupations, but the PC sees itself as the spearhead of the class struggle and in the front line of militant action at work. Where workplace cells are not in existence, there are local and rural cells. The members of the cell elect the leadership of the cell and conduct local party activities. The cells in a large factory, an industrial estate, a locality or perhaps a large social housing development are grouped into Sections. Cell delegates form the Section Conference. This elects the leadership of the Section which coordinates Party activity in its area. The next higher level of the Party is the *département* Federation. Its Conference is composed of Section delegates and elects the Federal Bureau. The Federation has an office and permanent staff, and the Federal Secretary is a very important figure in party organisation and his appointment must be ratified by the Central Committee. Federal delegates attend Party Congress, the supreme national body of the Party, which meets at least every three years (1987 was the twenty-sixth Congress since the Party's foundation in 1920). Congress proclaims important changes in the party line – such as the deletion from party objectives in 1976 of the Leninist notion of 'Dictatorship of the Protetariat' or the closing of the 'Union of the Left' period in 1985. It also elects the Central Committee, the supreme governing body between Congresses. At the time of writing, there are 136 Central Committee members, all elected almost unanimously from a list of 136 candidates (although *L'Humanité* of 7 December 1987 did note that 'two votes were cast for our comrade Claude Fischer, and as for Martial Bourquin he obtained the votes of two delegates'). The Central Committee elects from among its members the real leadership of the Party, the *Bureau politique* (currently twenty-three members, four of them women), the Secretariat (eight members, one a woman), and the Secretary-General (it has been Georges Marchais, aged seventy in 1990, since 1972). The members of the *Bureau politique* and the Secretariat have specific areas of responsibility: party organisation, international relations (these two jobs are always assigned to key secretariat members); liaison with Federations and the Parliamentary groups; publicity and communication, local councils and elections, the party newspapers, party education, party activity in different sectors: intellectuals, factories, immigrants, women, the young; economic and social policy, party finance, the Institute for Marxist Research, and so on. The Secretary-General of France's largest Union organisation, the CGT (General Confederation of Labour – in 1990 led by Henri Krasucki), is invariably a member of the *Bureau politique.*

French political parties have a long tradition of making exaggerated claims about their membership. In 1979, before the catastrophic decline in its electoral support, the PC claimed 700,000 members, two-thirds of them men, half of them working class, 60% under forty-five – this writer would be astonished if they actually had half that number of members. However, the great strength of the Party over the years has lain in the existence of a core of several thousand dedicated activists, trained and disciplined, capable of working in a most efficient and organised manner. In May 1968, when the whole country was in the grip of a general strike, Communist militants were able, within a few hours of *Bureau Politique* decisions, to put up posters nationwide indicating the new party line.

Many writers have commented on the 'total character' of Communist Party membership. Annie Kriegel has analysed the PCF as a '*contre-société*' or 'counter-community',[6] a private world with its own party schools, leisure activities, youth groups, books and newspapers, protecting its members against contamination from outside or assimilation. Edward Upward in his novels about life in the British Communist Party[7] in the 1930s paints a similar picture of Communist activity filling his entire life including marriage and personal relationships. Gabriel Almond, in *The Appeals of Communism*,[8] written in the 1950s, linked this total immersion to abnormal personality traits like exceptional feelings of hostility or self-rejection. A famous collection of essays called *The God that Failed*,[8] written by prominent intellectuals who eventually abandoned Communism, repeatedly recalled the 'emotional fervour and intellectual bliss'[9] of being admitted to a world of total certainty and all-demanding dedication. However, one should not be misled into supposing that the PCF is simply an army of disciplined robots or a closed secret sect. The job of explaining the correctness of the party line to members has always been taken seriously and, if it involves such matters as local tactical alliances with noted anti-Communists, can result in long and stormy meetings. There have been considerable debate, dissent and tension in the Party ever since the decision to abandon the

Union of the Left was taken in 1978, with important individuals and even Federations (like the Haute-Vienne in the Limousin region) refusing publicly to toe the line.

Some of the most important institutions in this private and all-embracing world, if that is what it is, are the schools for the education of activists. Federations run evening classes but there is a central party school at Choisy-le-Roi near Paris, which runs one-month and four-month courses. A 'four-month-school' activist is marked out for higher responsibilities. The students work intensively on Marxism, the history of the PCF and the Soviet Communist Party, party policy, and also art, literature and science as presented by the Party's leading intellectuals. Of 1,700 delegates at the 1987 Congress, over 300 (including fifty-one women) had done the four-month school, 450 the one-month school, and 650 Federation or 'elementary' schools.

The headquarters of the Party is at Place du Colonel Fabien (named after a Communist wartime Resistance hero) in the XX *arrondissement* of Paris (the east end). It is a remarkable curving glass and concrete building, suggesting the Hammer and Sickle, by the famous Communist Brazilian architect Oscar Niemeyer. Paris City Council includes tours of the building among tourist activities on offer – although the tour is accompanied everywhere by a party worker and kept away from the offices: it is strictly architectural, but very interesting.

The published accounts of the PCF – and at least, unlike other parties, they publish something – claim central income and expenditure in 1986 of Frs 124 million about half of which is spent on staff including members of Parliament. The most important element of income is what is called the *ristourne des élus*. Communist members of Parliament, Parliamentary assistants, secretaries and Group officials, and many Communist Councillors receive substantial salaries from the state or local council. They hand these salaries over to the Party and in return are paid the salary of a skilled manual worker. In 1986 the Party received Frs 66 million from this source and paid out Frs 24 million. The Party employs several hundred permanent staff at national and Federation level but most of these are in reality on the payroll of a union, a local authority (perhaps in the Mayor's *cabinet*), or some other body. That is one of the reasons why it has been so important for the PCF to make pacts with the Socialists to preserve Union of the Left local Councils. There is no mention in the published accounts of the companies owned or controlled by the PCF in publishing (the party newspaper *L'Humanité*, for example), in property development or trading consortia that deal with Communist councils, or in East-West trade. The Party, despite its reduced electoral circumstances, was initially opposed to any suggestion of state finance for political parties – an idea being actively considered by the Socialist government in 1989 – but then supported it.

The other elements of income, according to the Party's own publications, are membership subscriptions and special fund-raising efforts like the famous annual *fête de L'Humanité*. This, held in a gigantic park in the Paris suburbs in early September, is well worth a visit. You get a keynote speech from the Secretary-General, pop concerts, stands from all international fraternal organisations from the Communist parties of Eastern Europe to Sinn Fein, and stands from all the Federations in France, the latter frequently in the form of regional restaurants. If you want to enjoy a glass of excellent champagne, try the Federation of the Marne, for *omelette aux cêpes* the Federation of Corrèze. The avenues between the stalls were named, in 1989, after heroes of the French Revolution so that one would hear announcements that the retrieval point for lost children was in the Avenue Robespierre. Incidentally one of the many things that makes the PCF different from other parties is that it alone reveres Robespierre, the dictator during the Terror – a name that was not allowed even to be mentioned during President Mitterrand's bi-centenary extravaganza of July 1989.

The PCF is linked to various associated organisations. The CGT, France's largest union movement with about 1.5 million members and a presence in all branches of industry and public services, is often described as 'the Communist union' or as being under Communist control. The PC has indeed fought very hard to control the CGT, and in 1947 split it in order to do so. However, French unions, unlike British ones, are not affiliated to political parties. Nevertheless, Communist members are expected to join the CGT and they are the preponderant element among the activists, and the CGT leader, in 1990 Henri Krasucki, is always a member of the *Bureau politique* of the PCF. The daily Communist paper *L'Humanité* always gives out the CGT/party line on any industrial dispute in progress. There is an organisation of small peasant farmers – MODEF – linked to the PCF, and there are peace organisations, youth movements (*Jeunesse Communiste*), students' and women's organisations. It is traditionally dominant in the primary teachers' union SNI.

The Communist Party publishes a number of newspapers, monthlies and quarterlies. There is the Central Committee's daily *L'Humanité*, which it is a prime function of party activists to promote, and which probably sells over 100,000 copies and the weekly *L'Humanité Dimanche*, glossier and lighter. *L'Humanité* is crammed with communiqués from the Central committee, Soviet CP declarations, resolutions and motions. It gives the party line on domestic, industrial and foreign issues. There are Communist regional dailies too: *La Liberté* in the north, *La Marseillaise* in Marseille, and *L'Echo du Centre* (Limoges). It has an agricultural weekly *La Terre* (the party is traditionally strong among the small peasant farmers of the centre and south) and a theoretical monthly *Cahiers du Communisme*. Finally the publishing house Editions Sociales Messidor publishes the writings of Marx, Lenin and other prophets, books by party leaders and intellectuals, books on party policy and CGT handbooks; in short it satisfies almost every need for political, practical, literary, economic, philosophical, even musical material that an activist might feel.

Communist support

Table 8.2. (overleaf) says it all. Just as big ice creams and small ice creams melt at the same rate, Communist support has faded steadily, rapidly and more or less evenly across the country in strong areas and in weak ones. The loss has been most dramatic from the Party's point of view in the Paris region, the Communist heartland. Everything written in this chapter about party organisation and party finance belongs, in a way, to the past – the PC retains the trappings and the apparatus of a major party but it has ceased to be one.

The traditional areas of strength for the PCF have been primarily the zones of heavy industry in the north, the east and the Paris region; also, by contrast, the rural areas of the centre and south-west where the small peasant farm has always predominated, where the Catholic Church has been weak, where there is a historic tradition of left-wing voting (the Limousin has voted for the left since universal suffrage began in 1848), and where the Communists distinguished themselves in the Resistance. These are, of course, exactly the sectors where one would expect to see decline. Traditional heavy industries like coal and steel have greatly reduced in size, industrial workers form a diminishing percentage of the population, the peasant farmer is ageing and disappearing, memories of the Resistance have faded, and the popular Communist notables of that period are dead. The table shows clearly how the Communist vote has held up best in the more backward rural areas (parts of Limousin and

Table 8.2. COMMUNIST PARTY – TWO DECADES OF
DECLINE

	1967	1978	1981 (Marchais)	1986	1988 (Lajoinie)
	%	%	%	%	%
Paris Region (Île de France)	30 (2)*	24	17	10	7
North	27 (6)	28	22	15	11 (2)
Picardy	28 (4)	28	21	13	9 (5)
Upper Normandy	27 (6)	26	18	11	8
Lower Normandy	12	11	9	5	4
Brittany	17	15	11	7	5
Loire	14	12	9	6	4
Champagne	23	23	16	11	6
Lorraine	19	17	14	7	5
Alsace	9	7	5	2	1
Franche-Comté	15	15	12	6	4
Burgundy	21	18	14	9	6
Centre	22	21	15	10	7
Poitou	20	17	13	9	6
Limousin	31 (1)	30	23	19	12 (1)
Auvergne	20	19	15	11	10 (3)
Rhône-Alps	21	19	14	8	6
Aquitaine	18	19	15	9	7
Midi-Pyrénées	16	18	15	8	7
Languedoc	29 (3)	28	22	14	10 (3)
Provence – Côte d'Azur	28 (4)	27	21	12	9 (5)
Corsica	12	16	16	9	8
France	23	21	15	10	7
By social category					
Men		24	17	19	7
Women		19	14	7	6
Manual workers		36	30	20	12
Under-25s		28	24	6	9
Retired		17	12	11	7
No religion		49	39	20	19

*Strongest regions in brackets.

Auvergne) and among the elderly, and declined most in the economically dynamic regions (Paris, Normandy, Rhône) and the younger age
groups.

Against this catastrophic loss, within a decade, of half the electors
that voted Commmunist (5.8 million at the Parliamentary election

of 1978, 2.8 million at the Parliamentary election of 1988), there are two positive points for the PC. One is the very slight improvement in the electoral situation since the disaster of the Presidential election of 1988 – an increase to 11% (on a low national turnout) at the Parliamentary election that followed it (see chapter 13), the retention of enough seats to have a Parliamentary group (and the staff to go with it), and the retention of most Communist town halls in 1989. The European Parliament elections of 1989, however, saw the Party back under 8%. The other positive point, already alluded to, is the survival of a large part of Communist municipal power, which is the life-blood of the party machine. There are Communist mayors in sixty-eight of the 390 large towns (over 20,000 population) in the country and many in smaller ones. In the 'red belt' – the inner ring of industrial suburbs round Paris, which has been the most important element of Communist support ever since the 1930s – the Party retains thirty-seven out of 123 town halls (they had fifty-four in 1977). They have two *conseil général* (county council) Presidencies, powerful sources of power and patronage since the Decentralisation laws of 1982 (see chapter 14) – both are in the 'red belt' – and ten of their twenty-seven remaining Parliamentary seats are there too.

Municipal power is vital to the PCF. France has a somewhat clientelist political culture in which well-entrenched local notables maintain a personal vote through services rendered – including effective local administration. Government ministers have staff in their *cabinets* specifically to look after constituency and local matters. Much of Communist electoral success is achieved through the popularity and local reputation of municipal leaders – an excellent example is Jacques Rimbault, Central Committee member, Mayor and *député* for Bourges (Centre region). Additionally, there is what is known as the 'Communist system': the maintenance of the party machine and electoral support through control of municipal services (allocation of housing and jobs, council grants to Communist-related organisations – in particular support for the CGT), the employment of permanent party staff as mayors, *maires-adjoints* or members of the mayor's staff. Municipal employees can be directed to a variety of tasks. In 1985 there was a strike at SKF in the Paris suburbs, with some violent demonstrations. Most of those arrested were employees of a Communist council (not the local one), and municipal vehicles had been used to transport the men and projectiles used in the protest. In recent years the grim determination of the PCF to hang on at a municipal level has been revealed in various ways from its willingness to carry on at local level the Union of the Left alliance rejected at national level to increasing instances of electoral fraud, especially in the 'red belt', where a number of results favourable to the Communists have been annulled.

What kind of party?

The PCF is an old-fashioned Stalinist party. If it had been in power in Eastern Europe it would, one senses, have been like the parties in East Germany or Czechoslovakia before they collapsed rather than the more liberal Hungarians. There has been no *perestroika*. The Party is always right and no dissidents are tolerated. The basic elements of its doctrine have always been unwavering support for, and admiration of, the Soviet Union, a belief in the superiority of Socialism and a conviction that capitalism is in crisis and doomed to fail (the latter point illustrated by statistics on drugs, crime, discrimination and poverty in Western countries, especially the United States). Its admiration for the Soviet Union has not always been completely uncritical. During the 1960s and the Union of the Left phase in the 1970s it occasionally criticised Soviet persecution of intellectuals, and once, when there were some pictures on French television of a Soviet labour camp, went as far as to say:

> If reality corresponds to the broadcast pictures and if no public rebuttal is forthcoming from the Soviet authorities, the *Bureau politique* will express its most profound surprise and its most formal disapproval. Such unjustifiable acts can only prejudice Socialism and the renown which the Soviet Union has justly acquired in the eyes of the workers and peoples of the world . . .

During the Union of the Left period, the PCF also declared that the Soviet Union was not a model for the kind of socialism it wanted to introduce in France. Criticism of the Soviet Union, invariably wrapped around with protestations of admiration for its achievements and condemnation of 'anti-Sovietism', is normally intended as a signal to opinion in France that the Party is in a cooperative phase. Statements of uncritical support signal the return to a more isolationist phase. A word of warning, however: this was very clear and easy to read in the days of the orthodox Brezhnev dictatorship, whereas in the Gorbachev period there is much less that Western opinion expects to see criticised and much more which Western opinion expects to see admired.

The extraordinary events of 1989 in Eastern Europe and the Soviet Union left the PCF almost literally speechless. As the revelations of corruption, inertia and repression multiplied, the Party's line has been to say that it was not told about it ('We were duped'), and that Brezhnev bears a heavy responsibility for the difficulties the socialist system is experiencing, but that the crisis of socialism is a crisis of development whereas the crisis of capitalism is a crisis of the system itself and that the future still lies with socialism not social democracy or capitalism.[10] There is increasing challenge to this orthodoxy from within the Party, but open debate, even in 1990 after all the development of free expression in former Communist states, is still blocked. There has been no attempt to respond to the collapse of Communism abroad and electoral decline at home, as the Italian Communists have done, with new ideas and a new name.

The PCF is a Marxist party in the sense that it accepts the Marxist analysis of the class struggle as the fundamental social reality and the basic element of historical change. It is Leninist in that it has a Leninist view of itself as a revolutionary party, the 'vanguard of the proletariat'. An ever more exploited, ever more numerous, ever more class-conscious proletariat will, with absolute inevitability, one day rise up and cast off the shackles of its oppressors, the owners of capital. This can only be the work of the working class itself, but its revolutionary destiny requires the leadership of a disciplined party consisting of committed professional revolutionaries. The importance of the leadership of such a party that does not compromise with the bourgeoisie explains the lengths to which the PCF goes to retain its municipal power-base and such peculiarly Communist manifestations as the virtual unanimity of every vote in the Party. Most non-Communists regard diversity as the hallmark of healthy debate and unanimity as evidence of intimidation. For Communists, however, it demonstrates 'profound unity'. Why not have amendments and critical debates at Congress? 'We would be taking precious little interest in leading to success the struggle of the working class if we acted like that. The workers . . . need a party which gives force and effectiveness to their struggle.' In 1976, at the height of the PCF's commitment to the Union of the Left and therefore to improving its image in the eyes of moderate opinion, the Party Congress voted to drop the Leninist notion of 'dictatorship of the proletariat' from party statutes, but it was made clear that this did not involve 'any attenuation of the directing influence of the working class and its Communist Party'.

The American writer Roland Tiersky has written of 'the four faces of French Communism'.[11] If the Party is in a conciliatory phase it stresses its social role as 'tribune' (acting on behalf of the underprivileged to obtain better housing, better working conditions etc.) and its political role as party of government, willing to play a responsible part in municipal government, in Parliament, in elections and in a possible coalition government of the left. It has been the predominance of these roles for much of the time that has led many writers, notably Georges Lavau,[12] to stress that the PCF is not a destabilising force in French politics, and in many ways helps the system to function better. If, however, the Party is in an isolationist phase – the code word is 'seeking unity *à la base* (among the workers)' instead of 'at the top' – the other two faces are more visible: the social role of 'vanguard of the proletariat', joining the workers' struggle at industrial level, and the political role of 'revolutionary party' denouncing pacts and compromises, drawing closer to old-fashioned East European Communism.

The great debate in the 1970s was about Eurocommunism (the more liberal model favoured by the Italian and Spanish Communists in particular, which was especially critical of the Soviet dictatorship of the time) and whether the PCF 'has really changed' or retains some dark purpose, but this is somewhat irrelevant today. It appeared then that the PCF would come to power in France as an important part of the Union of the Left. Consequently its attitudes to participation in liberal democracy – for example, whether it would want to suppress other parties or agree to leave office if the electorate voted it out, whether it really aspired to a revolutionary seizure of power – were much discussed. It was difficult at the time not to conclude that it would have to change – to abandon the Stalinist mentality of the past, but this proved to be wrong: everything else changed while it remained as it was. The Soviet Union changed. French society changed. The Communist vote collapsed and the Socialists came to power without really needing an alliance with the PC.

NOTES

1. 'The French Communist theory of power', *Government and Opposition*, 1967, pp. 255–6.
2. *The Rise of the French Communist Party 1920–1947*, London: Faber and Faber 1984, ch. 6.
3. Ibid., pp. 300–6.
4. Ibid., p. 371.
5. *The State of France*, London: Secker and Warburg 1955, p. 161.
6. 'The French Communist theory of power', op. cit., p. 257.
7. *In the Thirties* and *Rotten Elements*, London: Heinemann 1962 and 1969.

8. Princeton University Press, 1954.
9. Arthur Koestler in Richard Crossman (ed.), *The God that Failed*, New York 1950, p. 19.
10. Report by Maxime Grenetz to the Central Committee, Jan. 1990.
11. *French Communism, 1920–1972*, New York: Columbia University Press 1974, esp. chapter 12.
12. 'Le Parti Communiste dans le système politique français' in F. Bon *et al.*, *Le Communisme en France*, Paris: Cahiers de la FNSP 1969.

9

THE GREENS

In the spring of 1989 the Greens throughout Europe seemed at last to have struck a chord. In West Germany, ahead of the rest of us in this as in so much else, the *Grünen* had been an effective and well-organised political force for some years, during which it had faced the problem of political purity and political realism. The *Grünen* first won seats in the Bundestag, under the Federal Republic's electoral system of proportional representation, in 1983. They have maintained their position, won representation in a number of provincial parliaments, and entered a 'Red-Green' coalition with the SPD in Hesse in 1986. In Britain the Greens, never having previously obtained more than a handful of votes, astonished everyone by achieving 2 million votes and 15% in the European Parliament elections of 1989 – but no seats thanks to the British electoral system. France comes between the two: the French Ecology Movement (now the Greens) has made fluctuating progress throughout most of the 1980s, usually managing 4 or 5% where they presented a candidate, building up to the occasional local 10%. In March 1989, 1,400 Green councillors were elected and in June 1989 at the European elections the Greens had 2 million votes (10.6%) and nine MEPs elected. Although part of this, particularly in Britain, can be dismissed as a generalised anti-government protest vote, this remarkable Europe-wide success in 1989 springs from a desire, often in better-educated and younger people, to place the environmental problems of the planet (the ozone layer, global warming, pollution of the atmosphere, the destruction of Amazonia, the threat of nuclear accidents, the threat to nature) in a prominent place on the political agenda.

The Greens used to be called Ecologists but were formed as a political party – *Les Verts* – in 1984 from a merger of the Mouvement d'Ecologie Politique and the Confédération Ecologiste. The former was a kind of think-tank deliberating on global environmental problems, the latter based more in community action and on associations like Friends of the Earth (*Amis de la Terre*). The first ecology candidate for President was René Dumont in 1974 (supported by the explorer Jacques Cousteau), but they had no great electoral successes in the 1970s (except

106

perhaps Paris-Ecologie which obtained 11% of the vote in Paris in the Council elections of 1977). They also experienced some severe setbacks: at the big anti-nuclear demonstration at the Creys-Malville fast-breeder reactor site in 1977 they met the full force of the French state with one demonstrator being killed and several injured, and in the first Euro-elections of 1979 they fell just short of the vital 5% threshold which would have averted financial ruin by triggering repayment of election expenses. In the early 1980s the problem was internal conflict. Brice Lalonde, supported by Friends of the Earth, became Presidential candidate in 1981 amid accusations of ballot-rigging. In the election his score was an honourable 4%; he did not endorse Mitterrand for the second ballot but, feeling that things would change for the better under a Socialist government, most of his voters did. At the founding conference of the Greens in 1984 Lalonde, who in 1988 in fact became Minister of the Environment in the Rocard government and is regarded by Greens as having completely sold out, tried to get agreement on a list for the 1984 Euro-elections with him as leader and with unilateral nuclear disarmament (a veritable heresy in France, but not so to the Greens) taken out. This proposition was vigorously rejected. Lalonde, with some left–of–centre personalities, presented a rival list (Entente Radicale Ecologiste) to the official Verts-Europe-Ecologie list. Lalonde's got 3.3%, while the Greens got 3.4% and, more importantly, established themselves as a structured party.

The political problem for the Greens is whether to ally themselves with the PS or not. Some of the leading Greens, particularly in the West of France where one, now an MEP, actually had the endorsement of the 'Presidential Majority' at the 1988 Parliamentary elections, argue that an alliance would make political sense: a government of the left would be more receptive to Green themes than one of the right, the Greens would achieve some concrete results, and the alternative is isolation. In other words, half a loaf is better than no bread. There is, however, a strong majority against this approach. The Greens were very disappointed by the Socialist government of 1981-6, which continued to develop nuclear power and nuclear defence and to pursue nature-damaging and resource-depleting unrestrained economic growth. Many Greens are active in local conservation groups and spend their lives opposing the development plans of firms and the state (Socialist or RPR). When the Prime Minister Michel Rocard in 1989 made a pro-ecology speech, the Greens replied with a barrage of criticism of his government: the resumption of nuclear tests in the Pacific, the authorisation of a nuclear-powered aircraft carrier, the stepping-up of an already 'demented' programme of *Autoroute* construction, opposition to catalytic converters for automobiles, the restart of the fast-breeder reactor programme, exports of dangerous waste and other environmental horrors.

The leading advocate of an independent stance for the Greens was Antoine Waechter, a sober-suited biologist from Alsace, who became the Green candidate for the 1988 Presidential election (3.8%), an Alsace regional councillor, Mulhouse town councillor, leader of the Euro-election Green list in 1989, MEP and chairman of the European Parliament's Environment Committee. He would undoubtedly be the party's leader, if the Greens had leaders. As an independent force they are working to establish a presence on the political scene which will develop support for Green ideas, will involve no compromise on the nuclear issue, and on environmental issues will generally compel other parties to come to terms with them. This is a position which does not exclude working with others. For example, they decided to open their Euro-election list to a certain number of 'non-Greens', notably regionalist movements, because the Greens support regional self-government. Consequently the nine MEPs elected on the Green list in 1989 include Max Siméoni, the leader of the (non-violent) Corsican independence movement *Union du Peuple Corse*, and Djida Tazdaït, president of the Young Arabs movement in Lyon. Indeed the Greens are working hard to develop support among these and similar groups – independence movements in French overseas territories and immigrant organisations.

The Greens, in conformity with their notion of decentralised decision-making, allowed local groups to adopt their own second-ballot strategy in the 1989 Council elections. In most cases where they achieved the 5% threshold at the first ballot, Greens decided to contest the second ballot independently – and in most cases increased their first-ballot score. In a number of towns, however, the local group decided to merge with another list in exchange for positions of influence in council policy-making and agreement on policy. The most interesting case was the second-ballot alliance with the Union of the Left in Lille, a city whose mayor is the former Prime Minister and leader of the PS, Pierre Mauroy. Most of the alliances were with the left but in one or two small towns with the UDF.

After only one significant national electoral success so far (the European Parliament elections in 1989), we do not know whether there is a permanent green electorate yet. The evidence from the 1989 Euro elections and from the vote for Antoine Waechter in 1988 (3.4%) is that the young, the well-educated and those of medium-to-high socio-

Table 9.1.   THE GREENS IN ELECTIONS

	Million votes	Seats	%
1974 Presidential (Dumont)	.3		1.3
1977 Municipal elections		30	
1978 Parliamentary	.6*		2.1
1979 Euro-elections	.9		4.5
1981 Presidential (Lalonde)	1.1		3.8
1981 Parliamentary	.3*		1.1
1984 Euro-elections (Green List)	.7		3.4
(Lalonde/Radical list)	.6		3.3
1986 Parliamentary	.3*		1.2
1986 Regional Councils		4	
1988 Presidential (Waechter)	1.1		3.8
1988 Parliamentary†	–		–
1989 Municipal		1,400	
1989 Euro-elections	1.9	9	10.6

*Candidates not presented everywhere.
†'We do not have to participate in every election imposed upon us just to affirm our existence' (Waechter).

economic status are the most likely to vote Green. In 1989 the Green list scored approximately 11% but were supported, according to a SOFRES post-election study, by 16% of those who had received higher education, 14% of those with the highest incomes, 19% of voters in middle and junior management, 14% of the 18–24 age group, and 19% of the 25–34s. By contrast they only received the support of 4% of the over 65s, 6% of those with no more than primary education, and 6% of the lowest wage-earners. Over 80% of those who voted Green classified themselves as left or centre, especially left (55%). Over 80% of 1989 Green voters who had voted in the second ballot of the 1988 Presidential election had voted for Mitterrand. BVA found that those intending to vote Green in 1989 were left-of-centre in their attitudes on all social and cultural questions (unions, privatisation, the death penalty, multi-racial society etc.), and that they had a distinctive view, compared to the electorates of other parties, on certain issues: priority for defence of the environment, a ban on smoking in public places, a ban on traffic in cities, a lack of confidence in scientific progress.

The Greens are attempting to improve their organisation – not an easy task given the somewhat anarchic individualism of most activists. Members join their Regional association. At national level there is an inter-regional Council (CNIR), the main governing body of the party, composed of representatives elected by the Regions and the General

Assembly. The General Assembly is the party conference which meets annually to lay down party policy and give a mandate to the CNIR – for example, on whether the Greens should be independent or should seek alliances with the Socialists. Up till 1989 all members could attend the General Assembly and vote. This was not a problem when there were only 200 or 400 members. In 1989 the Greens had 1,400 councillors and claimed 5,000 members, so the intention was to change the rules so that the regions would elect voting members of General Assembly. The Greens, as in Britain and West Germany, have no leader or President. The CNIR appoints four *porte-parole* (spokespersons), a secretary and a treasurer. The main sources of party finance, other than individual subscriptions and donations, are the refunds of election expenses – from the European Parliament elections in particular (they still have not achieved the 5% threshold for refunds in a French national election) – and a substantial proportion of the salaries of their nine MEPs.

Green policy themes, extremely well-argued and presented, cover everything from agriculture to education and health, with particular emphasis on energy, transport and the protection of nature. On defence they are adamantly opposed to the concept of deterrence by nuclear or chemical weapons and in favour of non-violent civil defence – the most potent way, according to them, to render a country unattractive to a potential aggressor. They reject an economic system, capitalist or socialist, mainly composed of huge units wasting resources, dehumanising workers and chasing ever-higher levels of consumption, in favour of small 'convivial' units based on respect for individuals and the environment and producing what is genuinely useful. Energy and transport policies follow the same ideas – reduce the reliance on wasteful and harmful road transport, get rid of nuclear power and other generation methods which pollute the atmosphere, and turn to measures of energy conservation and to renewable sources. In health, they advocate a turn away from massive expenditure on and treatment by drugs towards alternative medicine (homeopathy, acupuncture etc) and in the world of nature, cleaner water, restrictions on the killing of animals for sport and in conditions of economic over-exploitation, reversal of the trend towards large mechanised, chemical-employing farms producing costly surpluses, help for developing countries to protect the world's environment and agriculture by not speculating in its resources or imposing on it Western products which destroy its self-reliance. With so radical a programme the Greens are right to resist absorption into an alliance with a conventional political party. Concern for the future of the planet is a growing constituency.

10

THE NATIONAL FRONT

The extreme Right in France

The extreme Right has a long history in France. An extremist weekly is still called *Rivarol* after the anti-revolutionary journalist of the 1790s. Its principal themes since the French Revolution have been decadence and plots – the moral and spiritual decadence of the nation, plots by freemasons, plots by Jews and high finance, plots by Communists to make the nation degenerate. The cause of the extreme Right was once the restoration of the monarchy; then it was to combat the influence of Jews and Communists; and today it is to stop the degeneration of France through immigration, AIDS and crime.

Up to the Second World War there were many violent and nationalistic anti-Jewish, anti-democratic, anti-Communist movements in France collectively known as the *Ligues* (Leagues). The most important was *Action Française* led by a remarkable polemical writer, Charles Maurras, who fulminated against all democratic ideas from the time of the great Dreyfus scandal in the 1890s in which a Jewish officer was wrongly accused and sentenced for treason and the right wanted to deny him reinstatement, to the Vichy dictatorship of Marshal Pétain in the 1940s, which Maurras enthusiastically supported. Maurras and *Action Française* were royalist so their violent activists were known as the *Camelots du Roi*. The inter-war years saw in France, as elsewhere, a great increase in political violence. The Jeunesses patriotes and the Croix de Feu both engaged in street fighting against the Communists and in the famous riots of 6 February 1934 against the Parliamentary Republic and its financial scandals. The *Croix de Feu*, led by Colonel de la Rocque, was dedicated to the task of 'smashing the internal enemies of our fatherland', had 60,000 members and was organised, like Oswald Mosley's gangs in Britain, on the paramilitary lines of Mussolini's Fascist Party in Italy which he admired. After the dissolution of the *Croix de Feu*, de la Rocque gave up street violence and founded the *Parti social français*, which built up a mass membership and won some seats in Parliament. Another party of the extreme right in the 1930s was the *Parti populaire français*, founded by Jacques Doriot, a populist and ex-Communist, indeed a former leader of the young Communists and

Mayor of the Communist stronghold of St Denis. Doriot's movement was much more like classic Fascism or National Socialism than was the more aristocratic Action française. Finally there were the sinister and violent *Cagoulards* (hooded men) who carried on political killings after the dissolution of the *Ligues*. The most famous *Cagoulard* act of terrorism was the murder in France of two leading Italian anti-Fascists, the Rosselli brothers, in 1937 (the event is commemorated by a memorial at the site of the killing, outside the spa town of Bagnoles de l'Orne in Normandy).

When the German tanks moved into France in 1940, the National Assembly voted full powers to Marshal Pétain, the eighty-four-year old 'victor of Verdun' and hero of the First World War. A treaty was signed with the Nazis under which the northern half of France was occupied by German troops and the southern half, 'independent' and neutral, was governed from Vichy by Pétain in an increasingly dictatorial and collaborationist fashion. Maurras, Doriot, Marcel Déat (who tried to introduce the idea of a single party of the revolution), Pierre Laval (a former Prime Minister of the centre-left) and all the activists of the extreme right helped him to achieve his 'National Revolution' aiming at a sort of spiritual regeneration in France of 'eternal certainties . . . virtue, patriotism, family, pride, the right and the duty to work'. *'Liberté, égalité, fraternité'* was changed to *'Travail, famille, patrie'*. Anti-Jewish legislation and a Commissariat for Jewish Questions appeared as early as 1941. After the Liberation in 1944 all this was swept away and the extreme right, marked by collaboration with Vichy and the Nazis, were more isolated than ever before.

In the post-war period the three streams of the extreme right have been the memories of Pétain's 'national revolution' and the hopes of its rehabilitation, the movement in defence of the small trader and his traditional values known as 'Poujadism', and the struggle to retain a French empire and in particular the violent opponents of Algerian independence known as the *Organisation de l'Armée Secrète* (OAS). The same individuals are to be found in all these movements, and the three streams flow into the Front National, a political movement that has been exceptionally effective in sustaining electoral success and organisation throughout the 1980s. The main mobilising theme of the Front National has been fear of immigration – especially the growth of the North African Arab population in France.

The various neo-Vichy clubs and committees, in which nearly all the people later to be prominent in the extreme right participated – Tixier-

Vignancour (Presidential candidate in 1965), Pierre Poujade, Jean-Marie Le Pen – produced a small political party (UNIR – Union of National Independents and Republicans) which won three seats in 1951 and fed into the CNI (National Centre of Independents), a branch of French conservatism that, although usually allied to the RPR, is still today very close to the extreme right. Le Pen was a CNI *député* after the collapse of the Poujadists in 1958. Some of the Front National activists infiltrated the CNI in the 1970s and a number of Front National candidates elected to Parliament in 1986 were CNI (for example, Frédéric-Dupont and Briant, who was actually Secretary General of the CNI).

The most important expression of the extreme right in the 1950s was Poujadism. Pierre Poujade, a shopkeeper from St Céré (Lot), led a local tax strike which rapidly developed into a mass movement of discontented small traders known as the UDCA (Union for the Defence of Traders and Artisans). At the 1956 election 2.5 million people (12.5%) voted Poujadist, attracted to a campaign in which every conceivable discontent was grouped under the slogan '*Sortez les sortants*' ('Throw the rascals out') and fifty-one *députés*, including the twenty-seven-year old Jean-Marie Le Pen, were elected. Poujadism has given a new word to the world's political vocabulary and it serves to express the periodic outbursts of protest by groups who feel left behind by economic progress and threatened by change in the modern world. It is reactionary in the genuine sense of the word: it seeks to put the clock back to a simpler world where the small grocer was not threatened by the supermarket, the small craftsman by mass production, the small farmer by bureaucracy and taxes, the small employer by unions and social legislation to encourage idleness, and every decent person by big business, the state, the squabbling and ineffectiveness of Parliamentary democracy, the corrupt politicians, and the parties doing deals and forgetting their promises. Poujadism lives on in the Fifth Republic in the form of occasional outbursts of violence by farmers, protesting at low prices by dumping thousands of tons of fruit on main railways, for example, or small traders sacking a local tax office – but the mass movement of the 1950s was very short-lived.

In the period that followed, the great cause of the extreme right was the Algerian war, and opposition – increasingly bitter and violent – to Algerian independence. Le Pen, who had served as a volunteer in the Parachute regiment (*Paras*) during the last stages of the French defeat in Indo-China, volunteered for Algeria although he was a Poujadist *député* at the time. He has been accused of participating in torture, employed against terrorism by the French army in Algeria, and he himself admits to the 'necessary obligations' of war. When it became clear that the object of de Gaulle's policy was self-determination for Algeria, the extreme supporters of *Algérie française* formed, as already mentioned, the OAS (*Organisation de l'Armée Secrète*) which carried out numerous terrorist attacks against Algerians and French political leaders involved in the 'sell-out' – notably the assassination attempt on de Gaulle himself at Le Petit Clamart in August 1962. Independence for Algeria in 1962 brought the resettlement in France of a million French people who had to give up their land and businesses in Algeria. It is this group, the *rapatriés*, who predominantly settled in the 'sunshine belt' along the south coast, which is the hard core of the electorate of the Front National today. Also, many of today's Front National élites were closely involved in the *Algérie française* struggle, and in some cases in the OAS. Pierre Sergent, for example, FN *député* for Perpignan 1986–8 and also associated with the CNI, was the home Commandant of the OAS. Pascal Arrighi, FN *député* for Marseille in 1986–8, led the famous 'invasion of Corsica' at the time of the army takeover in Algiers in 1958.

After the Algerian war there followed a lean period for the extreme right. Most of those now active in the FN helped organise the 1965 Presidential campaign of Tixier-Vignancour against de Gaulle. Tixier obtained 5% – mostly among the embittered *rapatriés* in the south. In 1969, however, the 'new right' began to appear. A body of intellectuals, of whom Alain de Benoist was the most prominent and effective, formed GRECE (Research and Study Group for European Civilisation – the initials spell the French word for Plato's civilisation and the original of European superiority: Greece) whose publications argue against the ideology of equality and take up the themes of socio-biology on the genetic origins of inequality between individuals and between races, from which it is just a step to condemn the immigration of alien races as a corrupting influence on European civilisation. In the orbit of GRECE the *Club de l'Horloge* was formed. In the 1970s and particularly when they were in opposition in the 1980s, supporters of the RPR or UDF formed numerous Clubs – rather as the left had done in the 1960s. L'Horloge was the most right-wing of the RPR Clubs and its leading members, notably its President Yvan Blot, have since played a prominent role in the development of the FN. *L'Horloge* called for no more centrism but instead a clear-cut right nationalist and, in the French sense of a free-market economy, liberal leader 'like Mrs Thatcher'.

Other intellectual circles involved in the extreme right were integrist Catholics who opposed the watering-down of Roman Catholicism by the reforms of the Second Vatican Council (1962–5) and who are attracted by the schismatic Archbishop Lefèbvre and his 'illegal' celebration of the traditional ('Tridentine') Latin mass.

The FN itself was formed in 1972 under the leadership of Le Pen. It skilfully weaves together many of the themes discussed above – Poujadist anti-Parliamentarism and rejection of politicians, nostalgia for the days of empire and of French Algeria in particular, anti-Communism, the cult of the leader, anti-semitism and the rehabilitation of Fascism, traditional values concerning order and the family, above all the nationalist theme of 'France for the French' and opposition to the degeneration of the country through immigration and its related infections AIDS, unemployment, drugs and crime. Much of this is coded language for the activists of the extreme right rather than for the general public – particularly the anti-semitic remarks and those denying or minimising the Nazi genocide. Indeed there is some evidence from opinion polls and election results that particularly distasteful remarks in this vein alienate the voters – though not, it seems, for long. Le Pen has described the Nazi persecution of the Jews as a 'detail', and made a disagreeable pun (in reference to the death camps) on the name of a Jewish minister in the government whose name contains the syllable '*four*', the French word for 'oven'. An octogenarian NF supporter elected to the European Parliament on the Front list in 1989, Autant Lara, said that the Nazis '*avaient raté la mère Veil*' ('didn't get old Mother Veil' – a reference to Simone Veil, leader of the centrist list in the European elections, who, as a Jewish child, was sent to the Nazi death camps and survived). Le Pen condemned this remark, but you only have to hear the way he pronounces the name Veil, emphasising the final 'l' – which of course is not done in French – to have no doubt about his deeper sentiments. But the general themes of degeneration and immigration have found an echo in public opinion. In the 1980s the Front had considerable electoral success – normally achieving about 10%, with 14.4% for Le Pen in the Presidential election of 1988.

The principal themes of the FN can be summed up in various well-known Le Pen pronouncements, 'France for the French' and the ideas of nation and roots: 'I love my daughters more than my cousins, my cousins than my neighbours, my neighbours than strangers, strangers than enemies.' The FN wants a motherhood pension for French families so that mothers can stay at home with their children and have more of them, jobs and social benefits to be reserved for French people, a policy of returning immigrants to their native lands, the return of the death penalty for 'criminals, drug-traffickers [two-thirds of whom, according to the FN, are foreigners] and terrorists', an end to left-wing control in schools and union monopolies, the regulation of public service strikes, a reduced number of civil servants, and the end of income tax.

Le Pen travels round Europe in the world of the neo-Fascist Right. With his violent past, the thuggish behaviour of his party's élites in the Parliament of 1986–8, his coded sentiments on the persecution of the Jews or on AIDS (isolation in 'sidatoriums'*) delivered at conferences where Nazi songs are sung, or where the Italian MSI welcomes him as a hero – the nature of his movement is clear.

Elections and the Front National

Le Pen stood as a candidate at the 1974 Presidential elections but only obtained 0.7%. The electoral successes of the FN did not begin until 1983. First they scored 11% in the XXe *Arrondissement* of Paris, the most working-class, in the municipal elections, and then at a municipal by-election in the Norman town of Dreux, which has a high proportion of immigrants from North Africa, the FN list scored 16.7% and, thanks to a pact with the RPR at the second ballot, won a post of *maire-adjoint* on the Council. By this time they were getting full attention in the media. The Front had over 9% at another municipal by-election in Aulnay-sous-Bois, an industrial suburb of Paris again with a high immigrant population, and Le Pen himself stood for a Parliamentary by-election in his native Brittany, where there are no immigrants, and scored 12%. At elections from then on the FN scores are shown in Table 10.1.

Table 10.3 shows how virtually all Le Pen's best results have since the early 1980s come from the south coast, where the *rapatriés* and large numbers of immigrants from Algeria, Tunisia and Morocco have settled. In the Presidential election of 1988 he was easily the leading candidate of the right in Provence–Côte d'Azur and Languedoc, with 28% in Marseille, 27% in Toulon, 26% in Nice, 23% in Aix-en-Provence and Avignon, and 21% in Montpellier and Nîmes. In 1987 the UDF in Grasse agreed to an alliance with the FN at a municipal by-election because the FN commanded over 20% of the vote and could not be ignored. In the 1989 Town Council elections this success was

*The French for AIDS is *SIDA*.

Table 10.1.   FRONT NATIONAL: ELECTIONS SINCE 1984

	Seats	%
European Parliament 1984	10	11.1
Cantonal (County) 1985	1	8.9*
Parliamentary 1986	35	9.8
	+ 137 Regional Council seats	
Presidential 1988 (Le Pen)		14.4
Parliamentary 1988	1	9.9
Cantonal (County) 1988	–	5.5
Municipal 1989	390 (in towns over 20,000 pop.)	†
European Parliament 1989	10	11.7

*10.4% where there were candidates.
†FN lists not presented everywhere.

Table 10.2.   FRONT NATIONAL: 1988 PRESIDENTIAL ELECTION
(results by region)

	Le Pen %
Paris Region (Île de France)	15.9
North	13.7
Picardy	14.8
Upper Normandy	12.1
Lower Normandy	11.1
Brittany	9.9
Loire	9.4
Champagne	14.6
Lorraine	17.1
Alsace	21.8*
Franche-Comté	14.6
Burgundy	12.6
Centre	13.2
Poitou	9.4
Limousin	7.2
Auvergne	11.0
Rhône-Alps	16.4
Aquitaine	11.5
Midi-Pyrenées	11.2
Languedoc	18.9*
Provence – Côte d'Azur	24.5*
Corsica	13.3
France	14.4

*Leading candidate of the right and centre.

Table 10.3.   FRONT NATIONAL: BEST DÉPARTEMENTS

	European 1984 %	Cantonal 1985 %	Parliamentary 1986 %	Presidential 1988 (*Le Pen*) %
Bouches du Rhône (Provence)	19.4 (3)	19.5 (2)	22.5 (1)	26.4 (1)
Var (Provence)	20.0 (2)	20.2 (1)	17.1 (5)	25.1 (2)
Alpes Maritimes (Provence)	21.4 (1)	17.3 (3)	20.9 (2)	24.2 (3)
Vaucluse (Provence)	16.4 (5)	15.3 (7)	18.0 (4)	23.2 (4)
Haut-Rhin (Alsace)	13.9		14.5	22.2 (5)
Bas-Rhin (Alsace)	11.5		13.1	21.9 (6)
Gard (Languedoc)	12.7		15.1 (7)	20.6 (7)
Pyrenées Orientales (Languedoc)	15.9 (7)	15.9 (5)	19.0 (3)	20.5 (8)
Hérault (Languedoc)	15.3 (9)	15.0 (8)	16.0 (6)	19.9 (9)
Seine St Denis (Paris)	16.0 (6)	17.3 (3)	14.5 (8)	19.8 (10)

continued: 25% at Perpignan, 20% at Toulon, 18% at Nice. It has been remarked that the towns on the south coast have become 'like Bab-el-Oued', the Algiers suburb where the lower–class whites used to live.

Le Pen and the FN, as the tables show, have not only done well in the south, however. While they continue to be weak in the west of France from Normandy to Aquitaine, their strong showing in industrial areas of the north and east in 1986 was confirmed and strengthened at the 1988 Presidential election. For example, Alsace-Lorraine, a part of the country with a Catholic tradition which traditionally votes for the moderate right, voted heavily this time for Le Pen. So did many of the traditionally Communist Paris suburbs in Seine St Denis, although there is no evidence that the decline in the Communist vote can be attributed to voters switching from Communist to FN; that notion is not borne out by the social composition of the FN electorate and would, if it were true, make the success of the Socialist Party over the 1980s difficult to explain. Le Pen was supported by 19% of manual workers in 1988, but he did best among the social groups which have traditionally been most susceptible to the appeal of the extreme right, as in the period of classic Fascism in Italy and Germany in the 1930s: small business and traders (31% for Le Pen in 1988 according to one exit poll, but see Table 10.4), clerical employees and shopworkers, the professions.

Table 10.4.   FRONT NATIONAL: VOTE BY SOCIAL GROUP

	Parliamentary 1986 %	Presidential 1988 %
France	10	14
Men	12	18
Women	7	11
Under 25	9	16
25–34	8	17
35–49	9	17
50–64	12	11
65 and over	9	12
Farmers	11	13
Small traders	14	27
Professions, top management	9	19
Junior management	10	12
Clerical employees	7	13
Manual workers	11	19
No occupation/retired	9	12
Educational level:		
Primary or none		15
Secondary		13
Higher		12
Students	5	

Sources: 1986 BVA exit poll; 1988 SOFRES post-electoral study.

The view among the people who have observed the FN phenomenon most closely is that there is now a permanent FN electorate (somewhere between 5 and 10%) and an effective organisation with established local and national élites in a way that earlier manifestations of the extreme right did not achieve. There is in addition an extra electorate made up of people who are not unresponsive to Le Pen's themes but who mainly wish to give a signal to the mainstream political élites that their anxieties and preoccupations are not currently receiving enough attention. Surveys of farmers worried about farm prices and the EEC, or of residents of small industrial towns in the east where the principal heavy industry has closed down, revealed in 1988 a fairly widespread intention to use a first ballot vote for Le Pen as a protest and a warning. '*Cohabitation*' was a factor: how does one express discontent if all the mainstream parties are perceived as having been jointly involved in governing the country in a kind of 'grand coalition'? One opinion survey (Jérome Jaffré, *Le Monde* 12 April 1988) showed that intending Le Pen voters were disillusioned with both the changes of government, in 1981 and 1986, and critical of the record of both Mitterrand and Chirac, put immigration first after unemployment in the list of priorities (eleventh for supporters of other candidates), were particularly inclined to connect immigration and unemployment, felt more pessimistic about the future than the electorates of the other candidates, and by a two-to-one majority wanted a candidate other than Le Pen actually to win!

The Le Pen Presidential campaign of 1988 was extremely interesting. He achieved real campaign momentum. His poster theme was 'the outsider' (just a horse-racing term in French, not a pun as in English) edging nearer to the winning-post. His election broadcasts on television showed family photos from his childhood, and repeated the 'outsider' theme by showing a racing board-game in which horses marked Mitterrand or Chirac would go back a few squares because those candidates had supported the abolition of the death penalty and the horse marked Le Pen would move up because that candidate supported discrimination in jobs and housing in favour of Frenchmen! It is difficult to recall election broadcasts ever having been used more effectively in any country. One of the most successful elements of Le Pen's campaign was his claim, repeated in the election broadcasts on television, that he alone had a policy programme fully in line with what public opinion wanted. He would produce lists of opinion poll findings showing majorities for the return of the death penalty, the sending home of immigrants, the abolition of income tax, popular initiative for referenda, and so on.

However, immigration appears to have been the crucial theme which won him the extra votes, certainly the one most stressed at meetings ('So long as we are alive, France will never be an Islamic state!' – Marseille football stadium, 17 April). A lot of people worried by crime and violence in cities, by AIDS and drugs, by unemployment, and by the pressure on the social security system and benefits seemed willing to blame it on immigrants – especially Arabs from North Africa, who, with their descendants (French citizens) are particularly numerous in the areas of worst housing and deprivation in the big cities. Nonna Mayer and Pascal Perrineau have written that the FN is the party of the discontented and the party of fear, especially in deprived urban areas where there are no active associations or organisations to integrate the inhabitants and work to improve the neighbourhood.

Two questions remain to be answered about the success of the FN in the 1980s. What has been its effect on the parties of the mainstream centre and right? How much of the FN's success is attributable to the introduction of proportional representation for the 1986 Parliamentary elections? The RPR is the party (and Chirac the Presidential candidate) that has suffered the most. Chirac's 19.9% in 1988 was the lowest score for the leading candidate of the right in any Presidential election. Although the right is in a majority in France at virtually every election – notably all those from 1981 to 1988 – he failed to win. Only about 60% of FN voters voted Chirac in the second ballot despite his efforts to retrieve them with nationalistic *coups de théâtre* (see chapter 12), which according to Jean-Luc Parodi's voter panel research produced some movement from first ballot FN voters intending to abstain, and his message during the face-to-face televised debate with Mitterrand that he would 'halt immigration'. About 20% voted Mitterrand and about 20% abstained. Many of the local activists that form an important part of the FN organisation as well as leading élites like campaign director Bruno Mégret, who came to the extreme right through the influential *Club de l'Horloge*, are former RPR members. The FN cuts into the RPR's natural constituency of the authoritarian right.

How should the RPR respond? If one condones or supports FN themes, one loses the support of moderates. If one condemns them, the ground on the authoritarian right is not recovered. Younger leading RPR figures like Philippe Séguin were for condemnation: voters who consider that France's problems stem from the presence of too many foreigners must not be told that we understand their anxieties but that they have got it wrong. Former Interior Minister Pasqua and others, on the other hand, affirm that the supporters of the FN and the RPR/UDF share 'common values' – nation, family, law and order. Chirac's approach in the 1988 second ballot was to attempt to '*désenclaver*' (de-isolate) the Front National electors. For the whole mainstream right the FN creates problems at local level: do RPR (and UDF) élites make pacts with the FN or lose their seats, their town halls and their Regional Council Presidencies to the left? Sometimes they make pacts: in the case of Dreux or Grasse mentioned above, or that of the Presidents of Corsica, Franche Comté and other Regional Councils, and the second-ballot deals to save Parliamentary seats in the south in 1988. When they do, however, they further alienate liberal and moderate opinion and increase divisions in their own parties. The Mayor of Grasse was expelled from the Radical Party's executive committee. Sometimes they refuse alliances. In 1985 there were very few deals at the Cantonal (County) elections. In consequence the FN stood most of its candidates down, and where it did not it attracted no votes at all. In the 1989 Town Council elections, there were hardly any deals.

Can the success of the FN in France be 'blamed' on proportional representation? PR was introduced by the Socialist government for the 1986 Parliamentary elections at which the FN obtained 10% of the votes and thirty-five seats. The 10% was entirely consistent, however, with their performance under various electoral systems in local and other elections in the 1980s. Winning seats certainly helped them to establish their organisation, their credibility and their élites – but it is doubtful whether one should ask the electoral system to abolish political parties which, however unpleasant their ideas, remain lawful and can win the support of one voter in ten. Another point: the two-ballot majority system, to which France has now returned for Parliamentary elections, may make it more difficult for a party with 10% support to win seats but it provides an opportunity for a strong first-ballot risk-free protest vote, as was demonstrated in the 1988 (non-PR) Presidential election.

The decade of the 1980s closed on an optimistic note for the FN – over 15% in opinion polls and important wins in a Parliamentary and a *conseil general* by-election. In the Parliamentary by-election at Dreux (again) in December 1989, the FN candidate (Mme Stirbois, widow of the party's 'no. 2', killed in a road accident) won 43% of the vote at the first ballot. The Socialists and Communists, eliminated by the 12½% rule, urged their voters to vote RPR at the second. Mme Stirbois, however, scored 61% and increased her first ballot vote by 7,000. At the local by-election in the FN's strongest region, the south coast, the FN candidate was only just ahead of the UDF with 23%. The UDF candidate pulled out, declaring that the real enemy was the left, and the RPR recommended 'freedom of vote' to its supporters. The FN candidate scored 51% at the second ballot.

The FN has a structure with a secretary-general (in 1990 Carl Lang), a *bureau politique*, and national secretaries responsible for every conceivable sector: demonstrations, health (of the French), employment (of the French), housing (of the French), the family (French), *rapatriés*, or defence of small traders and of French agriculture. It publishes a tabloid weekly called *National*. It is riven with bitter conflicts – at least four of the 1986 *députés* were expelled including the only one who was re-elected in 1988, Mme Yann Piat, so that Mme Stirbois in 1990 was the Front's only *député*. Le Pen is always in court or protesting at allegations against him by his ex-wife or his former associates – the most serious being that it was with alcohol that he persuaded an elderly supporter to leave him his enormous fortune and advanced the moment when he could inherit it. At all events the FN does not appear to be short of money. The party charges for admission to its rallies – an unusual feature, not to say a unique one. Truly – in a phrase so often used about the PCF – it is 'a party not like the others'.

11

ELECTORAL SYSTEMS AND ELECTORAL BEHAVIOUR

The next chapters deal with voters in the Fifth Republic – the system of voting, the characteristics of electoral behaviour and the various elections that have taken place: Presidential, Parliamentary, local and referendums.

Voting in France

Everyone aged eighteen and above has the right to vote if he or she is French (by birth or by naturalisation after five years), not mad and not bankrupt. Men aged over twenty-one have had this right since 1848, women only since 1944 (brought in by de Gaulle's provisional government after the Liberation), and those aged between eighteen and twenty-one since 1974 (a Giscard reform). Electors register in the town or village where they live, but many remain registered in the town which they regard as 'home' even if they move away. Voting in France is not compulsory, as it is in Belgium or Australia. In order to vote the elector goes to the local polling station with a *carte d'électeur* and proof of identity, picks up a selection of ballots (there is one for each candidate), goes into the privacy of the *isoloir*, puts one of the ballots in the envelope provided, seals it and puts the envelope in the urn when invited to do so by the presiding officer. Secrecy, therefore, is absolute. The only information about an individual elector that can be discovered, because it is publicly available, is whether or not he or she went to vote.

There are several admirable characteristics of the French system of voting. Following some scandals about occult sources of campaign funds, a law was introduced in 1988 whereby campaign expenses in national elections up to a legal ceiling are repaid by the state (in Presidential elections about Frs 30 million for a candidate obtaining above 5% of the vote, Frs 6 million for a candidate with less, in Parliamentary elections Frs 50,000 for every candidate obtaining 5%). For further details of the rules governing campaign finance see chapters 12 (Presidential elections) and 13 (Parliamentary elections). Secondly the elector in France, unlike the British elector who has to depend on communications from the political parties, is given a great deal of information by the public authorities. A leaflet from each candidate and sample ballots are sent free by the local council and the Post Office to every registered voter for all elections, local or national. A third admirable characteristic is that a voter can cast a positive abstention. If for whatever reason there is no candidate you wish to support, you can vote with an empty envelope or a deliberately spoilt paper. These are counted separately as *blancs et nuls* and a total recorded. In Britain such ballots are simply disregarded and the electors who spoil their ballots, perhaps because there is no candidate of the party they want to support, are just considered not to have turned out at all.

Finally, the votes are counted by ordinary members of the public and not by officialdom with all the annoying formalities about declarations of secrecy, appointment of counting agents and exclusion of the public that are a characteristic of British elections. The president of each polling station is a local citizen appointed to do the job, who recruits during the day twenty or so volunteers from the people coming to vote to return and help count the votes when the poll closes. The count at each polling station is entirely open to the public – indeed the greater the number of people who are present, the more readily it is believed that the result is genuine. The only place where this does not work very well is Corsica, with its ancient tradition of electoral fraud – but the results would be even more fraudulent if the votes were counted behind closed doors! An attempt to introduce fraud-proof voting machines in Corsica some years ago was frustrated by the presentation of thirty or forty candidates in each constituency – more than the machines had been designed to handle! Frauds in Corsica include a vast and fictitious postal vote (in 1988 a doctor in Bastia was arrested and remanded in custody for issuing on medical grounds an astronomical number of postal vote authorisations) and the stuffing of ballot boxes by 'voting' on behalf of electors who have not turned up. One small village in 1973 had a registered electorate of 165 yet one candidate received 5,998 votes there. (The mayor was found in hiding by the police and suspended!) Some Communist results were challenged and in some cases annulled due to the stuffing of boxes (though not on the Corsican scale) in 1988. In 1989 the Socialist government brought in new legislation controlling proxy and postal voting and requiring the elector to sign the electoral register at the time of voting. This should stop stuffing or at least make it much easier to detect.

The two-ballot electoral system

The two-ballot electoral system is a curious French variant of a system widely used in other countries for 'private' elections: the system of repeated ballots. Party nominating conventions in the United States, British Labour Party candidate selection procedures, the Roman Catholic College of Cardinals electing a new Pope – all use repeated balloting until one candidate emerges with the support of an absolute majority. The French system used in almost all public elections, local and national, in the Fifth Republic has only two ballots. If no candidate at the first ballot has an absolute majority over all others added together, a second ballot is held (a fortnight later in Presidential elections, a week later in all others) and the candidate who comes top is the winner whether obtaining an absolute majority or not. In Presidential elections (see chapter 12) only two candidates are allowed to proceed to the second ballot, so that the winner, in fact, does automatically have an absolute majority, but that rule does not apply in other elections: the Parliamentary (see chapter 13) and the local (see chapter 14). This electoral system was first used in Napoleon III's Second Empire in 1852 and became the Third Republic's system for all but ten of its seventy years.[1] It is odd that the anti-monarchist, anti-clerical Republic should have turned to the Papacy and the Empire for an electoral system.

In the Fourth Republic various versions of Proportional Representation were used, but the Fifth Republic has returned – again surprisingly, in view of the discredited past of the Third Republic – to the two-ballot system. The Socialist government introduced Proportional Representation for the 1986 Parliamentary election (see chapter 13, pp. 181–5), but this was regarded as a cynical attempt to save some seats for the PS when the government was unpopular, and was immediately abolished again by the Chirac government. The Socialists also introduced a proportional element into the two-ballot elections for town and city councils (see chapter 14). Proportional representation is used for Regional Council elections. This was introduced in 1986 at the same time as PR for Parliamentary elections but was not abolished by the Chirac government. It is also used for some of the seats in the Senate (Senators are elected not by the general public but by an 'electoral college' consisting mainly of local councillors – pp. 192–4) and for elections to the European Parliament (pp. 190–2).

The advantage of the two-ballot system is that electors can express a wide choice at the first ballot. They can vote for any candidate, however extreme, who takes their fancy knowing there is a chance for second thoughts. The large vote for Le Pen, the leader of the Front National, in 1988 was to a large extent a protest vote by people who did not want him to be President but who wanted to give a warning to the mainstream political leaders (see chapter 12). At the second ballot the electors can use their vote to prevent the victory of the candidate they dislike most. 'At the first ballot you choose, at the second you eliminate.' Second-ballot slogans are often negative: 'unite to stop communism' or 'all against personal power' (i.e. General de Gaulle). Politically, the two-ballot system has the effect of favouring non-extremist parties and candidates who can attract extra votes at the second ballot. This is why Le Pen and the Front National do not like it: the system helps them in the first ballot and penalises them in the second.

Gaullists hold strongly to the view that the two-ballot system is the lynchpin of the Fifth Republic's stability – hence their bitter opposition to the introduction of Proportional Representation by the Socialist government for 1986. It ensures, in their view, majority government. This is historically incorrect. The two-ballot system was what helped the traditional centrist or independent notables to preserve Parliamentary seats for themselves and ministerial instability for the nation throughout the Third Republic. What has happened in the Fifth Republic is new (and this is our main theme in this book): the emergence of political parties capable of winning a majority. The first to have this capacity was Gaullism, and the Socialists were the second. Once a party can achieve around 35% at the first ballot, the two-ballot system gives it a 'bonus' – a *coup de pouce majoritaire* – by putting it in a very favourable position to pick up a majority of Parliamentary seats at the second.

Interpretation and analysis

The results of French elections are usually presented in these terms:

Inscrits	(registered electorate)
Abstentions	
Blancs et nuls	(spoiled or blank ballots)
Suffrages exprimés	(valid votes)

Most figures for analysis and comparisons between one election and another are based on *suffrages exprimés*. Occasionally, however, it is important to consider *inscrits*, for example where turnout has fluctuated considerably in two elections which you want to compare. For example, in the 1969 Presidential elections Pompidou scored a record 57.5% at the second ballot and his successor Giscard d'Estaing in 1974 scraped in with 50.7%. However, there was massive abstention in 1969 (partly because the Communists campaigned for a second-ballot abstention), and a record turnout occurred in 1974. By comparing the percentage of the total electorate (*inscrits*) that supported the winner in these two elections, we find 37% for Pompidou and 44% for Giscard.

The national result of an election is derived, naturally enough, from the votes of the whole nation. In France this includes various tropical islands and other territories scattered around the globe from the Pacific Ocean to some islands off Canada (St Pierre and Miquelon) and in the Caribbean (Martinique and Guadeloupe), and to French Guiana in South America. These territories send *députés* to the French Parliament and even take part in elections to the European Parliament. For most comparisons of election results, however, the figures for metropolitan France only tend to be used. This makes sense for several reasons. First, metropolitan France contains about 98% of the electorate. Secondly, the overseas territories vote in a rather untypical way – in some cases, for example, producing exceptionally high votes for pro-government candidates. Indeed François Mitterrand, after the 1974 campaign, sent a commission to report on tribal and other pressures for a 'loyalist' vote. Thirdly, the map of overseas territories keeps changing as parts become independent: from Algeria in 1962 to the New Hebrides (now Vanuatu) in 1979.

Metropolitan France divides, as the map on page xiv shows, into twenty-two Regions, which in turn are composed of ninety-five *départements* (counties). Most detailed electoral analyses concentrate on the *département*, and one can distinguish rural *départements* from urban ones, or traditionally Catholic and 'moderate' ones from ones that traditionally vote for the left. One can go further: the way the votes are counted means that figures for individual polling stations are (as in the United States but not in Britain) available. You can therefore compare a single district (say a working-class neighbourhood) over a series of elections, build up figures for a single town, or extract results by Parliamentary constituency from the figures for a Presidential election. The availability of results by individual polling station within minutes of the close of voting has, incidentally, robbed election nights of their excitement. Most polling stations close at 6 p.m., but some, for local reasons, stay open till 8, and no result, even partial, may be announced until all have closed. What happens, therefore, is that the news organisations obtain actual figures from 200 or 300 representative polling stations throughout the country, feed them into computers where they are compared with data from those same polling stations at previous elections, and, at 8 o'clock precisely, give a national result (predicted but invariably accurate to within a decimal point) – while officials are still at a very early stage of collating results from the thousands of polling stations. Election-night television coverage therefore starts with the result and is no longer anything but interminable commentaries and 'declarations' by political leaders.

Changing parties and alliances present a further analytical difficulty. It is necessary to make sure that one is comparing like with like, or at least aware of the changes. For example in the late 1960s and early 1970s the 'opposition centre' (groups neither on the left nor part of the de Gaulle or Pompidou presidential majorities) varied widely in composition (see chapter 5) and so did the presidential majorities (chapter 3). Figures for the RPR/UDF alliance – which, with substantially the same composition, has fought all elections since 1978 – are not always easy to analyse. Sometimes there are 'primaries' (first-ballot contests between RPR and UDF), sometimes just a few, sometimes none. If there are 'primaries' in nearly every constituency, as in 1978, it is possible to determine the relative appeal of RPR and UDF. Even then one has to remember the 'notability factor': the candidate that nearly always does best in a 'primary' between RPR and UDF is the one who is best known locally. If there are scarcely any 'primaries', as in 1981 or 1988, the electors who want to support the RPR/UDF can only vote for whichever party has been allocated to their constituency, and a true comparison between the strengths of each is impossible.

To work out the gain or loss in share of the vote achieved by the parties, one must always use the results of the first ballot – having taken account of special factors of the kind referred to in the last paragraph. The first ballot is a snapshot of public opinion which can be compared with the first ballot in previous elections. The second ballot, however exciting, is quite different. The electors' choice is constrained in all kinds of ways; in some constituencies they have no chance to vote at all because there will have been a decisive result in the first ballot. There are more first-ballot wins when a party wins by a landslide (e.g. Gaullists in 1968 or Socialists in 1981), and when the RPR/UDF has decided not to have primaries (1981 and 1988 but not 1978) because that concentrates the vote for the centre and right on one first-ballot candidate.

Table 11.1. DÉPUTÉS ELECTED AT FIRST BALLOT

	1978	1981	1988
Communists	4	7	1
Socialists and allies	1	49	40
RPR	31	50	37
UDF	29	43	40
Other right	3	7	1
Total	68	156	119

In the constituencies that remain, many voters will have to choose a party that was not their first preference. Socialist voters in constituencies where the Communist candidate led the left at the first ballot will be urged to vote Communist at the second, and vice versa. What one can extract from an analysis of the second ballot includes the '*report des voix*' (transfer of votes). It is normal after the first ballot, indeed the disciplined rule in the Fifth Republic both on the left and in the RPR/UDF, for the candidates with the least votes to withdraw in favour of their better-placed allies. This is called *désistement*. Sometimes the voters respond, sometimes they do not. On the whole the 'moderate' parties of an alliance like the Socialists or the UDF, do better at the second ballot than the Communists or the RPR, especially the Communists. Indeed, as we observed earlier, one of the political features of the two-ballot electoral system is that it favours moderates. A study by the present author of the 1978 election (the last when the four political forces PC, PS, UDF and RPR were roughly equal in strength) showed that in PC/UDF second-ballot duels nearly a quarter of first-ballot Socialist voters preferred to vote UDF rather than Communist and 12% abstained, leaving 65% to vote Communist. However, only 10% of Socialist voters switched to RPR when the choice was PC/RPR, nearly three-quarters voting Communist and 17% abstaining. In PS/UDF second-ballot contests there was a very high level of transfer from PC first-ballot voters to PS (98%) and from RPR to UDF (83%) and also in PS/RPR contests, except that 13% of UDF first-round voters preferred to abstain rather than vote RPR.[2]

When predicting the likely result of the second ballot, it is customary to add up the votes distributed among the candidates of left and right and see which total is the greater. This is adequate as a starting point but, in addition to the problem of the differential capacity to achieve a good *report des voix*, studies have shown that the electors who vote at the second ballot are not the same as those who voted at the first: many who abstained at the first vote at the second, many who voted at the first abstain at the second.[3] Second-ballot turnout is affected by a number of factors, particularly the presence of an acceptable candidate in the second ballot (reinforcing the point about moderate candidates made in the previous paragraph) and whether the contest is likely to be close or not. In 1978 turnout increased at the second ballot over all, but not in obviously safe seats. It increased most in seats where the second-ballot candidates were PS/UDF, next-most in PS/RPR contests, next in PC/UDF contests, and least of all when the candidates were PC/RPR. In the last two categories a large increase in the number of spoilt votes was also noted.

Aspects of electoral behaviour

No-one knows why people vote for one party or candidate rather than another, but we can observe certain patterns of behaviour. More working-class people in France (and elsewhere) vote for the left than the right or centre. More churchgoing Catholics vote for the right and centre than for the left. However one must avoid turning this into some kind of sociological determinism: they vote left because they are working-class, they vote right because they are Catholics. All kinds of factors influence the way an individual votes: background and family tradition, work experience, attitudes, perception of issues and personalities, discontent with the government of the day, and the level of interest or lack of it in politics and public affairs.

There is a 'map' of voting in France (as in other countries). Certain regions and *départements* have traditionally voted for the left since manhood suffrage began in 1848 (parts of the south and south-west). Others have had a tradition of 'moderate' voting (centre and right) – notably the strongly Catholic *départements* like the Vendée in the west (where Catholics fought a war against the Revolutionary Republic in 1794) or Lozére and Cantal, pockets of Catholicism in the pagan south. The geography of voting is studied closely by French political science. Theories abound whereby people who live on granite vote differently from those who live on chalk, a tradition traced to patterns of landholding in the nineteenth century. There is a geography of abstention where certain rural areas always seem to have a high level of abstention and others a low one.

The tables in this chapter for votes by various social groups use the elections of 1978 and 1988. The first of these dates is an excellent benchmark because the four main parties put up separate candidates almost everywhere. The 1988 Presidential election is a less defensible choice because a Presidential vote is not quite the same as a party vote. In particular Mitterrand seeking re-election was a great deal more than a mere Socialist candidate, although in fact the characteristics of his first-ballot electorate are not all that different from that of the PS in 1986 (see chapter 7). It also has the lowest Communist score of any election so far. However, it has the advantage of separate 'UDF' and 'RPR' candidates (to be interpreted with caution because it is a Presidential not a normal party election) and it enables us to look at the characteristics of Front National supporters. Most of the tables demonstrate the point made in chapters 4 and 5 that there is no great sociological difference between the RPR and UDF electorates. The tables tell us nothing about the Green vote because the only national election in which they have done really well so far was the 1979 European Parliament election, and the high level of abstentions makes it too unsatisfactory to include. What it did tell us about the Green electorate was included in chapter 9.

Religion and voting. The map that traditionally gives the clearest picture of electoral behaviour is the map of religious practice. Where the Catholic church is strongest, the vote for the left is weakest. The map has endured for generations because it is a map of where the church retained its influence after the upheavals of the French Revolution – notably the west, Alsace-Lorraine and parts of the Massif Central. We have encountered several times in this book the link between intensity of religious practice and voting. Catholics who go to church regularly are much more likely to be supporters of the RPR/UDF. PS supporters are much more frequent among those who do not go to church. As Table 11.2 shows, this is the part of the population that has been growing so rapidly over the last two decades as France has become a modern post-industrial secular society. François Mitterrand and the Socialist Party have been able to win majorities in traditionally Catholic regions like Brittany – something unthinkable in the 1950s. The proportion of people who go to mass has fallen to below 30%, and the proportion who do not is now two out of three. Women are more religious than men, the old than the young, the rural than the urban, the upper and middle classes than the workers. Some recent research has suggested that one should rather divide 'nominal

Catholics' into those who believe (less likely to vote for the left) and those who do not (more likely to vote for the left). A relatively small number of voters belong to other religions: Protestant (.75 million) and Jewish (.25 million), but there is no marked correlation between religion and voting in the case of non-Catholics. Most of the Muslims in France (there are about 1.5 million North Africans and Turks – 3% of the population) are immigrants and have no votes.

Table 11.2.   RELIGION IN THE ELECTORATE

	1967 %	1974 %	1986 %
Catholics		87	83
Regular churchgoers	25	21	14
Occasional churchgoers	22	18	15
Non-churchgoers (nominal Catholics)	} 53	48 } 58	52 } 66
No religion		10	14
Other religions		3	5

Table 11.3.   RELIGIOUS PRACTICE BY SOCIAL GROUP (1983)
%

	RC (regular)	RC (occasional)	RC (nominal)	No Religion
Men	11	13	56	17
Women	17	20	47	12
Under 25	9	14	52	22
25–34	7	14	56	19
35–49	14	20	48	14
50–64	19	19	51	9
65 and over	24	15	52	7
Occupation (head of family)				
Farmers	22	32	41	4
Self-employed	12	22	49	13
Professions, top management	24	18	37	19
Junior management and professional	10	16	47	6
Clerical	7	21	47	19
Manual workers	6	13	62	16
Retired, etc.	22	14	52	10

Table 11.4.   VOTING BY RELIGION
(*first ballot %*)

| | 1978 Parliamentary | | | | 1988 Presidential | | | | |
	PC	PS	UDF	RPR	L	M	B	C	LeP
National total (%)	21	25	21	22	7	34	17	20	14
Catholics									
Regular	2	13	39	31	0	18	31	38	7
Occasional	11	20	28	33	4	26	17	31	16
Nominal	24	30	17	20	6	39	14	16	17
No religion	49	29	4	6	19	41	8	9	9

1988 candidates: Lajoinie PC, Mitterrand PS, Barre UDF, Chirac RPR, Le Pen FN.

Table 11.5.   ELECTORATE: SOCIAL STRUCTURE/OCCUPATION

	1962 %	1982 %
Farmers	12	6
Self-employed	8	6
Professions, top management	3	6
Junior professional and management	6	13
Clerical	14	21
Manual workers	31	26
Retired		24

Young Arabs born in France (about 400,000, known as *Beurs*) vote overwhelmingly for the left – if they vote at all.

Social class and voting.   Table 11.5 gives a rough guide to the social structure of the French by occupation. The most interesting changes over twenty years are the decline in the number of farmers and manual workers as a proportion of the population, and the increase in the white-collar occupations.

Voting is much more polarised by social class in France than it used to be, and indeed it is more significant today than religion. In the heyday of General de Gaulle, the Gaullist electorate was an almost perfect cross-section of the population, obtaining in particular its full share of the manual working class. However, since the 1970s a majority, usually a

Table 11.6. VOTING BY OCCUPATION
(head of family; first ballot %)

	1978 Parliamentary				1988 Presidential				
	PC	PS	UDF	RPR	L	M	B	C	LeP
National total (%)	21	25	21	22	7	34	17	20	14
Farmers	9	17	27	30	1	23	19	35	14
Self-employed	14	23	25	26	3	18	15	35	23
Professions, top management	9	15	27	30	2	24	23	23	17
Junior professional and management					9	34	20	13	10
Clerical	18	29	14	20	7	38	17	13	13
Manual workers	36	27	16	14	11	42	11	10	18
Public sector employees					8	41	14	12	11
Private sector employees					10	35	15	14	17

1988 candidates: Lajoinie PC, Mitterrand PS, Barre UDF, Chirac RPR, Le Pen FN.

large majority, of manual and clerical workers, especially in public-sector jobs like health and education which have grown enormously, vote for the left. The Communist Party has seen the erosion of its working-class support and the erosion of the manual working class itself as heavy industry disappears to be replaced by high technology and services. The Socialists have been particularly successful in the expanding white-collar occupations. The Front National candidate in 1988 did particularly well with manual workers and small traders (31% if one considers them alone rather than the whole group of self-employed and their families).

Gender and voting. Of all the social changes discussed in this chapter – decline of religion, decline of the blue-collar manual worker – none is more marked than the change in the situation of women. Far more women go out to work, and research by Janine Mossuz-Lavau has shown that working women are far more likely to vote for the left than those at home. Women are a big part of other changes too, such as the growth in higher education (52% of students are women) and the increase in professional and clerical jobs. In 1965 Mitterrand would have defeated de Gaulle if men only had had the right to vote. He received the support of 51% of men at the second ballot but only 39% of women.

The same happened against Giscard d'Estaing in 1974 – 53% of men but only 46% of women voted for Mitterrand. By 1988, however, things were very different. Not only did more women than men vote for Mitterrand, but the preference was particularly marked among women at work in manual and professional jobs, and young women. For instance 53% of women manual workers and 42% of women clerical employees voted for Mitterrand compared with 41% and 34% of men respectively. More men than women over sixty-five voted for

Table 11.7. VOTING BY GENDER
(first ballot %)

| | 1978 Parliamentary | | | | | 1988 Presidential | | | |
	PC	PS	UDF	RPR	L	M	B	C	LeP
National total (%)	21	25	21	22	7	34	17	20	14
Men (48% of population)	24	25	19	20	7	32	15	20	18
Women (52% of population)	19	25	22	24	6	26	18	20	11
Women at work					5	40	17	19	10
Women at home					6	34	18	21	15

1988 candidates: Lajoinie PC, Mitterrand PS, Barre UDF, Chirac RPR, Le Pen FN.

| | Left 1988 | | Right 1988 | |
	Men	Women	Men	Women
Under 25	39	50	57	44
25–35	52	57	42	38
35–49	48	48	49	48
50–64	37	38	61	59
65 and over	46	32	53	66
Manual workers	67	69	30	29
Clerical	51	55	46	42
Junior management and professional	46	53	48	42
Shopkeepers and self-employed	22	17	76	79
Retired	45	35	54	62
Students	35	49	61	43

Source: Bull BVA exit poll, J. Mossuz-Lavau and M. Sineau, *Le Monde*.

Mitterrand. More women than men over sixty-five voted for Chirac and Barre. Women are less willing than men to vote for the extremes of left and right. The Communist vote has always been more male than female, and the Front National vote is predominantly male.

Age groups. The general rule is that the left does better with the younger age groups and the right with the older groups. There have been some changes, however. The Communists used to be the strongest party among those under twenty-five – even in the 1981 Presidential election, generally considered a disaster for the PC. Now their support from the young is, if anything, even less than their support from older voters. Another change is that the Greens in the 1989 Euro-elections took, as we saw in chapter 9, quite a high share of the younger age groups, especially the better educated. As long ago as 1978 there was an observable *électorat critique* among the 18–20-year-olds, then voting in their first national election, which preferred the extreme left and the Greens to the orthodox parties. Finally an age group is composed of men and women and, as Table 11.7 shows for 1988, their voting behaviour is very different.

Abstention. The French are, on the whole, conscientious voters. In Presidential elections the turnout is usually around 85%, in Parliamentary elections between 78 and 80%, and even in Town Council elections about 75%. In the 1970s turnout steadily increased. In the late 1980s, however, it fell quite sharply – possibly from sheer electoral exhaustion. In fourteen months from April 1988 to June 1989 one could have

Table 11.8. VOTING BY AGE GROUP
(first ballot %)

	1978 Parliamentary				1988 Presidential				
	PC	PS	UDF	RPR	L	M	B	C	LeP
National total (%)	21	25	21	22	7	34	17	20	14
Under 25s	28	25	17	15	5	35	17	14	16
25–34	26	24	18	17	9	38	15	11	17
35–49	19	25	20	24	7	29	16	20	17
50–64	20	24	22	23	6	35	19	24	11
65 and over	15	25	27	28	9	33	15	29	12

1988 candidates: Lajoinie PC, Mitterrand PS, Barre UDF, Chirac RPR, Le Pen FN.

been asked to vote ten times, or twelve times if you lived where there was a by-election. Nevertheless commentators began to bewail the depoliticisation of the French people. The problem with 1988–9 was that electors felt they had made the really decisive choice right at the beginning – the Presidential election of April-May 1988. Some of the subsequent polling was felt to be unimportant – the New Caledonia referendum (Chapter 15), the Cantonal elections (county councils), the European Parliament.

There are many reasons for not voting in an election. Abstention can be a positive act. The Communists called for it in the second ballot of the 1969 Presidential election because they considered the choice between two candidates of the right unacceptable. The Socialists called for an abstention in the Referendum of 1972 on EEC enlargement because they felt it was merely a Pompidou popularity stunt. The RPR called for an abstention in the New Caledonia referendum of 1989 for political, if confused, reasons. In France, too, a voter can cast a blank ballot, which is counted as such, if he doesn't like what is put before him. When Georges Marchais, the Communist leader, was the only candidate in the second ballot in his constituency in 1978 (because the Socialist candidate who had been second withdrew under the terms of the PS/PC alliance), a third of those who took the trouble to vote cast blank ballots. Abstention can also of course be a negative act – the voter is not interested or not available.

Various political scientists in France have done studies of abstention – notably Alain Lancelot.[4] There is a geography of abstention. On the whole more people abstain in the south than in the north, with Corsica invariably having the worst record – perhaps because migrants to the mainland cannot get back to the island on polling day. These regional variations seem to be remarkably consistent as do 'micro-variations' from town to town, village to village. There is a sociology of abstention. The very young and very old abstain more than other age groups, the less educated more than the more educated, the working class more than the middle class. Those who are well integrated into society, do not occupy isolated or subordinate social roles and participate in associations are less likely to abstain. Is there a 'standing army' of permanent abstainers? In France this is something researchers can check by looking at the voters' lists after an election. Excluding the special factors motivating high abstention during the electoral epidemic of 1988–9, most studies have suggested that only about half the electorate always vote and about 5% never vote. The rest are occasional abstainers. One of the interesting findings of these studies is that although it appears from the voting figures for Parliamentary elections in many constituencies that almost exactly the same number of people have voted at the second ballot as at the first, they are not the same people. Around 30% of first-ballot abstainers vote at the second ballot. Around 30% of second-ballot abstainers voted at the first. Hence the importance of mobilising both your first-ballot voters and the first-ballot abstainers in a closely-fought election.

The principal 'political' explanation for abstention is the feeling that this election does not really matter. This is easily demonstrated by looking at the first-ballot turnout figures (%) for Parliamentary elections in the Fifth Republic:

1958	77	1978	83
1962	69	1981	71
1967	81	1986	79
1968	80	1988	66
1973	81		

The three where turnout was low (1962, 1981, 1988) were all elections where the decisive political choice was perceived just to have been made. The 1962 election followed on from the referendum on direct election of the Presidency, while the 1981 and 1988 Parliamentary elections immediately followed the election of the President. The elections in the 1970s during the period of the Union of the Left always had high turnouts because the choice was presented as a life-and-death matter where victory for the left would bring constitutional upheaval, Communism and so on. Indeed turnout started to increase at the second ballot as the parties of the right dramatised the starkness of the choice facing the people,[5] and this continued to happen in the 1980s:

	1st ballot	*2nd ballot*
1967	81	80
1968	80	78
1973	81	82
1978	83	84
1981	71	75
1988	66	70

The most exciting election – the Presidential election of 1974 between Giscard and the Union of the Left headed by Mitterrand, won by Giscard by less than 1% – had easily the highest turnout, with 85% at the first ballot, 88% at the second. The lowest turnouts are invariably at the European Parliament elections which are felt to have little importance for the government of the country. A further political explanation for abstention is dislike of the candidates on offer. It was noticeable in the 1978 election that abstention increased at the second ballot where the candidates remaining were Communist or RPR. In 1988 about 20% of Le Pen's first-ballot voters took refuge in abstention at the second ballot.

There are of course innumerable other aspects of electoral behaviour. There is the 'notable factor' whereby well-established local personalities have considerable electoral capital of their own. There is an element of clientelism in French political life. The mayor and *député* – often the same person; over three-quarters of *députés* are mayors of towns in their constituencies – control patronage and favours in their area. When the UDF and RPR have systematically run separate candidates, as in 1978, it was noticeable that it was the best-established local notable who nearly always won the first-ballot contest between the two.[6] There is the question of attitudes and 'vote motivation'. Research into supporters of the Front National has revealed the existence of something similar to the 'authoritarian personality' discovered in the classic post-war study by T.Adorno and others,[7] who were trying to find out why Fascism had such popular support in Europe before the war. FN voters are more favourable to the death penalty, against abortion, more critical of sexual deviation, more in favour of strong political leadership, and above all more inclined to stress immigration and crime as reasons for their electoral choice. We saw in chapter 9 that Green voters have a distinct set of attitudes on environmental issues. Communist voters were shown by some research in the 1950s to have distinctive and positive attitudes about the Soviet Union quite different from non-Communists.[8] However it is unclear whether such attitudes motivate or confirm political choice. It is better to stick to observing correlations than attributing causes.

NOTES

1. See Peter Campbell, *French Electoral Systems and Elections since 1789*, London: Faber and Faber, 1958.
2. J.R. Frears and J.-L. Parodi, *War Will not Take Place*, London: Hurst, 1979, p. 89 *et seq*.
3. Alain Lancelot, *L'abstentionnisme en France*, Paris: Armand Colin, 1968.
4. Ibid.

5. Jean Charlot (ed.), *Quand la gauche peut gagner* . . ., Paris: Moreau, 1973.
6. J.R. Frears and J.-L. Parodi, op. cit., p. 72.
7. *The Authoritarian Personality*, New York: 1950.
8. Pierre Fougeyrollas, *La conscience politique dans la France contemporaine*, Paris: Denoël, 1963.

12

PRESIDENTIAL ELECTIONS

Presidential elections by direct universal suffrage have become the most important in the Fifth Republic – in terms of deciding the configuration of power and in terms of public involvement and interest. However, they were not part of the original conception of the Fifth Republic and were introduced as a constitutional amendment adopted by referendum in October 1962. Many have argued that the amendment was adopted unconstitutionally because Article 89 specifies that Parliament has to agree constitutional changes before they are submitted to the people. However, the change was adopted by referendum, and because there is now an utterly overwhelming majority of people who prefer the direct popular choice of the President, it can be said to have legitimised itself. Of course, it is a change which has greatly altered the power of the Presidency, since the latter can now claim, as a direct expression of the popular will, a role as head of the executive that the constitution confers somewhat ambiguously.

The system of direct presidential elections began in 1965, when de Gaulle's first seven-year term expired. The General's original election as President in 1958 had taken place in the manner originally inscribed in the Fifth Republic Constitution, a manner which followed closely the constitutional doctrine of de Gaulle as outlined in his famous speech at Bayeux in 1946. The President of the Republic should be chosen by an 'electoral college which includes Parliament but is much wider than Parliament'. Thus it was. The 1958 electoral college consisted of all members of both houses of Parliament, *conseillers généraux* (*département* or county councillors), representatives of overseas territories, and a number of delegates from municipalities determined by size of commune and chosen by the municipal council. One of the arguments in 1962 for going over to direct elections by universal suffrage, according to Eric Roussel in his biography of Pompidou, was that such an electoral college comprising local councillors would probably have voted the next time for that old Fourth Republic conservative and symbol of financial orthodoxy, Antoine Pinay. The one 'indirect suffrage' presidential election of 24 December 1958 produced this result:

Electorate	81,761
Turnout	79,470

	%
De Gaulle	78.5
Marranne (Communist)	13.1
Chatelet (Union of Democratic Forces)	8.4

The constitutional amendment of 1962 has ensured that the successors of General de Gaulle possess an authority which in normal circumstances a President chosen by 80,000 local worthies could not expect. Some directly-elected Presidents fulfill an honorific and not a leadership role – in Austria and the Irish Republic, for instance – but in France the prestige of the office, its central position in the institutions of the Fifth Republic, and the further deliberately added lustre of direct elections make it inconceivable that Presidents of the Fifth Republic will, as in the two previous Republics, 'be content with opening flower-shows'.

The election of the President by direct universal suffrage, introduced by the constitutional amendment of October 1962, operates in the following way. It is a two-ballot election, with the second ballot a run-off between two candidates only. The election must, according to Article 7 of the constitution, take place not less than twenty and not more than thirty-five days after the expiry of the existing President's term of office or after a vacancy has been caused either by his resignation or by his death. During this brief interval between a President's resignation or death and the election of a new President, the President of the Senate becomes temporary Head of State. Senator Alain Poher had to do this twice: in 1969 after the resignation of General de Gaulle and in 1974 after the death of President Pompidou. Any citizen can be a candidate for the Presidency – in 1974 it seemed as though most were. Since 1974, however, a candidate has needed 500 signatures, collected from Mayors and other elected persons in at least thirty *départements*. This was designed to stop the increasing tendency for publicity-seeking '*fantaisistes*' to put up for election and get all that free air-time on television. The Presidential ambitions of the late Coluche, the famous clown, were brought to an end by the new rule. Candidates also pay a deposit of Frs 10,000 – refundable if they poll 5% of the vote. The constitutional council decides whether candidatures are valid, presides over the running of the election, can start the election again if a candidate dies or stands down, and declares the result.

In 1988 President Mitterrand, in the wake of a number of scandals involving election funds, instructed his Prime Minister Jacques Chirac to introduce a law limiting campaign finance and introducing state aid for it. A ceiling on campaign expenditure of Frs 120 million per candidate (Frs 140 million for the two candidates present in the second ballot) was introduced. The state repays all campaign expenses up to 25% of this ceiling to each candidate who receives more than 5% of the vote. Candidates receiving less than 5% are repaid their expenses up to 5% of the ceiling – so a minor candidate could spend Frs 6 million, at least covering the printing of an election address, and get it all back, and a major candidate (there were five in 1988) Frs 30m. The winner of the election has to make a declaration of his personal wealth and another at the time his term of office expires.

Like Britain but unlike the United States, France has no television commercials with air time paid for by candidates. Instead each candidate has an equal free allocation of broadcasting time on radio and television, and can use it personally to address the voters or share with supporters or indeed present a filmed 'commercial'. Thus in 1969 the Socialist candidate Gaston Defferre used to appear on television with the man he intended, if victorious, to appoint Prime Minister, Pierre Mendès-France. In the 1974 elections one of the Trotskyist candidates, Arlette Laguiller, who always starts her broadcasts with the words '*Travailleuses, travailleurs*', used to introduce revolutionary printing workers to intrigued viewers. In 1988 (see chapter 10) Le Pen, the candidate of the Front National, used the image of a horse race board game to present himself as the 'outsider' gaining on the other runners. The principle of equal broadcasting time is rigorously respected at presidential elections – unlike referenda, where supporters of '*Oui*' and '*Non*' have not always enjoyed equality. In 1969 one of the candidates was doing his military service; nevertheless Infantryman Second Class Krivine, A., representing a proscribed student revolutionary movement, was able to address the nation on the need for armed revolutionary struggle for one hour and forty minutes of free television and radio time which, like all the other candidates, he had been accorded. Let it not be said that there is no freedom of speech in France.

To be elected at the first ballot a candidate needs an absolute majority of votes cast (at least 50% + 1). If this does not occur, a second ballot is held a fortnight later – in France voting always takes place on Sunday. As in other elections for public office in the Fifth Republic, no new candidate may enter the contest after the first ballot, but unlike other elections, the constitution (Art. 7) lays down that there shall, in a presidential election, be only two candidates in the second ballot. This ensures that the President of the Republic will be the final choice of an absolute majority of those voting. The rule is that the only candidates allowed at the second ballot are the two who had the most votes at the first ballot. If either, for some reason, prefers to withdraw, then it is the candidate with the next highest first-ballot score who would contest the second ballot. At all events, the second ballot is a run-off between two – and only two – candidates. In America the successful presidential candidate has to carry a majority of states, or at least the most populous ones with a majority of electoral votes, and he could conceivably win without an absolute popular majority. Nothing analogous to this happens in France: each elector's vote counts towards one national total.

The President of the Republic is elected for seven years. Pompidou, shortly before his death, began the Parliamentary process of changing the term to five years to bring it into line with that of the National Assembly. The idea was not that Presidential and Parliamentary elections should take place together (impossible when the power to dissolve Parliament exists), but that the Presidential mandate would always be reasonably fresh. The shorter term would thus strengthen the President's authority. Mitterrand in his 1981 campaign promised to propose a similar constitutional change – either reducing the Presidential term to five years (re-eligible once as in the United States) or retained at seven years with no re-election. In the event no changes were proposed.

The 1965 election (5 and 19 December)

The 1965 presidential election aroused great public interest, and has been much analysed. It was the first 'television election' in the sense that ownership of sets was sufficiently widespread for the whole nation to participate in a national political event, and in the sense too that the public, thanks to the provision of equal time on the air, got the chance to have a good look at the opposition to de Gaulle. What were the issues and the incidents of the campaign is not important at this distance in time: the enduring interest centres on three things. First, it marked the turning-point from 'personal' Gaullism to the development of Gaullism as an organised party machine. Secondly, it marked the first relative success for the concept of a single candidate to represent all the left, and the making of François Mitterrand as a national figure. Thirdly, it revealed in the candidature of Jean Lecanuet the probable limits of centrist attempts to oppose both Gaullism and the left. Four years later, in the unusual circumstances of 1969, a centrist candidate, Alain Poher, was to obtain more votes than Lecanuet's total in 1965. In 1974 Giscard d'Estaing presented his candidature, backed by Lecanuet, as a centrist, but the anti-Gaullism of the Finance Minister who had served the General and President Pompidou was one of nuance rather than fundamental principle. The Lecanuet candidature seems to represent the Fifth Republic limits of an anti-Gaullist, anti-left movement.

The main issue of the campaign was the General himself. Despite his immense prestige he was vulnerable in terms of his age (seventy-five), the 'contemptuous impression' given by the apparent haughtiness of his candidature at the outset, and his foreign policy – most notably European policy. This was the period of the 'empty chair' when France simply refused to take part in European Community decision-making for several months until the other countries had agreed to drop demands for decisions to be based on majority voting, not unanimity. Opposed to de Gaulle were a *fantaisiste* candidate (Barbu); a senator with no party backing (Marcilhacy); a right-wing lawyer Maître Tixier-Vignancour who campaigned against de Gaulle's 'treachery' in selling-out Algeria and was supported by many of those who now lead the Front National; Jean Lecanuet, president of the MRP and Mayor of Rouen; and François Mitterrand. The last-named obtained the support of the Socialist Party (SFIO) and the Radicals, who grouped together to form the Federation of the Democratic and Socialist Left (FGDS; see chapter 6), and the Communist Party. He was thus the 'sole candidate of the left'. Both Mitterrand and Lecanuet presented their candidatures as representing a first step towards the creation of a new political movement. The creation of the Centre Démocrate and the alliance, six years later in 1971, of its persistent anti-Gaullist elements with Servan-Screiber's Radicals to form the Mouvement Réformateur (Reform Movement) was the outcome of Lecanuet's pledge. The FGDS and, six years later, the creation of the new Socialist Party under Mitterrand's leadership and the building of the Union de la Gauche with its joint programme of government agreed with the Communist Party – these were the ultimate developments of the Mitterrand candidature in 1965.

De Gaulle failed to win outright at the first ballot and this was regarded as something of a shock. His 10.4 million votes were almost 2 million less than the total of those voting 'Yes' at the October 1962 referendum on direct presidential elections. F.L. Wilson considers this as the decisive moment when the Prime Minister Georges Pompidou, seeing the need for organisation to supplement the waning of charismatic authority, turned himself into a party manager to direct the second-ballot campaign and subsequent parliamentary elections.[1] One must not exaggerate the de Gaulle 'failure'. He received more votes than the supporters of the Gaullist UNR party at the parliamentary elections of November 1962. He obtained a first ballot overall majority in thirteen *départements*, nearly all in Eastern France, Brittany and Normandy. Moreover, he polled very well in working-class industrial districts in northern cities like Lille and Communist suburbs of the Paris 'red belt' like Nanterre and Montreuil.

Mitterrand found most of his strength in the southern half of the country, where his first ballot exceeded the General's in twenty *départements*. His total of 7.7 million (32.2%) was still 3.5 million less than the combined parties of the left had obtained in the last parliamentary election of the Fourth Republic. A very large number of traditional left-wing supporters clearly preferred de Gaulle as President. The Lecanuet vote was concentrated in the old rural Catholic strongholds of the MRP, particularly in the west of France. This was support that would probably have gone to de Gaulle in the first ballot, but, having prevented his first-ballot re-election, two-thirds of it transferred to him at the second. Tixier-Vignancour polled fairly strongly

Table 12.1.   PRESIDENTIAL ELECTION, 1965

	1st ballot		2nd ballot	
Electorate	28.2m.		28.2m.	
Abstentions	15.0%		15.5%	
Spoilt votes	.2%		.7%	
	million votes	%	*million votes*	%
De Gaulle	10.4	43.7	12.6	54.5
Mitterrand	7.7	32.2	10.6	45.5
Lecanuet	3.8	15.8		
Tixier-Vignancour	1.3	5.3		
Marcilhacy	.4	1.7		
Barbu	.3	1.2		

among the white families, mainly on the south coast, who had been resettled in France after independence made them leave Algeria, but he got nowhere near the total of 1.8 million votes cast against Algerian independence in the referendum of April 1962.

The electoral turnout, 85%, was very high. The only vote in French electoral history that had attracted similar public interest was the 1958 referendum which consecrated de Gaulle's return to power and inaugurated the Fifth Republic. A final point to be noted on the 1965 vote is the General's success in the overseas territories (the results of which do not appear in Table 12.2). Of the half million overseas electors who voted, about 45,000 voted for de Gaulle at each ballot. This gives a final score at the second ballot of:

De Gaulle	13.1 million votes – 55.2%
Mitterrand	10.6 million votes – 44.8%

The 1969 election (1 and 15 June)

Of the six presidential elections that have taken place by universal suffrage so far in the Fifth Republic, the one in 1969 is the most peculiar. It took place in the strange circumstances of General de Gaulle's abrupt resignation at midnight on 28 April after his proposed reform of the Senate and the Regions had been defeated by referendum. The opposition forces were completely disunited, and in consequence there was no major challenger from the left. Indeed it is the only election from 1965 up till the time of writing that did not have François Mitterrand as a candidate. The great upheaval of May 1968 and then the Soviet invasion of Czechoslovakia in August 1968 had re-opened all the old hostility and mistrust between the Communist and non-Communist Left. The election defeat for the Left in 1968 had been heavy, the FGDS which grouped Radicals and Socialists had collapsed.

There are two points to retain from the 1969 election. The first is the smooth transition from de Gaulle's leadership to that of a less heroic figure. The prophecies of chaos were completely unfounded. The Gaullist electorate did not disintegrate; it remained cohesive and elected Georges Pompidou. The second is that, although presidential candidates like to appear 'above party', party organisation is critically important in a presidential election. The role of the UDR party in this smooth transition from heroic Gaullism was of capital importance.

Georges Pompidou campaigned on the admirably clear slogan '*continuité et ouverture*': continuity of the stability and achievements of the Fifth Republic, and an opening towards a more liberal approach in civil liberties, in European policy and so on. By this means the valuable support of Giscard d'Estaing and the Independent Republicans (which had been denied to the General in the April referendum) was secured, as well as that of some opposition centrists (though not Lecanuet), and the future presidential Majority was widened. Pompidou's principle opponent turned out to be the President of the Senate, Alain Poher, a centrist of MRP background, who had played a big part in the campaign to defeat the April referendum in which the virtual abolition of his beloved Senate had been proposed. The public had rather taken to this amiable figure, fumbling with his notes on television and putting on his glasses to read them better. It was an agreeable and reassuring contrast to the olympian General. After the resignation of de Gaulle, Poher, in conformity with Article 7 of the constitution, became the temporary President of the Republic, and early opinion polls placed him in a favourable position to win.

The left, in complete disarray, had four candidates. The romantic revolutionary left was represented by Michel Rocard (PSU) – later, as we have seen, to become very popular as a leader of the social-democratic moderates in the Socialist Party and in 1988 Prime Minister – and Alain Krivine, who had been active, and indeed was arrested, in the student revolt of May 1968. The Socialist Party after much dissension agreed to the candidature of Gaston Defferre, Mayor of Marseille. François Mitterrand stayed right out of it. No one believed that the Communist Party would present a candidate; it was supposed that electors who are quite happy to vote for a hard-working Communist mayor or Member of Parliament would not want a Communist President, and that the extent of their supporters' commitment to the Party would be derisorily revealed for what it was. However, the PCF did present a candidate, its jovial elder statesman Senator Jacques Duclos, and fought a well-organised and rather successful campaign. Finally there was the *fantaisiste* candidature of Ducatel.

According to R.G. Schwartzenburg,[2] the results in 1969 proved that three elements are essential to success in a presidential campaign – party support, credibility of policies and credibility of the candidate. The candidature of Alain Poher, whose star steadily declined as time went on, lacked all these elements. He and Gaston Defferre were extremely vulnerable to the charge that they would have no ministerial team which could command a parliamentary majority, and that they would be unable to continue strong government under presidential leadership, the essential feature of the stability of the Fifth Republic. Poher's emphasis on Gaullist abuses of power – control of television, secret police and so on – struck a progressively less responsive chord as the campaign developed. The only two candidates to have the support of a large and efficient party organisation were Pompidou and Duclos. Duclos, completely written off at the outset, received more votes than the Communist Party in the 1968 elections, and almost defeated Poher for a place in the second ballot. Pompidou polled only half-a-million fewer than de Gaulle in the first ballot of 1965. There were local campaign committees for Pompidou, giving an impression of wide support from different sectors, but the organisational effort was contributed by the UDR. In the words of Jacques Duclos: 'Behind the lace curtains of the campaign committees, it was the vast machinery of the UDR party that took on the heavy work.' Poher's campaign committees, by contrast, were no camouflage but all he had.

The election is difficult to analyse in terms of comparison with previous elections, mainly because of the collapse of the Socialist candidature. Hardly any of the electors who normally vote Socialist or Radical voted for Defferre. A very large proportion decided to support Poher on the grounds that the main object of the election was to defeat Gaullism. Poher, it was felt, had the best opportunity of gaining wide enough second-ballot support to do that, and one therefore voted Poher at the first ballot to ensure that he had a place in the second. This practice of the 'useful vote' at the first ballot was to become more and more a feature of elections in France – as the Communists discovered to their cost in 1981. Some Socialists, on the other hand, felt the need to vote for a genuine candidate of the left in the first ballot and supported Rocard or Duclos. The total vote for the left at 6.9 million was its worst result since the Second World War – three-quarters of a million fewer than Mitterrand on his own in 1965, 3 million fewer even than in the disastrous parliamentary elections of 1968.

Geographically Poher did best where Lecanuet had done best (Normandy and the Loire country) and in some of the old Socialist and Radical bastions of the south-west. Pompidou did not perform so well in industrial areas as de Gaulle, but in parts of the rural centre and south he actually did better, reflecting Gaullist gains in the 1968 parliamentary elections. Poher's second ballot vote was 4 million below the 'No' vote in the April referendum – partly, no doubt, because the Communist Party advised its supporters to abstain in the second ballot. Pompidou, in the second ballot, received 2 million fewer votes than de Gaulle in the

Table 12.2.   PRESIDENTIAL ELECTION, 1969

	1st ballot		*2nd ballot*	
Electorate	28.8m.		28.8m.	
Abstentions	21.8%		30.9%	
Spoilt votes	1.0%		4.5%	
	million votes	*%*	*million votes*	*%*
Pompidou	9.8	44.0	10.7	57.6
Poher	5.2	23.4	7.9	42.4
Duclos (PC)	4.8	21.5		
Defferre (Socialist)	1.1	5.1		
Rocard (PSU)	.8	3.7		
Ducatel	.3	1.3		
Krivine (Trotskyite)	.2	1.1		

second ballot of 1965, but about the same number as the referendum 'Yes' vote and the RPR vote in the 1968 parliamentary elections. The Communist candidate also polled his party's normal electoral score of between 4.5 and 5 million.

The turnout, even at the first ballot, was low for a presidential election. At the second ballot, the big increase of over 2.5 million in the numbers of people not voting or spoiling their ballot papers was due to the advice of the PCF to its supporters. The PCF takes elections very seriously and always tries to get its supporters to participate in the vote, but the 1969 second ballot was the one and only occasion when it has urged Communist electors to stay at home, and even warned that there would be Communist militants at the polling station watching to see that they did. Pompidou must have been very grateful. Only a massive switch by Communist voters to Poher could have defeated him. It has been maliciously suggested that the Soviet Union, which preferred the continuation of Gaullist foreign policy, played a part in the PCF's decision to deny its votes to the anti-Gaullist candidate. The low second-ballot turnout meant that the 10.7 million electors who finally chose Pompidou were only 37.2% of the total electorate.

The 1974 election (5 and 19 May)

The election of May 1974, provoked by the sudden death of President Pompidou on 2 April, was much more a war of succession than the 1969 contest. Pompidou, despite his dismissal as Prime Minister in June 1968, had been regarded as the natural successor to de Gaulle. In 1974 no individual had been anointed or declared to have a 'national destiny'. The first interesting aspect of the 1974 election is therefore the emergence of a champion of the outgoing Majority. The second aspect is the great success of the Union of the Left strategy in uniting Socialists, Radicals and Communists behind the single candidature of François Mitterrand, who came within 400,000 votes of victory in a poll of 26 million. The third point to retain is the immense public interest in the election – huge crowds at meetings and rallies, tremendous audiences for the television coverage, especially the second ballot face-to-face debate between Giscard and Mitterrand; and the record voting participation of almost 90% of the electorate.

The rivalry within the ranks of the government Majority for the presidential crown is a very interesting story. The first candidate to appear, before the late President was cold in his grave, was Jacques Chaban-Delmas. An ardent Gaullist since the wartime Resistance, Mayor of Bordeaux, Prime Minister under the Pompidou Presidency from 1969 to 1972, he was endorsed by the UDR Party where orthodox Gaullists, rather than Pompidou men, had gained the upper hand since the Party conference at Nantes in November 1973. He was challenged by Valéry Giscard d'Estaing, President Pompidou's Minister of Finance, and by Edgar Faure, President of the National Assembly and a Prime Minister from the Fourth Republic. The Prime Minister, Pierre Messmer, expressing the fears of those who thought that a division in the ranks of the government Majority would lead to a victory of the Left, invited all to withdraw in favour of himself. Jacques Chaban-Delmas was the first to refuse. In consequence Giscard retained his candidature – at least that was the explanation he gave. Edgar Faure withdrew. Two days later another minister, Jean Royer, Mayor of Tours – champion of family life, sexual decency and the small shopkeeper – announced his candidature. His brief and ineffective campaign never recovered from his first televised meeting when a number of nubile students took their clothes off. The sole significance of the Royer candidature was that it appeared to cut into the support for Chaban-Delmas, thus enabling a large gap to open in the opinion polls between him and Giscard d'Estaing. That gap never closed, and Giscard, increasingly judged to have the best second-ballot chance against François Mitterrand, grew ever stronger at the expense of the Mayor of Bordeaux.

There were two important pointers to the eventual success of Giscard d'Estaing in rallying an enlarged Majority to his banner. The first was the support of Jean Lecanuet, candidate against de Gaulle in 1965. This was important because his party – the *Centre Démocrate* which, together with part of the Radical Party, was a component of the *Réformateurs* – had been an opposition party during the Pompidou Presidency. The second was the declaration of 'the 43' on 13 April. 'The 43' were four ministers – most notably Jacques Chirac, Minister of the Interior and protégé of President Pompidou – and thirty-nine members of Parliament, mostly UDR. Their declaration made it clear that many influential people in the UDR, especially the new men who represented '*Pompidolisme*' rather than the orthodox heroic Gaullism, had reservations about the Chaban-Delmas candidature. They declared that they would support whoever appeared best placed to safeguard the fundamental principles of the Fifth Republic and defeat any 'Socialo-Communist' candidate – a message in code meaning support for Giscard.

In policy terms Giscard's campaign was very similar to that of Pompidou in 1969: '*continuité et ouverture*'. He would continue the policies of the late President in the spheres of economic and foreign policy, especially European integration. In constitutional matters, in dealings with the opposition and with Parliament and over civil liberties such as freedom from telephone tapping he would be more liberal. Chaban-Delmas tried desperately to conjure up the genii of heroic Gaullism, constantly invoking the General's name, national prestige, the Resistance. He even visited the Île de Sein, a bleak, rocky and almost unpopulated islet off West Finistère, which in 1940 had sent all its men to join General de Gaulle and fight for Free France. The failure of the Chaban-Delmas campaign marks the end of heroic Gaullism as an electoral force.

In contrast to the division within the Majority and those within the left at the time of the previous Presidential election, the parties of the left were speedily united behind Mitterrand's candidature. Agreement was reached on 5 April; the special conference of the Socialist Party adopted him unanimously on the 8th; the same day the PCF, at its most conciliatory and cooperative throughout the campaign, announced that it would not present a separate candidate; and a statement signed by the PS, the PCF and the MRG (Left-wing Radicals) declared Mitterrand to be the common candidate of the Left. This term was a concession to the PCF, since 'sole candidate' would have implied that he was the socialist candidate who happened to be supported by the other parties.

In addition to the rival candidates of the Majority and Mitterrand,

there was an unusually large number of *fantaisistes*. There were two
Trotskyists from rival chapels, the veteran presidential candidate Alain
Krivine and Arlette Laguiller (Workers' Struggle); an 'ecological'
candidate – still not called 'green' – René Dumont; an extreme right-
wing nationalist who had been a Poujadist *député* in the 1950s, but was
to become much more prominent as the leader of the *Front National* in
the 1980s (Jean-Marie le Pen); a royalist (Renouvin); an anti-
Communist Socialist (Emile Muller); and two European Federalists
(Sébag and Héraud) – twelve candidates in all.

The final result was remarkably close – only 400,000 between the
two candidates out of 26 million counted. Mitterrand was the
beneficiary of the biggest-ever vote for the Left. Some observers saw
the election as re-constituting the old division of the country into the
right and the classic left as the left-wing sympathisers of Gaullism and its
right-wing opponents returned to their traditional camps. This view
underestimates Mitterrand's success in urban areas and among working-
class voters in parts of the country traditionally associated with the
Right. Reims, Beauvais, Le Creusot or Le Mans provide examples.
Mitterrand improved on his 1965 performance predominantly in the
industrial areas of the north and east, where de Gaulle used to have such
electoral appeal.

Table 12.3.   PRESIDENTIAL ELECTION, 1974

	1st ballot		2nd ballot	
Electorate	29.8m.		29.8m.	
Abstentions	15.1%		12.1%	
Spoilt votes	.8%		1.2%	
	million votes	%	*million votes*	%
Mitterrand	10.9	43.4	12.7	49.3
Giscard d'Estaing	8.3	32.9	13.1	50.7
Chaban-Delmas	3.6	14.6		
Royer	.8	3.2		
Laguiller (Extreme Left)	.6	2.4		
Dumont (Green)	.3	1.3		
Le Pen (Extreme Right)	.2	.8		
Muller (Socialist dissident)	.2	.7		
Krivine (Trotskyist)	.1	.4		
Renouvin (Royalist)	.04	.2		
Sébag (European Federalist)	.04	.2		
Héraud (European Federalist)	.02	.1		

The 1981 election (26 April and 10 May)

Virtually the same people and parties had governed France for twenty-three years. Presidents de Gaulle, Pompidou and Giscard d'Estaing had been supported by coalitions of Gaullists and Centrists. In 1981, for the first time in the Fifth Republic, power passed to the opposition. Prophecies that a victory for the Left would bring chaos were unfounded as a perfectly peaceful transfer of power took place, followed incidentally by a continuation of the national consensus on political institutions, defence, foreign policy and other fundamentals. It was also the first time that the electors had got rid of an apparently all-powerful incumbent President at a normal election.

As well as the outstandingly important fact of the first peaceful alternation of power, there are two other interesting aspects of the 1981 election. The first was the collapse of the Communist vote to 15%, their worst score since the 1930s though only the beginning of an ever greater decline as the 1980s went on. The second was the contribution to the defeat of Giscard d'Estaing by his former Prime Minister and leader of the Gaullist RPR, Jacques Chirac.

There were no great surprises among the candidatures. The Communist party had long declared its intention to present a candidate and had been in a mood of intensely anti-Socialist hostility since the break-up of the Union of the Left in 1977. Its candidate was Secretary General Georges Marchais. President Giscard d'Estaing declared himself a candidate and was supported by the UDF. Gaullism was somewhat divided. Michel Debré, de Gaulle's first Prime Minister in 1958–62 and one of the historic Gaullists, decided to stand. So did Marie-France Garaud, one of the formidable duo, Garaud and Pierre Juillet, from Chirac's private staff when he was Prime Minister and when he set up the RPR, who had been so influential in urging a tough line against anyone thought of as 'wet' or liberal or sympathetic to Giscard d'Estaing. The RPR, however, supported its leader Jacques Chirac.

The Socialist Party in France is the only one which has a democratic procedure for selecting its candidate for the Presidency, and it looked for a time as if it would actually have to operate. François Mitterrand's star had been on the wane since the failure of his strategy of the Union of the Left and the defeat of the Left at the Parliamentary elections of 1978, and it was not certain that he wished to be a candidate again. Michel Rocard, leader of the social-democratic wing of the party and critic of Socialist 'archaism', always ahead of Mitterrand in popular opinion as measured by the polls, and Jean-Pierre Chévènement, leader of the left wing of the

PS declared themselves candidates for the nomination, but they also declared that they would stand down if the party leader François Mitterrand wished to stand. At the last moment, Mitterrand said he would, so the special party congress was a rally and not a selection.

There were four other candidates, left or left-inclined: Michel Crépeau, leader of the MRG (Left Radicals) – a party that had been closely allied to the Socialists since 1972; Huguette Bouchardeau of the small left-wing party the PSU (whose leader before 1974 had been Michel Rocard); the Trotskyist veteran of the 1974 campaign Arlette Laguiller; and the Green candidate Brice Lalonde, who polled over 1 million votes. The first two of these were to become ministers in the Socialist government of 1981–6, and Lalonde (no longer regarded as a true Green) a minister in the Socialist government of 1988.

The first factor in the success of Mitterrand was the unpopularity of Giscard: the relaxed and informal style, for which he had been known as Minister of Finance in the 1960s and with which he began his Presidency, had long since disappeared and given place to a more distant and high-handed manner. There had been the affair of the Bokassa diamonds – he was said to have received a costly gift from the dictator of one of France's client-states in Africa – in which he disdainfully declined to explain himself to the French people. He had not achieved his aim of making France a more liberal society, and power was just as concentrated in the hands of the President as when he criticised de Gaulle for the 'solitary exercise of power' in 1967. Mitterrand did not have to campaign very hard. His posters reassuringly presented him as '*la force tranquille*'. It was the thought of another seven years of Giscard d'Estaing, making fourteen years in all, that was decisive.

Another main factor in the success of Mitterrand was the collapse of the Communist vote. Mitterrand had always championed the policy of the Union of the Left as the only winning strategy. However, at successive national elections in the 1970s (1973, 1974, 1978) the Right had always been able to make the fear of Communist domination its principle electoral weapon against the Left. With the Communist vote down to 15%, who could pretend that the Communists would dominate? Furthermore, it put them in no position to make demands, and consequently Marchais joined the other first-ballot candidates of the Left in urging a second-ballot vote for Mitterrand.

The third element was the contribution of Jacques Chirac to the defeat of Giscard, the man he had helped to become President in 1974 when urging Gaullists to abandon the sinking ship of Jacques Chaban-Delmas. His virulent attacks on the state of the nation under Giscard included the following: 'France is growing weak. Its currency is shaky, its position in the world is crumbling . . . lassitude and doubt . . . process of degradation.' So bad was Giscard's record that it did not lead 'the majority of us spontaneously and joyfully to give him a new licence for seven years'. Above all was the statement which Mitterrand used with great effect in the television face-to-face debate before the second ballot: 'We are in an extremely worrying situation which requires a complete change of policy, and one does not change policy by keeping the same men.' As if this was not enough, Chirac did not endorse Giscard for the second ballot other than saying he would personally vote for him, and did not campaign for him. It has been estimated that about 1 million of the 6 million non-Giscard first-ballot votes for the Right went to Mitterrand at the second ballot.

At the first ballot Mitterrand did well. His 26% was the best total ever achieved by a Socialist party in France up to then. One of the reasons why the Communist vote was so low was that many

Table 12.4. PRESIDENTIAL ELECTION, 1981

	1st ballot		2nd ballot	
Electorate	36.4m.		36.4m.	
Abstentions	18.9%		14.1%	
Spoilt votes	1.4%		2.5%	
	million votes	*%*	*million votes*	*%*
Mitterrand (Socialist)	7.5	25.9	15.7	51.8
Marchais (PCF)	4.5	15.4		
Crépeau (MRG)	.6	2.2		
Laguiller (Trotskyist)	.7	2.3		
Bouchardeau (PSU)	.3	1.1		
Total left	*13.6*	*46.9*		
Lalonde (Green)	1.1	3.9		
Giscard d'Estaing	8.2	28.2	14.6	48.2
Chirac (RPR)	5.2	18.0		
Debré (Gaullist)	.5	1.7		
Garaud (Gaullist)	.4	1.3		
(Total right and centre)	*14.3*	*49.2*		

Communist electors had already chosen Mitterrand as the only credible champion of the left. Even so, the total left-wing votes came to only 46%. At the second ballot, the turnout was much higher (87%), and Mitterrand gained extra support, as well as the lion's share of the first ballot green vote, the disciplined support of the Communist voters and, as we have noted, many of Chirac's votes too. Mitterrand gained in every region of the country, as compared with 1974, except Provence. The gains were particularly marked in the traditionally Catholic regions like Brittany and Normandy, where the left has always been weakest. Mitterrand carried seventeen out of twenty-two regions against only ten in the close election of 1974.

The 1988 election (24 April and 8 May)

The 1988 Presidential elections marked the end of *'cohabitation'* – at least of the Fifth Republic's first experience of it. Ever since the opposition came close to winning an election in 1967, the possibility of a President facing a Parliamentary majority composed of his political adversaries became the dominant issue at almost every parliamentary election – 1973, 1978, 1986. In 1986 it finally happened. President Mitterrand, like the Queen in Britain, sent for the leader of the largest Parliamentary group, Jacques Chirac, and asked him to form a government. Presidential supremacy, the principal characteristic of government in the Fifth Republic for twenty-eight years, melted away. Policy leadership passed to the Prime Minister and the government. What was not generally recognised was how far this process went between 1986 and 1988. In foreign affairs and defence, for example, traditionally regarded as Presidential domains, the flow of information to the Presidency was substantially reduced, and more and more decision-making passed to the Prime Minister's diplomatic and military policy unit. Nevertheless public expectation of Presidential leadership and the high prestige of the Presidency continued. Consequently, the most interesting aspect of the 1988 Presidential election was the struggle between Presidential legitimacy and Prime Ministerial power, which reached its inevitable climax in the second-ballot contest between Mitterrand and Chirac. The other significant features of the 1988 election were the remarkable success of Le Pen, the leader of the Front National, and the lowest-ever score of the PCF.

In the pre-election period interest had centred on two points: the carefully contrived uncertainty over the candidature for a second term of

President Mitterrand himself, and the rivalry between Chirac and Raymond Barre. Barre – Prime Minister under Giscard in 1976–81 – had stood high in the opinion polls during the *'cohabitation'* period, mainly because he had always refused to accept *'cohabitation'* and therefore could distance himself from unpopular government policies, but his position was inherently weak. He did not have that inspirational quality miscalled charisma. The leading members of the UDF, which officially supported Barre, were mainly ministers in the government and committed to supporting it. Some – like François Léotard the leader of the Republican Party (see chapter 5) – could scarcely conceal their preference for Chirac, and ex-President Giscard d'Estaing, for some extraordinary reason, refused to declare which of his two former Prime Ministers he was supporting, despite the fact that Chirac had contributed massively to his defeat in 1981. Barre's main problem, however, was the agreement he made with Chirac not to criticise the government. The reason he did so was because both men saw the need to avoid what happened in 1981: the hostility of Chirac to Giscard contributed to a very poor transfer of votes to Giscard at the second ballot and the victory of the Socialist candidate. Once Chirac and Barre were in the field as candidates, with Barre and the UDF ministers loyally refraining from criticising the Prime Minister's record, Chirac's greater energy, his ability to use governmental power and resources and his better organisation all meant that he established an immediate lead as the more credible candidate. In the event Barre, with 16.5%, did well to avoid *'Chabanisation'* – the fate of marginalisation that can so easily overtake whomever is perceived, like Chaban-Delmas in 1974, as the minor candidate of the right and centre coalition.

The PC selected not Georges Marchais but its National Assembly group President, André Lajoinie, not well-known outside his own rural constituency in the Auvergne. There was also a dissident Communist candidate, Pierre Juquin – the leader of the liberalising *Rénovateurs* who had been for many years a member of the Central Committee, and two candidates of the extreme left. One was Arlette Laguiller, fighting her third Presidential election, and the other Pierre Boussel, an elderly representative of an obscure organisation called MPPT (Movement for a Workers' Party) which appeared to be engaged in some private internal conflict.

Mitterrand's campaign was Presidential, Chirac's Prime-Ministerial. The theme of Mitterrand's poster campaign was national unity (*La France unie*). He wrote a 20,000-word 'Letter to all French people', placed as a paid advertisement in regional and national dailies. It set out his vision for a united Europe, a new 'Marshall Plan' for the Third World, the maintenance of democratic freedoms and stable institutions, the priority of education and the elimination of poverty. He spoke, alone on a platform decorated only with the national *Tricolore* gently ruffled by an air-blower as the *Marseillaise* was played, at huge meetings in a number of major cities. The Socialist Party and its leaders played virtually no role in the campaign.

Chirac's campaign was notable for its astonishing exploitation of the resources of government power. In the few days before the decisive second ballot, he had the remaining French hostages released from the Lebanon, the French gendarmes held by rebel forces in the French territory of New Caledonia released in a commando operation, and the last of the French secret service operatives, still held in detention after the 'Greenpeace affair' (the sinking of a pacifist vessel in New Zealand in 1985 by the French secret service – a patriotic deed in the eyes of French public opinion) released by the French government in breach of an international agreement. The traditional face-to-face televised confrontation between the two final-found contestants was very revealing of the President's grim struggle to maintain the influence of his office, especially in this amazing moment:

> *President*: I feel obliged to say that I remember the circumstances in which you sent back Gordji [an Iranian diplomat wanted for questioning by a *juge d'instruction* in Paris] to Iran after explaining to me, in my office, that the evidence against him was overwhelming and that his complicity in the murders that covered Paris with blood in 1986 was clearly demonstrated.

In other words, the President – however much he disapproved, even in a matter involving international relations and the security of the state – had no power to stop the Prime Minister doing what he had decided to do. Mitterrand referred to his fellow-candidate only as 'Prime Minister' because it was the use and abuse of Prime Ministerial power that he saw as his adversary.

The Le Pen phenomenon was analysed in chapter 10. The 14.4% obtained by the Front National in the 1988 Presidential election was the high point of its remarkable success in the 1980s. Le Pen's campaign was exceptionally skilful. He made the best use of the free television broadcasts, and his posters showed him as '*l'outsider*' (in racing terms) gaining on the more fancied runners. Le Pen was strongest in the 'sunshine belt' along the south coast, home to most of the French settlers repatriated from Algeria – the bedrock of electoral support for the extreme right. He was the leading candidate of the right in most towns in the south (Marseille 28%, Toulon 27%, Nice 26%). More surprisingly, he was the leading candidate of the right in Alsace, with its long tradition of moderate – especially Christian-Democrat – conservatism. The momentum generated by his campaign enabled him to pick up a vast protest vote, especially on the theme of immigration. Le Pen voters were also disillusioned with the changes of government in 1981 and 1986, were critical of the record of both Mitterrand and Chirac, and felt more pessimistic about the future than other voters. Surveys of farmers worried about EEC prices, or of residents of small industrial towns in the east where the principal heavy industry has closed down, revealed a widespread intention to use a first-ballot vote (risk-free in a two-ballot election – a two-to-one majority of Le Pen voters wanted another candidate to win!) to give a signal to mainstream political élites that their anxieties required attention.

What was the effect of the Le Pen success on the other parties? One theory is that the rise of the Front National and the decline of the Communist vote are directly inter-related: protest votes switching directly from extreme left to extreme right. It is true that the FN does exceptionally well in the PC's traditional industrial and working-class areas, that Le Pen was supported by 16% of manual workers in 1988, and that about a fifth of his 1988 voters switched to Mitterrand at the second ballot (another fifth abstaining, and three-fifths voting Chirac). However, such a theory leaves out the amazing rise of the Socialist Party in the 1980s. The PC's real problem is that it has been steadily losing votes to Mitterrand and the Socialists. About 19% of manual workers supported Lajoinie on 24 April, and about 40% supported the President. Furthermore, the decline of the PC has occurred at a constant rate in areas where the FN does well and those where it does badly (see chapter 8). The success of Le Pen has been profoundly destabilising to the mainstream right, from which he took most of his votes. Both RPR and UDF are divided over how to respond to it. Does one borrow Le Pen's themes (as leaders like Pasqua advocate) and alienate moderates? Or does one condemn them (the approach of Philippe Séguin) and fail to win back lost votes? Does one make an electoral pact at local level with the FN or risk losing one's seat or control of the Council? The high score of Le Pen, by contrast, actually helped Mitterrand. It cut into the right and, above all, it provided a rallying point for the whole left in the second round. Communists and the extreme left were lukewarm about recommending a second-ballot vote for Mitterrand until the success of the FN because apparent. One

Presidential elections

even saw the germ of a Popular Front response to Le Pen's Paris rally of 1 May: 'Not one vote for Chirac and the right'.

Chirac's first-ballot score (19.9%) was the lowest-ever for the leading candidate of the centre and right, and the lowest for any candidate getting through to the second round, only just better than his own score in 1981 against Giscard. In the second ballot he did significantly better than the 1981 performance of Giscard only in his own electoral kingdoms of Limousin and Paris. Raymond Barre's performance was respectable in that he avoided the virtual submergence that can happen to the candidate of the centre-right who is perceived as being the minor one. De Gaulle had a big working-class electorate, but Barre and Chirac

Table 12.5. PRESIDENTIAL ELECTION, 1988 – RESULTS BY REGION

	1st ballot					2nd ballot	
	Mitt. %	Chirac %	Barre %	Le Pen %	Lajoinie %	Mitt. %	Chirac %
Paris Region (Île de France)	31.1	22.6*	14.9	15.9	7.2	*51.6*	48.4
North	38.5	14.8	15.0*	13.7	10.8	*62.1*	37.9
Picardy	37.5	17.3*	14.1	14.8	8.7	*59.8*	40.2
Upper Normandy	38.2	17.6*	16.1	12.1	7.8	*59.2*	40.8
Lower Normandy	35.4	21.8*	19.4	11.1	3.6	*52.4*	47.6
Brittany	36.6	20.3*	19.3	9.9	4.6	*55.1*	44.9
Loire	35.0	21.5	21.7*	9.4	3.7	*52.3*	47.7
Champagne	35.1	19.7*	16.4	14.6	6.4	*54.9*	45.1
Lorraine	34.4	16.8	17.3*	17.1	4.9	*56.1*	43.9
Alsace	28.8	17.4	18.4	21.8*	1.4	49.1	*50.9*
Franche-Comté	35.4	20.1*	15.8	14.6	4.3	*54.5*	45.5
Burgundy	37.3	20.3*	16.1	12.6	6.3	*55.3*	44.6
Centre	35.1	19.5*	17.6	13.2	6.7	*54.8*	45.2
Poitou	38.1	20.3*	17.7	9.4	5.6	*55.9*	43.0
Limousin	34.1	29.0*	8.7	7.2	12.1	*57.0*	43.0
Auvergne	32.1	22.2*	16.6	11.0	9.6	*53.5*	46.5
Rhône-Alps	30.4	18.4	19.5*	16.4	5.8	*51.9*	48.1
Aquitaine	37.0	21.2*	15.5	11.5	6.5	*55.2*	44.8
Midi-Pyrénées	38.2	19.5*	14.7	11.2	6.5	*57.4*	42.5
Languedoc	31.8	17.3	13.7	18.9*	10.0	*54.2*	45.7
Provence – Côte d'Azur	26.5	18.5	15.0	24.5*	8.6	46.9	*53.1*
Corsica	28.8	31.0*	13.0	13.3	8.1	45.7	*54.3*
France	34.1	19.9*	16.6	14.4	6.8	*54.0*	46.0

* Leading candidate of the right and centre.
Figures in italics = 2nd ballot winner.

each got the support of only 7% of manual workers (Le Pen got 16%). Chirac did best among farmers (71% at the second ballot), the self-employed (69%) though he lost a lot who had voted for Le Pen in the first ballot, the over sixty-fives (57%) and churchgoers (67%). The right and centre were in the majority at every election in France from 1981 till May 1988.

The 1988 result was a triumph for Mitterrand, who thus became the first President to be elected twice by universal suffrage. He and the Socialist Party over the previous ten years had become a genuinely national political force. The days when they could get few votes in the traditional right-voting Catholic regions of the north-east and north-west have gone. Mitterrand's vote in the first ballot was close to his national average in every part of the country, and at the second he carried virtually every region (see Table 12.5), making his greatest gains in the Catholic regions like Brittany and the Loire, actually losing ground in the old republican, socialist and anti-clerical south. He had the support of 74% of manual workers at the second ballot, 65% of people aged 25-34, 70% of teachers and health service workers, and 74% of nominal, non-churchgoing Catholics, a group which had grown to become a majority of the whole population. Of Le Pen voters who voted in the second round (20% stayed at home) 20% voted for Mitterrand; of Barre voters 14% did so, of Green voters 79%, of Communist and extreme left voters almost all.

The electoral victory in 1988 was the victory of a man whose party

Table 12.6   PRESIDENTIAL ELECTION, 1988

	1st ballot		2nd ballot	
Electorate	38.0m.		38.0m.	
Abstentions	18.5%		15.8%	
Spoilt votes	2.0%		3.7%	
	million votes	*%*	*million votes*	*%*
Mitterrand	10.4	34.1	16.7	54.0
Chirac (RPR)	6.1	19.9	14.2	46.0
Barre (UDF)	5.0	16.5		
Le Pen (FN)	4.4	14.4		
Lajoinie (PCF)	2.1	6.8		
Juquin (PC – diss.)	.6	2.1		
Laguiller (extreme left)	.6	2.0		
Boussel (extreme left)	.1	.4		

and policies had been defeated two years earlier, whose powers in 'Presidential' areas of policy were under systematic attack from a most 'voracious' opponent (in the expression most commonly used). Like civilisation in the Dark Ages, Presidential power came near to being wiped out. Mitterrand, however, turned relative powerlessness into an advantage. He distanced himself from the government's actions, used the prestige of the Presidency's twenty-eight years of supremacy to intervene and to address the nation when he chose, and placed himself 'above politics' to enunciate the 'higher values' of fraternity and national unity. It was enough on 8 May to slay the dragon.

NOTES

1. 'Gaullism without de Gaulle', *Western Political Quarterly*, 1973, pp. 485–506.
2. *La guerre de succession*, Paris: PUF, 1969.

13

PARLIAMENTARY ELECTIONS

National Assembly elections (élections legislatives)

The National Assembly is the lower house of the French Parliament and its members (*députés*), unlike the Senators in the upper house, are elected by universal suffrage. Its elections take place every five years unless the President under Article 12 of the Constitution dissolves the Assembly. If he does this, there can be no further dissolution for at least twelve months. There is a historic suspicion of dissolution in France since President MacMahon tried it in 1876 in the hope of bringing back a royalist majority and with it the monarchy. In the Fifth Republic dissolution is clearly back as one of the weapons in the President's armoury, but the tradition seems to have been established that dissolutions contrived purely for party advantage, as is now the practice in Britain, do not occur. Dissolutions in the Fifth Repulic have occurred either because there is a genuine crisis or because a new President has just been elected. Since Presidential leadership is only possible with a Parliamentary majority in support of the President, it is normal that the electors who have just chosen a President should have the opportunity to give him a Parliamentary majority too. The following are the elections that have taken place in the Fifth Republic up to the time of writing:

1958   New Constitution
1962   Dissolution following defeat of government by motion of censure
1967   Expiry of five-year term
1968   Dissolution – 'Events of May' crisis
1973   Expiry of five-year term
1978   Expiry of five-year term
1981   Dissolution after election of President Mitterrand
1986   Expiry of five-year term
1988   Dissolution after re-election of President Mitterrand

There are 577 seats in the National Assembly. From Algerian independence in 1962 (when the Assembly lost its Algerian members) to 1986 the membership varied between 485 and 491. When the Socialist government brought in proportional representation for the 1986 election, it sharply increased the number of seats and the new, higher

165

number was retained by the Chirac government when it reintroduced the old two-ballot electoral system. Of the 577, mainland France and Corsica are represented by 555, and the French Overseas territories from the West Indies to the Indian Ocean and the South Seas by twenty-two. The smallest Overseas territory consists of the islands of St Pierre and Miquelon off the south coast of Newfoundland. Its *député* represents only 4,000 electors. On average the French *député* has around 70,000 electors.

—The electoral system

The electoral system used for every Parliamentary election in the Fifth Republic except 1986 is the single-member constituency two-ballot system. When this was introduced by de Gaulle in 1958, it surprised people because this was the system used in the discredited Third Republic before the Second World War and it had never 'produced' stable majority government. However, it was preferred because proportional representation was associated with the Fourth Republic, which the constitution-makers were reacting against, and was expected to give the Communists, who had been capable of winning 25% of the vote in the 1950s, a regular quarter of the seats. It was also preferred to a single-ballot system like the British because that too would have given the Communists extra seats where they lead the field at the first ballot but find everyone united against them at the second. One of the surprises of the Fifth Republic has been the emergence of political parties with, as the French say, a 'majority vocation' – that is to say, capable of attracting between 35 and 40% of the vote at the first ballot. This was true of Gaullism in the 1960s and of the Socialists in the 1980s. A party with this level of support gets a bonus from second-round standdowns, and can win a majority of seats. The other surprise has been that electoral alliances for the second ballot are maintained in Parliament after the election as in the long-standing alliance between Gaullists and the UDF. So the two-ballot system has played its part in 'producing' stable majority government, but the fundamental point has been the change of behaviour by the electors.

Candidates who wish to contest the election pay a deposit of Frs 1,000 which is returnable to them if they receive 5% of the votes cast. The state repays certain campaign expenses to candidates obtaining 5%: posters for official notice boards, distribution of the election address, printing of ballot papers (all candidates produce their own, according to a standard format, for electors to place in the voting envelope). In addition the 1988 law on party and election finance (see chapter 11) limits candidates' campaign expenditure in their constituencies to Frs 500,000. The state repays to any candidates obtaining 5% of the vote what they have actually spent up to a limit of 10% of the Frs 500,000 ceiling.

If in a constituency no candidate wins an overall majority at the first ballot, a second ballot is held the following Sunday. No new candidates are allowed (unlike in the Third Republic), and no candidate from the first ballot may continue without having received the votes of at least 12.5% of the registered electorate – usually about 18% of votes cast. This hurdle is very high – and it sometimes has peculiar effects. If all candidates except one are eliminated by the 12.5% rule, the candidate who came second is allowed to contest the second ballot. More often all but two allies are eliminated, and the one with the lower score, in conformity with their parties' electoral pact, withdraws leaving only one candidate. For example, in the constituency of Georges Marchais, the Communist leader, all candidates in 1978 and 1981 were eliminated by the 12.5% rule except Marchais and the Socialist candidate. The Socialist candidate withdrew, and thus Marchais was the only second-ballot candidate and, in 1978, nearly 20,000 voters went to the polls to cast spoiled votes. Candidates who are unable or choose not to enter the second ballot may simply withdraw from the contest or 'desist' in favour of some other candidate, urging their supporters to transfer their votes.

—Elections in the Fifth Republic

1958 (23 and 30 November).   The 1958 elections were the last of the old and the first of the new. That they were the last of the old is reflected in the vast number of Independents and 'Moderates' and local notables who were elected, in the numerous party labels and groupings, and in the division of the left. They were the first of the new in that one national issue, the return to power of General de Gaulle and the New Republic, dominated the elections. It was the beginning of the 'nationalisation' of French politics and of the growth of Gaullism as a disciplined majority which was to have such a profound effect on the Fifth Republic's party system. The election was a disaster for the Communists. They had been the only political party to call for a 'No' vote at the referendum in September 1958 at which the Fifth Republic Constitution was adopted. At 3.9 million their first-ballot vote was their lowest since the war. Furthermore, the new two-ballot electoral system proved catastrophic for them because they could not attract extra voters at the

Table 13.1.   PARLIAMENTARY ELECTION, 1958

	1st ballot		*seats*
Electorate	27.2m.		
Abstentions	22.9%		
Spoilt votes	2.3%		
	million votes	*%*	
Communists	3.9	19.2	10
Socialists	3.2	15.7	44
Radicals	1.7	8.3	32
Total left	*8.8*	*43.2*	*86*
MRP and Centre	2.3	11.1	57
Gaullists (UNR)	4.0	19.5	199
Independents (CNI *et al.*)	4.7	22.9	133
Other	.6	3.3	
(Algeria and Sahara)			(71)

second ballot. From 150 seats in the outgoing Parliament they dropped to ten. By contrast, the success of Gaullism at the first ballot established its credentials as a 'serious' party and voters flocked to support its candidates at the second round. Well-known political figures like Gaston Defferre, Mayor of Marseille, were defeated by unknown Gaullist candidates.

1962 (18 and 25 November). The 1962 elections resulted from a remarkably timed dissolution by de Gaulle, the circumstances of which were described in Chapter 2. The ending of the Algerian war, a dramatic summer which included an assassination attempt on the President, the proposal to submit to referendum the idea of perpetuating Presidential legitimacy by direct election, the motion of censure carried by traditional parliamentarians against this proposal, the dissolution of Parliament, the victory for 'Yes' in the October referendum – all created the conditions for a remarkable Gaullist electoral victory in November. The UNR won almost 6 million votes at the first ballot, was joined by a further 1.75 million at the second, and, with 233 seats out of 482, almost won a majority on its own – without even the help of its perfectly dependable allies, the *Giscardiens*.

The year 1962 marks the emergence of Gaullism as a majority party, the first such ever seen in Republican France. The Independents and

Moderates who were not prepared to give support to the government were electorally destroyed. Opponents of direct Presidential elections, most Independents had voted for the motion of censure that defeated the government in September and campaigned unsuccessfully as part of the forlorn and divided '*Cartel des Non*' in the October referendum (see chapter 15). This symbolic attachment to the past was severely punished by the electors in November. Most of the Independents who survived were, by contrast, those who had supported the government (perhaps, like Giscard, actually being members of it) and had campaigned for 'Yes' in October. After the election those pro-government Independents who formed the Independent Republicans were to be a loyal and disciplined (if not always unconditional) component of the Majority, on whose Parliamentary support President and government depended.

A second group that felt the full force of the Gaullist tide was the MRP. In their Fourth Republic Catholic strongholds, electors, having voted 'Yes' to direct elections against the advice of the MRP, transferred their allegiance to the UNR. In the northern, more Catholic half of France the MRP lost half their seats. A third group to feel the effect of a marked popular preference for the new political order were the dissident Gaullists who had not accepted independence for Algeria. Official UNR candidates were run against even the best-known dissidents, and beat them. Discipline, appropriate to a new majority

Table 13.2.   PARLIAMENTARY ELECTION, 1962

	1st ballot		seats
Electorate	27.5m.		
Abstentions	31.3%		
Spoilt votes	2.1%		
	million votes	%	
Communists	4.0	21.7	41
Extreme left	.4	2.4	–
Socialists	2.3	12.6	66
Radicals	1.4	7.8	39
Total left	*8.1*	*44.5*	*146*
MRP and Centre	1.7	9.1	55
Gaullist (UNR)	5.9	31.9	233
Giscardiens (RI)	1.1	5.9	35
Majority	*7.0*	*37.8*	*268*
Other right	1.6	8.6	13

party in a new political order, was upheld, and that was the way the voters wanted it to be.

A final noteworthy feature of the 1962 elections was the first attempt, albeit grudging and ill-organised, by the parties of the left to collaborate at the second ballot as an alternative to slaughter. There were a number of frosty pacts to eliminate competition between left-wing parties at the second ballot, and even Guy Mollet, the anti-Communist leader of the Socialists, advised electors to vote Communist at the second ballot if to do otherwise would favour the election of a Gaullist. The left picked up no extra votes between ballots – in fact there was a further haemorrhage of 250,000 – but by reducing fratricidal competition it increased its parliamentary representation over 1958.

1967 (5 and 12 March).   Between 1962 and 1967 was a period of prosperous calm. The turbulence of the Algerian war and its settlement was over and the solitary crisis-leadership of General de Gaulle which had accompanied that phase was attenuated. It was a period of grandiose and prestigious diplomatic initiatives – reconciliation with Germany, rapprochement with the Soviet Union, the French departure from NATO, attacks on American hegemony in nuclear defence, money and technology, and of France as friend of the developing world and the Arabs. Throughout the period France had one President, one Prime Minister and one Foreign Minister. The 1967 elections were held at the expiry of a five-year term. In an atmosphere free from crises the electorate had an opportunity to judge a stable government and consider the alternatives.

Unlike the previous two elections it is the campaign rather than the result, close and exciting though that was, which today retains our interest. It does so for two reasons: first, the campaign had a strong presidential character, and secondly, the process of party realignment to a bipolar party system was demonstrated in a very marked way.

The campaign was a long one – indeed, that is a feature of elections that come at the end of a full five-year Parliament (1973, 1978 and 1986 were all very long campaigns). It was a continuation of the 1965 Presidential election and was personalised in a presidential way. Posters featured the three main presidential candidates – de Gaulle, Mitterrand and the centrist Lecanuet. The Mitterrand leadership of the Left led on, as we saw in chapters 6 and 7, to the alliance with the Communists, the creation of the FGDS (Federation of the Democratic and Socialist Left), the relaunched Socialist Party, and the Union of the

Left in the 1970s. The Lecanuet candidature led to the creation of the Centre Démocrate, the Reform Movement and ultimately the UDF (chapter 5). The Prime Minister, Georges Pompidou, directed the campaign for the government majority – another innovation – and played the leading public part.

The Mitterrand strategy was to build a strong and united federation of the non-Communist left, which would be in a good position to negotiate a pact with the Communist Party and extract guarantees from it on respect for democratic liberties if an alliance of the left should win. The Communist Party, still led by Waldeck Rochet, was in a conciliatory mood, and the alliances on the left worked very well – indeed, 1967 and 1973 were the two best Parliamentary elections for harmonious cooperation between the parties of the left. The Radicals, the Socialists and Mitterrand's 'Convention of Republican Institutions' (the collection of left-wing 'clubs') cooperated to designate a single FGDS candidate in 413 constituencies out of 487. In the remainder they endorsed the PSU (Mendès-France in Grenoble, for example) or a vaguely Radical non-party notable (like former Prime Minister André Marie) or no-one at all. Of the 413, 216 were Socialists, seventy-nine Radicals, twenty-one of no particular party, and ninety-seven, after some frantic head-hunting by Mitterrand's staff, from the Convention (including some who were not even members, two of whom actually won seats). The FGDS, the PSU and the Communists all agreed that every candidate of the left would withdraw in the second ballot in favour of the one 'best placed'. In subsequent elections that was always interpreted as the one with the most votes in the first ballot. In 1967, and only in 1967, the Communists agreed to withdraw some candidates who had run ahead of the Socialists on the grounds that in a close second ballot a Socialist would have a better chance than a Communist. However, the Communists refused to support centrist or right-wing anti-government candidates even where the left had been eliminated: 'We refuse to choose between cholera and the plague'! The FGDS backed that old right-winger Frédéric-Dupont (later Front National and then back to RPR) in order to defeat the Foreign Minister Couve de Murville, and thus, according to Pompidou's biographer Eric Roussel, prevented de Gaulle from carrying out his plan to make Couve Prime Minister.

In the government majority, there were to be none of those difficult decisions about who would withdraw for whom because there would be only one official 'Fifth Republic' candidate in each constituency.

Pompidou announced this to the UNR National Council in June 1966. A sub-committee of the 'Action Committee for the Fifth Republic' was formed to decide centrally on candidate adoptions. Not all *députés* were readopted. There was some conflict here and there. The 'Fifth Republic' endorsement was given to 407 UNR/UDT (201 eventual winners) and to seventy-nine RI (forty-two eventual winners). In the 1970s the practice of having 'primaries' gradually came in (first ballot contests between Gaullists and *Giscardiens*) – but not in 1967.

The Centre Démocrate, created by Jean Lecanuet after his relative success in the 1965 Presidential election, presented 390 centrist candidates against both Gaullism and Socialism – 133 former MRP, ninety-seven former Independents, and twenty-nine Radicals, thus prefiguring the Reform Movement, which as an alliance of Radicals and Centre Democrats would contest the election of 1973. The Centre Democrats' modest 13% in the 1967 election, however, was an eloquent indicator of the way the party system was going. The viability of an 'opposition centre' was increasingly in question. By 1969, many of those who had contested the 1967 election as Centre Democrats had been absorbed into Georges Pompidou's Presidential majority. In 1974,

Table 13.3.   PARLIAMENTARY ELECTION, 1967

	1st ballot		seats
Electorate	28.2m.		
Abstentions	18.9%		
Spoilt votes	1.8%		
	million votes	%	
Communists	5.0	22.5	73
PSU	.5	2.1	4
FGDS (Socialists and Radicals)	4.2	19.0	116
Total left	*9.7*	*43.6*	*193*
Opposition Centre			
(CD)	3.0	13.4	41
Government Majority	8.5	37.7	245
(UNR)	(7.3)	(32.2)	(201)
(RI)	(1.2)	(5.5)	(44)
Other	1.1	5.4	8

Lecanuet and the rest of the centre joined the Presidential majority of Giscard d'Estaing. Since then there has been no separate centre at all.

It was a simplified party system that fought the 1967 election. Under the label 'Fifth Republic', the Gaullists and their allies fought a well-organised and disciplined campaign, won a close victory (overall majority of one seat), and remained in government as a cohesive majority, so confirming the innovation of majority party rule. The parties of the left also found an effective and disciplined alliance profitable. Although the overall vote for the left was slightly down (43.6% against 44.5% in 1962), effective cooperation at the second ballot (in which the voters cheerfully played their part) increased the left's parliamentary representation by fifty seats.

The close result reawakened executive suspicion of Parliament. One legislative consequence was the recourse to special powers, under Article 38, to enact unpopular measures by decree and not by legislative process in Parliament. This executive high-handedness provoked a number of demonstrations in the spring of 1967 – the opening chords of May 1968. Pompidou stayed on as the Fifth Republic's longest-serving Prime Minister, to acquire the national stature through those Events of May to be de Gaulle's natural successor in 1969.

1968 (23 and 30 June).   The extraordinary Events of May provoked this election and dictated the result: a landslide victory for the Gaullists on a platform of order and anti-Communism. The student revolt, the general strike, the occupations of factories, the demonstrations, the police charges, the breakdown of supplies and services, the near-collapse of the regime itself all produced the inevitable reaction: the fear of chaos, the vote for crisis leadership in the shape of General de Gaulle and his government. Parliament was dissolved by de Gaulle in his radio broadcast of 30 May, and the campaign was brief.

The parties of the left maintained their pact, but the crisis had strained relations (chapter 6), and the spirit of cooperation, present in 1967 and 1973 and necessary for a good transfer of votes at the second ballot, was absent. The left lost a million votes. The spirit of unity was less marked in the government majority as well. Giscard d'Estaing had indicated some sympathy for the frustrations that had led to the Events of May, though not of course identifying with the unruly behaviour. His Independent Republicans challenged Gaullists in 'primaries' in some constituencies in an attempt, pursued in the 1970s and 1980s, to build an independent electoral following – and Giscard's lieutenant Michel Poniatowski had an official Majority candidate against him.

Table 13.4.   PARLIAMENTARY ELECTION, 1968

	1st ballot		seats
Electorate	28.2m.		
Abstentions	20.0%		
Spoilt votes	1.4%		
	million votes	%	
Communists	4.4	20.0	34
PSU and extreme left	.9	4.0	–
FGDS (Socialists and Radicals)	3.7	16.5	57
Other left	.2	.7	–
Total left	*9.2*	*41.2*	*91*
Opposition Centre (PDM)	2.3	10.3	33
Government Majority	9.9	44.7	360
(UDR)	(8.2)	(37.0)	(296)
(RI)	(1.7)	(7.7)	(64)
Other	.7	3.5	3

The Majority had scored a remarkable success – after the turbulent events of recent weeks it was baptised with the initials UDR (Union for the Defence of the Republic), later to be taken over by the Gaullist party as Union of Democrats for the Republic. The Gaullists on their own won 296 seats – the first time in Republican history that a single party had, independently of its allies, won an overall majority in the National Assembly. Its allies, Giscard's Independent Republicans, became the second largest Parliamentary group with sixty-four seats. Giscard's future allies – the centrists, still in the opposition – experienced a further decline.

The Majority made gains in every part of the country – in particular breaking new ground in the old left-wing strongholds of the south coast, the Pyrenees and the Limousin. It was particularly successful against Communist candidates, and anti-Communism was to be the basis of the next electoral victory of the same Majority in 1973.

Georges Pompidou, regarded as the architect of restored order in 1968 and of the massive electoral victory that followed, was dismissed by de Gaulle after the election; Couve de Murville was appointed Prime Minister in his place. Pompidou remained in the public eye, however, and was the natural Gaullist choice for President when de Gaulle resigned in 1969 (chapter 2). It was the 1968 election victory that provided the foundation for the 'UDR state' – the total dominance of Parliament, government and public services by Gaullists in the Pompidou Presidency (1969–73).

1973 (5 and 11 March).   The 1973 election was in many ways similar to that of 1967 and can be compared with it. Both were non-crisis elections held at the expiry of a full five-year term. With Giscard back in the government under President Pompidou, the Majority was cohesive and well-organised. François Mitterrand was back in the leadership role on the left that he had played in 1967. The alliance between Socialists and Communists was once again working harmoniously; the *Programme Commun* joint manifesto had been signed in 1972, and the parties fought the election as the Union of the Left. It was also, like 1967, a long campaign and a close result.

What makes 1973 particularly interesting is that it was the first election in the Fifth Republic which the opposition was thought to have a chance of winning. It was therefore the first of many elections in which the question of a Parliamentary majority opposed to the President, and the supposed threat to the stability of the regime, was an issue. Commentators endlessly evaluated what the President's options would be. As we now know from the *'cohabitation'* of 1986–8, policy leadership passes from the President to the leader of the Parliamentary majority, but stability is not a problem.

The only party to improve on its 1967 share of the vote was the Socialist Party. Relaunched with Mitterrand as leader in 1971, and now in alliance with the MRG (the fragment of the Radical Party that preferred to stay with the left as the remaining Radicals joined the centrists), the PS was moving strongly towards supplanting the Communists as the leading party of the left. The PS also started to do well in the Catholic regions of France where the left had tradition-ally been weak – Normandy, Brittany, Alsace-Lorraine. This factor, connected to the decline in the active churchgoing population and the increase in the white-collar sector, was the germ of the great Socialist successes in the 1980s. The PCF topped 5 million votes – the sign of a good year – but its share of the vote was slightly down on 1967, and its decline was particularly marked in its strongest areas like the Paris suburbs. Nearly two-thirds of manual workers voted for the left in 1973 compared with less than a half in the days of de Gaulle.

Table 13.5.   PARLIAMENTARY ELECTION, 1973

	1st ballot		seats
Electorate	29.9m.		
Abstentions	18.7%		
Spoilt votes	1.8%		
	million votes	*%*	
Communists	5.1	21.4	73
PSU and extreme left	.8	3.3	1
UGSD (Socialists and MRG)	4.9	20.8	101
Other left	.1	.3	1
Total left	*10.9*	*45.8*	*176*
Opposition centre	3.1	13.1	34
(Reform Movement: CD and Radicals)			
Government Majority	8.5	36.0	268
(UDR)	(6.1)	(25.7)	(183)
(RI)	(1.6)	(6.6)	(55)
(CDP)	(.9)	(3.7)	(30)
Other	1.2	5.1	12

The government majority would have been unable to win without the seats won by the CDP, the former opposition centrists who had decided to join the Presidential majority during Pompidou's election campaign in 1969. The rest of the centre – the Radical Party led by Jean-Jacques Servan-Schreiber and Lecanuet's Centre Democrats – remained in the opposition under the label of 'Reformers', but agreed to help the government at the second ballot by withdrawing candidates where their presence might favour the election of a Communist or a Socialist. In return, the government majority withdrew enough candidates to give the Reformers the thirty seats necessary to form a Parliamentary group. In 1974, as we know, the Reformers joined the Giscard Presidential majority. The evidence is that already by 1973 this is what their electors wanted. Whereas in 1967 45% of centrist electors were prepared to vote Socialist at the second ballot to stop a Gaullist from winning, in 1973 this proportion was only 22%. The Majority's share of the vote was lower than in 1967 but, because the anti-left forces were more united, their margin of victory was greater. At the second ballot the Majority did much better – collecting some 2 million votes which had gone elsewhere at the first. President Pompidou spoke on television of the threat to freedom and to people's homes and property that would immediately follow a victory by the left. Fear of the left was a powerful mobilising theme.

The electors of the left behaved in a reasonably disciplined manner at the second ballot. The PCF, unlike in 1967, insisted on its right to present a second-ballot candidate wherever it was the leading party at the first. In more and more cases, however, the lead candidate was a Socialist – 220 compared with only 184 Communists (in 1967 the figures had been 205 FGDS and 267 PC). This trend became very unfavourable indeed for the Communists, and was a factor in the decision in 1977–8 to break off the Union of the Left. In 1981 half the Communist *députés* lost their seats – not to the right but to Socialist candidates in whose favour they had to stand down at the second ballot.

1978 (12 and 19 March).   There was keener interest in the 1978 election than in any other Parliamentary election so far in the Fifth Republic, and it produced a record turnout – almost 84% at the second ballot. It was the last of the 'choice of society' elections: this was to be the election in which the Union of the Left – the alliance of Communists and Socialists with a joint programme of government – would come to power. This 'threat to freedom' had been, as we saw, an important theme in 1973. However, the 1978 election came at the end of a period in which the left had made sweeping gains in by-elections and local elections. Union of the Left lists won power in 159 of the 221 large towns, seventy-two with Communist mayors (see chapter 14). The Socialist Party, from its relaunch at Epinay in 1971, had become, in the opinion polls, the leading party of France. It was also the election in which the Fifth Republic constitution would be put to its ultimate test: would it work if the President faced a Parliamentary majority composed of his political adversaries? In the end none of these things happened in 1978 because the left did not win. The left eventually did win an election in 1981, and freedom and stability were not abolished. The constitution had its test in 1986 and '*cohabitation*' worked.

In relation to what were perceived as the two great issues (Communist participation in government, the testing of the constitution), the significant events occurred well before the election rather than during the campaign. The first was that President Giscard d'Estaing, from 1976 on, made it clear that he would stay in office if the left won the 1978 election. In particular he made a speech at Verdun-sur-le-Doubs in

January 1978 which had a big impact. In it he said: 'You can choose the *Programme Commun* That is your right. But if you choose it, it will be applied. Don't imagine that the President has, under the constitution, the means to stop it.' He therefore hoped that the electors would think carefully and make the 'right choice'.

The second, and most extraordinary, event was the decision by the Communists, six months before the election, to break up the Union of the Left (see chapter 6). The problem for the Communists was that they were being eclipsed by, and losing electors to, the rising star of the Socialist Party. On the pretext of a breakdown of negotiations over the updating of the 1972 *Programme Commun*, they declared that the Socialists had 'veered to the right' and, for the crucial six months up to the election, turned all their guns on the Socialists. Indeed they did more than that. If a Union of the Left strategy is to succeed, the Communists must do everything they can to reassure public opinion (as in 1967 and 1973, for example). On this occasion the Communists went out of their way to be as aggressive as possible: 'Yes, there will be communist ministers!' said the posters, and 'We will make the rich pay!'

As for the actual election, 1978 is interesting as the one occasion when the government Majority partners, Gaullists and *Giscardiens*, systematically had 'primaries' in almost all constituencies – not quite in all because there were ministers and other leading figures whom it would have been impertinent to oppose. We have seen how the practice of having 'primaries' had been growing: in 1967 there was one official candidate of the Majority in each constituency (no 'primaries'), in 1973 there were sixty-one 'primaries', in 1978 there were 354. A 'primary' is where the parties of the Majority each present a candidate at the first ballot with an agreement to withdraw in favour of the best-placed at the second – in other words, exactly how the Union of the Left worked. In order to make the best possible showing against the Gaullists, the parties that supported Giscard united (see chapter 5) to form the UDF. The UDF endorsed one non-Gaullist candidate of the Majority in each constituency. The most interesting fact about the 'primaries' was that in almost all constituencies it was the best-known local figure, the best-established local *notable* who won the first ballot. Only eight RPR *députés* seeking re-election and six from the UDF were eliminated in 'primaries'. This is why one cannot identify a distinctive Gaullist or 'liberal' electorate. The electors of the centre and right tend to vote for the best-known local candidate whether RPR or UDF.

Table 13.6.   PARLIAMENTARY ELECTION, 1978

	1st ballot		seats
Electorate	34.4m.		
Abstentions	16.6%		
Spoilt votes	1.8%		
	million votes	*%*	
Communists	5.8	20.7	86
Extreme left	.8	3.1	–
Socialists and MRG	7.0	25.0	114
Other left	.1	.5	–
Total left	*13.9*	*49.3*	*200*
Greens	.6	2.1	–
Other opposition	.2	.7	–
UDF	6.0	21.4	138
(PR)			(69)
(CDS)			(36)
(Radicals)			(8)
(other UDF)			(25)
RPR	6.3	22.5	150
Other Majority	.6	2.0	2
Total Majority	*12.9*	*45.9*	*290*
Extreme right	.1	.5	–
Other	.4	1.5	1

On the left the Communists limited the damage for themselves by retaining, or very nearly, their 1973 share of the vote, and gained thirteen seats to achieve their highest Parliamentary representation in the Fifth Republic. The writing was on the wall, however, in the serious decline in their share of the vote in the Paris region, the Communist heartland. The Socialists became the leading party of in France with 25% – and the leading party of the left for the first time too. The second-ballot transfers did not work well in 1978 because of the disunion that had characterised the parties of the left in the six months preceding the election. In 1973, when there was a climate of unity, the left were picking up seats at the second ballot where they had been in a minority at the first. This did not happen much in 1978, and was more than offset by losses in seats where the left had a majority at the first ballot. The groundswell for unity was no longer there. Where the second ballot candidate was a Communist the losses were greater. Socialists were second ballot candidates in 264 constituencies compared with 220 in 1973 and 111 in 1967. Once again for the Communists, the writing was on the wall.

1981 (14 and 21 June).   One of the first actions of the newly–elected President Mitterrand, as he predicted during the Presidential election, was to dissolve the National Assembly. The 1981 Parliamentary election was entirely dominated by the fact that the country had just given itself a new President, and its first taste of a change of power from government to opposition in twenty-three years. The Socialist Party got 38% of the vote – on a par with Gaullist scores of the 1960s – and, like the Gaullists in 1968, a majority of seats on its own.

The event long feared by the Communist Party actually occurred. After the poor showing of Georges Marchais in the Presidential election (15% – see chapter 12), they meekly accepted a second-ballot pact with the Socialists and lost half their Parliamentary seats, not to the right but to the Socialists. They only got 16% at the first ballot, and in forty-two of the eighty-six seats they won in 1978 their *député* was beaten by the Socialist candidate and, by virtue of the pact, had to stand down. After the election Mitterrand gave the Communist Party four junior ministries in the government – the first Communist ministers in France, or indeed in any other major Western state, since 1947.

The Gaullists and the UDF, despite the venomous feelings generated by the contribution of Jacques Chirac to the defeat of Giscard d'Estaing, hastily agreed to try and save as many of their *députés* as possible by returning to the method of one joint candidate in most constituencies and having this time only eighty-eight 'primaries' (as against 354 in 1978). They chose the curious label 'UNM' (Union for a New Majority) and became very much the new minority, losing 130 seats between them.

The rate of abstention was very high in this election – nearly 30% at the first ballot, almost a record. There are two explanations for this. First, as in the elections of 1962 and 1988 (the latter holding the record for abstentions in a Parliamentary election in France), the electors felt the important choice had already been made. In November 1962 it was the October referendum on direct Presidential elections. In June 1981, and again in June 1988, it was the previous month's Presidential election. The other explanation is the demobilisation of electors of the right and centre. François Goguel has shown that the left's share of the

Table 13.7. PARLIAMENTARY ELECTION, 1981

	1st ballot		seats
Electorate	35.5m.		
Abstentions	30.1%		
Spoilt votes	1.4%		
	million votes	%	
Communists	4.0	16.1	44
Extreme left	.3	1.3	–
Socialists and MRG	9.4	37.8	285
Other left	.1	.6	4
Total left	*13.8*	*55.8*	*333*
Greens	.3	1.1	–
RPR/UDF	10.0	40.1	
RPR	(5.2)	(20.9)	86
UDF	(4.8)	(19.2)	66
Other right and centre	.8	3.1	7

total electorate was the same in 1981 as in 1978, but the right's share was down by a quarter and abstention was considerably up.

One odd fact about the vast army of 285 Socialist *députés* in the new Parliament is that 150 of them were teachers!

1986 (16 March). March 1986 was the '*cohabitation*' election: the one that finally produced a Parliamentary majority opposed to the incumbent President and obliging the two to coexist. The event over which a flood of ink had been expended speculatively in 1973, 1978 and 1986 had finally come to pass. Another interesting point about the 1986 election was that it was a consensus-politics election. The Socialists had been in power for five years; they had manifestly upheld the national consensus over institutions, nuclear defence and foreign policy, and in economic matters had become a rather pragmatic management party rather than being a programmatic Socialist one. So it was not a 'choice of society' election – freedom or the jackboot; elections in the 1970s had always been presented in this light. In 1986, 75% of the votes were cast for mainstream consensus parties.

There are some particular features of 1986 that are important. The first was the electoral system. This was the Fifth Republic's one experiment with proportional representation for the National Assembly.

Because it was believed to have been introduced for purely partisan reasons by the Socialists, it was immediately abolished again by the new government (which had won under it). The Socialists have always included PR in their programme on the grounds of fairness. However, the Socialist government finally introduced it at a time (in 1984–5) when it looked as though the Socialist Party, because of government unpopularity, would be lucky to get 20–22% of the vote. This would have meant, under the two-ballot system, the loss of most of the Social-

Table 13.8.　ALLOCATION OF SEATS BY 'HIGHEST AVERAGE'

(Dordogne – 4 seats – 1986)			
Communists	38,983	16.3%	
Socialists	78,528	32.7%	2 seats
RPR/UDF	104,503	43.7%	2 seats
Front National	13,823	5.8%	
Extreme left	2,344	.9%	eliminated*
Other right	1,442	.6%	eliminated*
Total	239,353		
Quotient	239,353/4	= 59,838	

* Under 5%.

The 'highest average' system result is 2 seats for RPR/UDF, 2 seats for Socialists, obtained as follows. The vote for each list is divided by the quotient: RPR/UDF obtains 1 seat, PS obtains 1 seat. The vote for each list is then divided by the number of seats it has so far obtained plus 1. The next seat goes to RPR/UDF whose original total is now divided by 3 (34,834) so that PS now has the 'highest average' and obtains the

Communists	38,983/1	= 38,983
Socialists	78,258/2	= *39,129*
RPR/UDF	104,503/2	= *52,252*
FN	13,823/1	= 13,823

fourth seat. (The 'highest remainder' system, by comparison, would have given 2 RPR/UDF, 1 PS, 1 Communist). First seats go to parties obtaining the quotient as above: 1 RPR/UDF, 1 PS. Remaining seats allocated according to the remainder (original vote less quotient):

Communists	*38,983*	
Socialists	78,258	– 59,838 = 39,129
RPR/UDF	104,503	– 59,838 = *44,665*

ist seats, including some leading members of the Party. With PR, on the other hand, they would 'save the furniture' even in an electoral disaster. The system chosen – party lists in multi-member *départements* and allocation of seats by highest average – had been used in France before, though with some important variants sometimes permitting alliances of lists, from 1919 to 1927 and from 1945 to 1956. The number of seats in a *département* depends on its population: Paris had twenty-one, Nord twenty-four, Hautes-Alpes two. Each party list has as many names as there are seats in the *département*. The elector votes for a whole list with no cross-voting allowed. A list with under 5% is eliminated. The seats are allocated by the 'highest average', starting with the top name on the list, as Table 13.8 shows. This system favours large parties in two ways. First, two-thirds of the ninety-six *départements* have six or fewer seats (over a third have three or fewer). This means that in most areas a party needs 15–25% to have a chance of winning a seat. The 5% threshold, except in big *départements* like Paris, is irrelevant. The second is that the highest average system leaves more of a party's original vote 'available' for redistribution than other alternative methods like 'highest remainder'.

Because of the advantage to larger parties, it was calculated that a party or alliance winning 43% of the national vote could expect to have a majority of seats in the new Parliament. That is precisely what happened: the RPR/UDF and allied independents got 43.1% and 291 seats out of 577.

A rather undemocratic feature of this type of PR is that the candidate's position on the party list is everything. In a country like France, where the political parties are not very democratic, this means that the party leadership has the patronage to place whom it wants in 'electable' positions. This of course is not true of all PR systems, nor is it true in countries where candidates are selected by the votes of a party's local members. Another consequence of the electoral system was the arrival of the Front National in Parliament. This sounds, to anyone who dislikes racist parties, like a serious indictment of the system. However, it is a legal party and it did obtain the support of 10% of the voters. Who is to say that they should be denied representation?

Another interesting feature of the election was the catastrophic result achieved by the Communist Party – less than 10%, its lowest score since 1932. Participation in government had not helped it electorally; and its return to the opposition and denunciation of the Socialist government did not help it either. More than half of its 1978 electorate lost, especially in the vital industrial regions of Paris and the north, home to a dwindling manual working class: the election posed some serious questions for the Party, as we saw in chapter 8.

A third feature, already alluded to, was the success of the Front National. This was the best performance by the extreme right since the Poujadists won more than fifty seats in 1956, and is analysed in chapter 10. As early as 1965 there was a strong vote in that region for Tixier-Vignancour, the extreme-right candidate against de Gaulle.

Fourthly, the Socialist Party, with 32%, had its second-best result ever – and this after its government had passed through a deep trough of unpopularity from 1983 to 1985. Projecting a reassuring image with blue posters depicting sky and a country church, and led by the Prime Minister Laurent Fabius, a technocrat in the mould of Giscard d'Estaing, the party warned the country not to take any risks – like trying '*cohabitation*'. There was no alliance with the Communists. The Union of the Left was dead anyway, and because there was no second ballot this time, there was no need for a pact of any kind.

Finally, the RPR/UDF alliance fought the election as an alliance, won, and governed as a coalition. Under proportional representation its component parts could have decided to fight the election separately. After all, in 1978, as government partners, the RPR and UDF presented separate candidates in most constituencies – but with a second-ballot pact and an agreement to govern together. In 1986 the RPR and the UDF presented joint lists in sixty-one of the ninety-six home *départements* and competing lists in the other thirty-five. The decision whether to have a joint or separate list was dictated by the local situation, in terms of personalities and the negotiations over 'electable' places on joint lists, and by the tactics of the electoral system. Basically it made sense to present separate lists in large *départements* and joint lists in small ones. In twenty out of twenty-nine *départements* with seven or more seats there were separate lists. In fifty-two out of sixty-seven with six seats or less, the parties presented joint lists. List leadership went to the RPR in forty-one of the sixty-one joint lists, but the UDF had a similar proportion of list leaderships in the Regional Council elections the same day (see chapter 14). The total electoral performance of the RPR/UDF was the same whether the lists were joint or separate. If the RPR came out as slightly the larger party, it is because of its tendency to do better in Paris and the overseas territories. The only prominent personality from the RPR/UDF considered to have had a poor election was former Prime Minister Raymond Barre. He had declared right from the start that he would have nothing to do with '*cohabitation*'. Thus, the rather poor performance of his list in Lyon was considered to be a rebuff from the electorate. That did not prevent him coming back strongly within a few months as a Presidential candidate, his hands clean from non-involvement in the Chirac government.

Table 13.9. PARLIAMENTARY ELECTION, 1986

			Seats
Electorate	36.6m.		
Turnout	78.5%		
Spoilt votes	2.0%		
	million votes	%	
Communists	2.7	9.7	35
Socialists and allies	8.8	32.1	216
Other left	6	2.2	–
Total left	*12.1*	*44.0*	*251*
Greens	.3	1.2	–
RPR/UDF and allies*	11.8	43.1	291 (RPR 151, UDF 130, Ind. 10)
Front National	2.7	9.8	35
Other right	.5	1.9	–

*Includes independents or dissident lists resulting from difficulties over candidate selection.

1988 (5 and 12 June).   The 1988 Parliamentary election was the third of the Mitterrand Presidency. It was like 1981 in that it followed immediately after victory in the Presidential election and a dissolution. It also marked a return to the two-ballot electoral system used in every Parliamentary election in the Fifth Republic except 1986. The reason for this was that the Chirac government, considering the introduction of proportional representation in 1986 to be a socialist attack on the stability of the Fifth Republic's institutions (see chapter 11), had enacted a return to the old system. It retained the 577 seats and division between *départements* of 1986 but had them re-arranged by the Minister of the Interior and former RPR functionary, Charles Pasqua, into new constituencies. The election was very unlike 1981 in that it did not produce a dramatic confirmation of the Presidential election in the form of a landslide for the party of the President.

The brief campaign was dominated by two questions. The first was *ouverture* and the other was relations between the Front National and the RPR/UDF alliance (baptised 'URC' – *Union du Rassemblement et du Centre* – for the occasion). François Mitterrand said constantly during the Presidential election that he wanted *ouverture*: a coalition between Socialists and centrists from the former Majority. When he appointed Michel Rocard, from the modernising social-democratic wing of the PS, as Prime Minister, everyone expected some sort of coalition. Ex-President Giscard d'Estaing was much in view – but his idea was not to join the government but simply to refrain from systematic opposition by judging each issue on its merits. He called on the President to show his spirit of *ouverture* by refraining from a dissolution. Rocard failed to get any of the elements of the UDF, other than a few isolated ex-ministers from the pre-1981 era like Lionel Stoléru, to join a coalition, and appointed a government that was virtually a copy of the last Socialist government of 1984–6. The cry from the right was that *ouverture* was a sham, while from the left it was claimed that no-one was willing to respond to *ouverture*. The election was thus fought, like all the elections of the previous twenty years, as a straight contest between left and right. The bipolar party system of the Fifth Republic had become deeply entrenched: how can centrists opt for *ouverture* and coalition with Socialists when they have been elected by supporters of an alliance of the right?

Relations between the Front National and the URC received much attention and generated a considerable amount of humbug. The problem centred on the constituencies of the south coast where the URC would risk losing to the left if the FN candidates declined to withdraw from the second ballot and the nine constituencies (eight in the Marseilles area and one in Var) where the FN had polled more votes than the URC candidate at the first ballot. The inevitable agreement took place: the nine URC candidates and almost all the FN ones in the other constituencies were withdrawn. Jean-Claude Gaudin, the leader of the UDF in Marseille, denied that there was an agreement and received all the blame for it. Raymond Barre, Simone Veil and some of the younger Gaullists (Michel Noir and Philippe Séguin – the latter only retaining his seat in the Vosges by 75 votes after the FN called for an anti-Séguin vote at the second ballot) condemned it. Giscard and Chirac said nothing.

President Mitterrand asked the electors to give him a 'clear but not excessive' Parliamentary majority. They gave a subtle response. Turnout at the first ballot was the lowest for any French Parliamentary election – 65.8% – increasing to 70% at the second. In 1981 it had been low as well (70.4%), indicating that there is naturally a higher rate of abstention at a Parliamentary election coming straight after what is viewed as the much more important Presidential one. In addition, there was the expectation that as in 1981 it would be a walkover for the Socialists. The vote for the left as a whole was substantially down on 1981 – for the Socialists it was about the same as in 1981, for the PCF much less – and millions less than the vote for François Mitterrand at the second Presidential ballot a month earlier. However, the electors managed collectively to achieve a result – not quite an overall majority for the Socialists – which gave the President whom they had just re-elected a workable Parliamentary situation, and which left on the table the requirement that parties should work together (*ouverture* to replace *cohabitation* which had been popular).

The Front National, a month after the great success of its leader Jean-Marie Le Pen at the Presidential election (14.4%, 4.4 million votes), managed only 9.9% and 2.4 million votes. Under proportional representation in 1986, the same percentage had won them thirty-five seats. This time, under the two-ballot system, they won only one: Mme Piat (Var), who incidentally was expelled from the party a few months later. The fluctuating performance of the FN is sometimes quoted as an argument against proportional representation – indeed Le Pen himself blamed his party's disappointing showing in June 1988 on the return to an unfair majority system where a vote for the FN is a 'wasted' vote. Obviously a party that can get about 10% in a Parliamentary election will win more seats under a proportional than a majority system. The argument that the system affects the size of their popular vote, however, is rather dubious. If the motive for voting FN is to cast a protest vote as a warning to the country's political leaders (see the section on 1988 in chapter 12), then a two-ballot election where there is no 'risk' that the FN will actually win is an ideal opportunity. The Presidential election of 1988 (two-ballot) has so far been the FN's high point in terms of the popular vote. At all events the desire of many voters to cast a protest vote seems to have been limited to the Presidential election. They achieved over 20% in twenty-nine constituencies, twenty-four of them in Provence, and over 30% in two, both in Marseille where Le Pen was a candidate and said he would stand for Mayor in 1989 – a pledge unfulfilled.

The Communist Party enjoyed a mild success in June 1988. After falling steadily and steeply at every election for ten years, reaching only 6.7% for the Communist Presidential candidate André Lajoinie in April 1988, the Communist vote actually went up. They beat the FN with 11.3%. Their score of 2.8 million votes was the same as they had achieved in 1986 (on a much higher turnout), and they returned to Parliament with twenty-seven seats, only eight fewer than in 1986 and much better than the slaughter they had feared after April. There was a second-ballot pact with the Socialists which worked well from the point of view of the transfer of votes, although nearly all Communist candidates, including leading party figures like Charles Fiterman, Roland Leroy and Maxime Gremetz, had to withdraw in favour of Socialists who had run ahead of them at the first ballot. There were only twenty-four Communist candidates in the second round. After the election, the PC found that it actually held the balance of power in Parliament – so the new Parliamentary majority was rather like the old Union of the Left.

Table 13.10.   PARLIAMENTARY ELECTION, 1988

	1st ballot		seats
Electorate	37.8m.		
Abstentions	34.3%		
Spoilt votes	1.4%		
	million votes	%	
Communists	2.8	11.3	27
Socialists and allies (MRG and Presidential majority)	9.2	37.5	277
Total left	*12.0*	*49.2*	
URC (RPF/UDF alliance)	9.7	40.5	270
(RPR)	4.7	19.2	128)
(UDF)	4.5	18.5	130)
(Other URC)	.7	2.9	12)
Front National	2.4	9.9	1
Others	.1	.4	–

—By-elections (élections partielles)

There are occasions when a vacancy in a Parliamentary seat has to be filled. In Britain by-elections usually occur as a result of the death, ennoblement or resignation of the sitting member. In France a *député* who dies or accepts some office which is a bar to membership of the Assembly is automatically replaced without a vote. Under the 1986 proportional system, the new *député* was simply the next unelected name on the previous *député*'s party list. Under the two-ballot system he is replaced by his *suppléant* or substitute whose name appeared on the ballot at the previous election as running-mate.

In France there are basically only two reasons for a by-election. The most common in recent years – especially since June 1988 – has been the annulment of the general election result in a constituency because of irregularities. In earlier years more interesting ones were caused by the resignation of ministers from the government. Under Article 25 of the Constitution a *député*, when appointed a minister, has to resign his seat and be replaced by his *suppléant*. However, if he is dismissed or resigns he naturally wants to regain his parliamentary seat and is usually able to prevail on the *suppléant* to resign and produce a by-election. That is why there is always a flurry of by-elections after a government reshuffle – in 1974, for instance, or after the resignation of the Chirac government in 1976. Sometimes ex-ministers cannot prevail upon their *suppléants* to resign. Couve de Murville in 1969 could not, and another member sportingly offered the former Prime Minister his seat. In the famous by-election that followed, Couve was beaten by Michel Rocard, at that time leader of the PSU. At the subsequent general election Couve exercised his right to stand for his original constituency, and thus the insubordinate *suppléant* did not last long. On another famous occasion the Prime Minister in office had to contest a by-election. In 1970 the *suppléant* of Jacques Chaban-Delmas died. Chaban-Delmas contested the by-election in his Bordeaux constituency, although he knew that as Prime Minister he would have to give up the seat again to his new *suppléant* as soon as he had won it! To stress the ridiculous nature of these rules, the chief opponent of the Prime Minister was another candidate who would not have been able to take his seat either because he was already *député* for Nancy – the Radical Party leader and media tycoon Jean-Jacques Servan-Schreiber!

By-elections, as in Britain, are regarded as a live opinion poll on the popularity of government and opposition, often with the added spice of a well-known public figure seeking to regain an influential role in public life after resignation or dismissal from government. The spectacular by-election victory of Jaques Chirac in rural Corrèze in 1976, for instance, when the Socialists were making gains everywhere else, was a splendid launching-pad for the December rally at which the RPR was created with Chirac as its undisputed chieftain. It was at a by-election in 1984 that ex-President Giscard d'Estaing made his return to political life.

European Parliament elections

In France, as in most other European Community countries, interest in the European Parliament and its elections is very low, and the elections are regarded mainly as a live opinion poll on the internal standing of the different political parties and their leaders. There is very little discussion of community affairs. The electoral system employed to elect the eighty-one French members is proportional representation – but of the least satisfactory kind. The country is one vast constituency – so there is no regional representation, and this encourages the nationalistic notion that French members go to represent France. The parties put up lists containing eighty-one names with the order determined by the parties themselves. Since French political parties are not particularly democratic, this essentially means that the party leadership determines the order of names and, effectively, the ones that will be elected. The whole system gives tremendous – and quite unnecessary – powers of patronage to the party leaders. The party leaders themselves often get elected to the European Parliament, but they play no part in it. Some party leaders, like Jacques Chirac, even decree that members will retire in rotation and permit list members not elected by the public to have a turn.

The June 1979 European election was dominated, in France, by the rivalry inside the two principal alliances. Chirac ran an extremely nationalist campaign. He made a vehement attack on President Giscard and his supporters, calling them – in a statement given the idiotic title 'Appel de Cochin' because it was issued from his bed at the Cochin hospital in February – the 'foreigners' party'. The Communists also ran a nationalist campaign to try to win back some support from the Socialists. Only 60% of the French voted (compared with 30% of the British) and the pro-Giscard list led by the popular Health Minister Simone Veil, who became President of the European Parliament after the election, did best. This was considered to be a vote of confidence in the President. Chirac's list did badly. The Socialists' 1978 leadership over the Communists was reduced, but the Communists continued to lose ground in their Paris region heartland.

June 1984 also served as a mid-term opinion poll on the popularity of the President and government – this time Socialist. The left did disastrously badly. The Socialists reached their lowest point in the 1981–6 period with only 21%, but the Communists hit a spectacular new low with only 11%. From 1984 to 1986, however, the Socialists picked up, but the Communist decline continued. The RPR/UDF fought the election on a united list led by Simone Veil. The aim was to show a clear 'win' for the anti-Socialist alliance. In fact many observers think that the UDF was outmanoeuvred by Chirac because a separate UDF list, especially with Simone Veil, might well have won more votes than the RPR and established itself more clearly as a major force and not a satellite of Chirac.

Apart from the collapse of the Communist vote, the most interesting phenomenon of the 1984 election was the 11% won by the Front National. This was the big breakthrough which kept them in the public eye and around the 10% mark in the 1985 local elections and by-elections, and the 1986 Parliamentary elections.

The 1989 Euro-elections in France were, as always and as in all countries of the Community, entirely preoccupied with internal politics. The main point of interest was the rivalry within the RPR/UDF. It was thought possible at one time that a list of *Rénovateurs* – the leading younger figures in the two organisations such as Philippe Séguin and the newly-elected Mayor of Lyon, Michel Noir – might stand against the official RPR/UDF list. It did not happen. The only split in the opposition was the presence of a Centrist list, led by the ever-present Simone Veil. The list only scored 8% and probably ended Mme Veil's hopes as a national political figure. The RPR/UDF list was led by Giscard himself. It came top in the elections, and the ex-President was considered to have made something of a comeback, though not sufficiently to make him a realistic candidate for his old office in 1993. The Socialist government was not as severely censured as in 1984. Communist marginalisation was confirmed. The Front National's 11% in the 1984 Euro elections was confirmed. The most significant element in the result, and part of a Europe-wide phenomenon, was undoubtedly the high score of the Greens (chapter 9), who obtained representation in the European Parliament for the first time.

Table 13.11. EUROPEAN PARLIAMENT ELECTIONS
(*France – 81 seats*)

Parties and list leaders	1979 Seats	1979 %	1984 Seats	1984 %	1989 Seats	1989 %
Abstention		39.3		43.3		51.1
Extreme left	–	3.1	–	3.7		2.0
Communists						
1979 Marchais	19	20.5				
1984 Marchais			10	11.2		
1989 Herzog					7	7.7
Socialists and allies						
1979 Mitterrand	22	23.5				
1984 Jospin			20	20.9		
1989 Fabius					22	23.6
Greens	–	4.4	–	3.4	9	10.6
1989 Waechter						
RPR						
1979 Chirac	15	16.3				
UDF	25	27.6				
1979 Veil						
RPR/UDF						
1984 Veil			41	42.7		
				(RPR 20, UDF 21)		
1989 Giscard					26	28.9
						(RPR 12, UDF 12, Other 2)
Centrists						
1989 Veil					7	8.4
Front National	–	1.3	10	11.0	10	11.7
1984/1989 Le Pen						
Other	–	3.3	–	3.7	–	7.0

Senate elections

It is often overlooked that the French Parliament has an elected second chamber. The Senate is important for the part which it plays in the legislative process, and it has often been more disposed than the National

Assembly to be critical of the government. That was certainly the case when de Gaulle was President as it was from 1981 to 1986 when there was a Socialist government but a non-Socialist majority in the Senate. The two Presidents the Senate has had so far in the Fifth Republic have made themselves far more of a nuisance to the Executive than the *députés*. Gaston Monnerville had the audacity to invoke the Constitutional Council, which the President of the Senate has the right to do, to test the constitutionality of the October 1962 referendum on direct Presidential elections. Alain Poher, whom we have already encountered in this narrative, campaigned against the referendum on Senate reform in 1969, and during the two brief periods when after de Gaulle's resignation and again after the death of Pompidou he became, as the Constitution requires of the President of the Senate, interim President of the Republic, he sacked various highly-placed Gaullist officials and took steps to end electoral corruption in the overseas territories.

The Senate is important but its elections attract little interest, mainly because they do not involve the general public. The Senators are elected by indirect suffrage – that is to say by an electoral college composed of parliamentarians and councillors who have themselves been directly elected. The term of office is nine years, but one-third of Senators retire every three years so there is a Senate election every third year. There are two electoral systems – proportional representation by lists and highest average for the more highly-populated *départements* which have five or more Senate seats (for an explanation of how this system works see the section above on the 1986 Parliamentary election), and the two ballot list system for the smaller *départements*. In the first case the electors just vote for a list, while in the latter case candidates can be individuals or lists and the electors can cross-vote for individuals on different lists. The people who form the electoral college in a *département* are the *députés* (regional councillors) and *conseillers généraux* (county councillors), and a number of town councillors. Town council delegates are elected by their councils, the smallest villages choosing just one Councillor and the largest cities their whole council membership plus some extras (one for every 1,000 inhabitants over 30,000). In addition there are twelve Senators representing French people living abroad. They are elected by the Higher Council of French People Abroad, which is itself elected by its constituents – the French nationals living overseas.

The Senate is not very representative of public opinion. First, its electorate of local worthies is not exactly a cross-section of the populace, and, secondly, the composition of its electorate considerably

Table 13.12.   PARTIES IN THE SENATE

	1980	1983	1986	1989
Communists	23	24	15	16
Socialists	69	70	64	62
Democratic Left	39	39	35	23
Centre Union	67	71	70	68
UDF	52	58	54	52
RPR	41	58	77	91
Other	13	5	4	5

over-represents small villages and rural areas. Furthermore, since senators are elected by local councillors, Senatorial elections tend, if anything, to reflect what public opinion was when the last Town Council
elections took place. The Senate elections of 1986 continued to reflect
the successes of the right at the Municipal elections of 1983.

The Senate remains a haven of traditional French parliamentarism
where the new party system has hardly taken root. Many of the senators
are still Independents or Moderates, or centre-left. In the country as a
whole the Radicals are split between those who have allied themselves
with the Socialists (and were therefore in the opposition after 1986) and
those who are in the UDF and were members of the 1986–8 government
coalition. In the Senate, however, both wings sit quite happily together
in a group called 'Democratic Left'. The elections are getting gradually
more politicised, and in 1989 the RPR, with its policy of outright
opposition to the Socialist government, made gains at the expense of
moderates and centrists. The Senate has a sense of tradition. The seat at
the front on the extreme left has brass nameplates to show that it was
once occupied by Victor Hugo and later by Clemenceau. It is now
occupied by the leader of the Communist Group.

14

LOCAL ELECTIONS

At first sight it seems strange that in a country with so strong a tradition
of centralised government, local elections and local government should
be so important. This was true before the Decentralisation Laws were
introduced by the Socialist government of 1981–6. Previously, the
préfet, a central government official rather like a colonial governor, had
exercised powers of *tutelle* (somewhere between supervision and control)
over the local authorities. Today he still reviews all local authority
decisions and has the power to refer them to administrative law courts
or regional audit courts. The *recteur*, appointed by the Minister of
Education, still administers all local schools and universities. The
Minister of the Interior and the Minister of Defence still control all the
police.

There are three reasons for the importance of local elections and of
local government. The first is that local government is very presidential.
The mayor of a large town and the president of a regional council
or of a *conseil général* (the equivalent of a British county council) have
important executive powers and considerable scope for local initiative.
Oversimplifying slightly, one may say that if they can get the money for
something they can do it. In a British local authority this is much less so.
The main local fiscal effort in Britain is directed towards doing things
that cannot be avoided – like paying teachers' salaries. In France that is
all taken care of by the state, and local authorities can get on with doing
local things. The mayor of a town is leader of his party's list; he is in
office for six years, and is the most prominent local personality. He has
considerable resources at his disposal, and, once the budget has been
voted, is not subject to much day-to-day scrutiny or control.

The second reason is that, partly for the reasons given above, national
political figures keep their positions in local government. About three-
quarters of the *députés* in the National Assembly are mayors or local
councillors. Pierre Mauroy remained Mayor of Lille when he was Prime
Minister (1981–4), and Jacques Chirac remained Mayor of Paris when
he was Prime Minister (1986–8). Until 1985 politicians could 'accumu-
late' mandates – mayor, *conseiller général*, regional councillor, *député*,
minister, Member of the European Parliament, all at the same time.

Now the number of such posts that can be held at the same time is
limited to two. The combination *député* and mayor remains very preva-
lent, and the *député-maire* has been described as the pivot of the whole
French political and administrative system – with the opportunity for
'general political control of the political system including its local sub-
system' (Gremion).[1]

Why is it worthwhile for a national political leader to remain involved
in local affairs? In the first place, it is electorally profitable because local
attachments are an important electoral factor. The French tend to vote
for prominent local personalities rather than systematically following a
party ticket, and they are suspicious of candidates 'parachuted' in from
Paris. Electors vote for Jacques Chaban-Delmas in Bordeaux or for
Jacques Chirac in the Corrèze (where he has his Parliamentary seat)
against the trend outside. A prominent local notable is also better placed
to win a 'primary' against his alliance partners in a two-ballot Parliamentary election. In 1978 the great majority of RPR/UDF first-ballot
'primaries' were 'won' by the best-known local personality.

Secondly, leadership roles in local government are satisfying in
themselves. Local power is a reality in France, and a local notable – the
mayor of a large town, for example, or president of a *conseil
général* – has the standing, the resources – office, personal staff, a car, a
budget – and the opportunity for tangible local achievement to build a
national leadership role. Pierre Mauroy, Gaston Defferre (who found
being Mayor of Marseille much more satisfying than being a *député*) and
Jean Lecanuet, Mayor of Rouen and President of the UDF, all owed
their national leadership roles largely to their prominence as city and
regional leaders. Becoming Mayor of Lyon in 1989 gave a considerable
boost to the national leadership ambitions of Michel Noir (RPR).
Députés who do not have a local mandate feel incomplete. Jacques Chirac
as Mayor of Paris has a huge personal staff, many of whom, like Edouard
Balladur (Minister of Finance) or Denis Baudouin (Prime Minister's
spokesman), went straight into government as senior ministers or into
the Prime Minister's personal *cabinet* after the election victory of 1986.
He was able to act almost as a head of state, receiving foreign leaders at
the town hall and making overseas visits, and used the office to stay in
the public eye and build up an electoral clientele. Philippe Séguin, an
important minister in the 1986–8 Chirac government, was an official in
a ministerial *cabinet* before 1978. He won the Parliamentary seat of
Epinal (Vosges) in 1978, consolidated it by becoming mayor in 1983,
and retained this office as a government minister, with an official in his
cabinet to deal with local Vosges matters.

The presidential character of local elections, especially municipal or town council elections, often linked to a prominent and even national personality with considerable local power, explains the great interest they generate. Voter turnout of around 75% (78% in 1983), even higher in small communities, is normal, as compared with around 40% in Britain. There are 500,000 local councillors in France, nearly 1% of the population – a very significant figure for participation in government.

Town and City Council elections (élections municipales)

All the cities, towns and villages of France vote for their local municipal council on the same day every six years. It is at this level that local government has the most meaning to the citizen. Elections are on a two-ballot list system: lists are presented by political parties, alliances or local groups (there are innumerable non-party local action lists). Councils vary in size according to population, ranging from nine members in villages with less than 100 inhabitants to sixty-nine for cities over 300,000. The three largest cities – Paris, Marseille and Lyon – have a special system described below. Lists presented have as many names as there are seats on the council. In small towns and villages where the population numbers less than 3,500, the elector may cross-vote by voting for individuals on different lists, and in the very small villages one may even write in the name of an individual who is not a candidate. In the remaining larger towns (only 2,000 out of 36,000 councils) the elector just votes for the whole list. The leader of a list is that list's candidate for mayor, although strictly speaking it is the newly-elected council that appoints the Mayor and not the electorate directly. In this respect it is rather like a British general election: the Prime Minister is not directly elected by the people, but everybody knows that the leader of the party winning a majority will hold that office.

Under the 1982 Decentralisation Laws some important changes to the electoral system for the larger towns were introduced. Before that date the list that won the election won all the seats on the council. This meant that in large cities, where council elections are highly politicised, there was no opposition on the council itself. This left the party in power, and in particular the mayor, very free from scrutiny and accountability indeed. The Socialist government in 1982 introduced a change, which has meant that the opposition lists do now win some seats. It is complicated, and tries to combine the majority principle and the proportional principle. The winning list gets half the seats (majority principle) and the other half are distributed, in proportion to votes received, to all the lists including the winning one – so the winning list usually ends up with about 80% of the seats on the council. Lists obtaining under 5% get no seats. It is a two-ballot election, so that if no list wins an absolute majority at the first ballot, a second ballot is held. Any list with 10% at the first ballot may stand at the second. First-ballot lists may combine into merged lists for the second ballot if they wish.

Paris, Marseille and Lyon have their own separate model. These cities are divided into districts, each of which has its own list election as if it were a separate town. The winners from each district collectively form the city council. Paris has twenty districts and a council membership of 159, Marseille has nine and 101, Lyon six and seventy-three. Of course the main parties present lists in every district, so that in Paris, for example, electors voting for the RPR list in any of the twenty districts would know that they were voting for Chirac even though Chirac himself was only a candidate in the Fifth district. To make matters more complicated, each district in the three cities has its own local district council (*conseil d'arrondissement*) with limited powers and the right to be consulted over local matters. The original idea of the Socialist government in proposing these was to create something like the London boroughs, and cut back the power and status of the Chirac-controlled Paris City Council. However, this transparently political

Table 14.1.   LOCAL COUNCIL ELECTIONS
(LILLE, GRENOBLE, STRASBOURG, 1989)

LILLE

	First ballot		Second ballot	
Abstentions	43%		44%	
Union of the Left	43.1%	Left Union + Greens (merged list)	54%	46 seats* (24 PS, 8 PC, 5 Green, 9 other left)
RPR/UDF	34.4%	RPR/UDF	46.1%	13 seats* (5 RPR, 8 UDF)
Greens	8.4%	(merged with Union of Left)		
FN	7.9%	(eliminated)		
Others	6.2%	(eliminated)		

*59 seats on Council, so winning list gets half (30) and the remaining 29 divide 16 for the winning list and 13 for the loser.

GRENOBLE

	First ballot		Second ballot
Abstentions	36%		
RPR/UDF	53.3%	46 seats (9 RPR, 8 UDF, 29 other)	
Union of the Left	31.7%	9 seats (6 PS, 2 PC, 1 other)	
Greens	8.5%	2 seats	
FN	6.5%	2 seats	

*55 seats on Council, so winning list – overall majority at first ballot – gets half (28). The remaining 27 are divided (roughly) proportionally between all four lists: 18, 9, 2, and 2. No list was eliminated by the 5% rule and there was no second ballot for mergers to be arranged.

STRASBOURG

	First ballot		Second ballot	
Abstentions	42%		35%	
UDF/RPR	31%		36.3%	11 seats (5 UDF, 5 RPR, 1 other)
Socialists and allies	30.1%		42.7%	45 seats (33 PS, 12 other)
FN	14.5%		12.1%	3 seats
Greens	12.8%		8.9%	2 seats
Dissident RPR	5.2%	(withdrew)		
Dissident UDF	4.1%	(eliminated)		
Communists	2.2%	(eliminated)		

*61 seats on Council, so winning list gets half (31). The remaining 30 are divided proportionally 14, 11, 3, 2, to the lists present in the second ballot. No mergers.

move aroused such a storm of protest that the government was compelled both to water it down and to extend it to Gaston Defferre's socialist stronghold of Marseille. Those who win places on the city council also serve on the district council, so that today when you get off the bus at the impressive *Mairie du XIIIe Arrondissement* you can reflect that it is now the seat of an elected Council and no longer just an administrative office for matters like births, marriages and deaths.

Local elections have become more and more politicised in the 1970s and '80s. The results have come to be interpreted as a live national opinion poll on the standing of the parties, with most interest centred upon the 400 or so large towns with populations above 20,000.

1977. There was a particularly interesting set of city council elections in 1977 – mainly because of the 'battle for Paris' and the great success nationally for the Union of the Left. Until 1977 Paris was the only town in France not to have its own Mayor. So many governments in history have been overthrown in the streets of Paris and so many Republics proclaimed from the town hall balcony that it has been thought that a Mayor of Paris might be a rival to the government itself. President Giscard d'Estaing restored its Mayor to the City of Paris – the first since the 1871 Commune. He probably came to regret it, because this enabled his carnivorous rival Jaques Chirac, who had resigned as Prime Minister in 1976 and formed the RPR, to acquire a magnificent power-base from which to operate. As we noted above, Chirac as Mayor of Paris amassed a huge personal staff including most of those he was able to appoint as senior ministers in the 1986 government. Giscard rather clumsily designated his own candidate for mayor, Michel d'Ornano, one of the leading *Giscardien* faithful. Chirac flung his hat into the ring. The Chirac lists in the eighteen sectors (as there were then) totalled 26% at the first ballot, the d'Ornano lists 22%. Because merging of lists between ballots was not allowed in 1977, but there was a second-ballot pact between Gaullists and *Giscardiens* against the left, the d'Ornano lists had to stand down in eleven sectors. They finished with a mere sixteen councillors out of 109 against Chirac's fifty. The left got the other forty-three.

   The parties of the left in 1977 presented joint Union of the Left lists in 200 of the 221 large cities. In the election of 1971 there had merely been a second-ballot pact whereby the less successful first-ballot list would stand down in favour of its partner. In 1977 there were tough negotiations over the composition and leadership of joint lists. In retrospect, however, the 1977 elections stand out as the high point of the Union of the Left, and the united lists that won control of 156 of the 221 cities governed in a united way in most cases for many years after – even though the Union of the Left, as we have seen, broke down in late 1977. The electors in March 1977 were prepared to vote for the Union of the Left whether local list leadership was Communist or Socialist. New Communist mayors came to power in important cities like St Etienne or Le Mans. Cities in Catholic heartlands like Rennes or Reims fell to the left. In Marseille, the Socialist leader Gaston Defferre accepted his party's nationwide policy of severing former municipal alliances with centrists, but refused to have Communists on his lists. They opposed him in every sector, but he still won.

1983. In 1983, at a period when the Socialist government was beginning to lose its popularity, the local elections reversed the results of
1977. Once again the two most interesting features were the battle for
Paris and the performance of the left. In Paris, as we have seen, the
Socialist government had made a clumsy attempt to undo the 1977
reforms by creating twenty separate district councils – a crude attempt
to clip Chirac's wings. Chirac successfully made himself the champion
of keeping a proper city council for Paris. In the Paris elections this time,
and indeed in almost every city in France, the RPR and UDF presented
joint lists at the first ballot – this despite the new electoral law
allowing the merging of lists between the ballots. Chirac's joint
RPR/UDF lists won every district in Paris.

The Union of the Left principle was retained by the Socialists and
Communists. Despite the problems of 1978–81, the Communists were,
after all, still partners in government – they only left in 1984. There
were disputes about list composition and leadership in those cities where
there was a Communist mayor but which had gone Socialist in the 1981
Parliamentary elections. In eleven cities they could not agree, and presented separate lists. The left lost control in thirty-one cities including
Grenoble (a high-tech Socialist showcase), Nîmes (a solid Communist
bastion of the deep south), and two Socialist strongholds in the north,
Roubaix and Tourcoing. They hung on, however, in some cities which
they expected to lose – notably Marseille and some towns in strong
Catholic regions with a weak Socialist tradition, which had been won in
1977, such as Rennes and Angers.

The tactic of unity on the right worked well. The only serious case
of division was Lyon where the outgoing Mayor, supposedly non-
political but in reality UDF, was challenged by one of the RPR 'young
Turks', Michel Noir, subsequently a rather outspoken minister in the
Chirac government. The outgoing Mayor of Lyon, Senator Francisque
Collomb, was re-elected. Nationally, united lists enabled the Gaullists,
less a party of local notables than the UDF, to win some more town halls
and the UDF to run less risk of being crushed by the Chirac steamroller.

1989. The City Council elections of March 1989 were good for the
Socialists, for the Greens and for trouble-makers. In a mid-term election the government party can normally expect to suffer from a protest
vote, but this emphatically did not happen to the PS in 1989. Its candidate, appropriately a *Rocardien* Catherine Trautmann, even won in

Strasbourg, the very heartland of Catholic centrism, and became the first
woman mayor of a major city.

There were two main types of trouble-maker or heretic that did well
in 1989. There was the impatient young thoroughbred, best typified by
Michel Noir (RPR) in Lyon. He is one of the *Rénovateurs* of the RPR,
well to the left of the *Chiraquien* leadership, and always one of the first to
denounce any idea of a pact with the FN. The well-established if ageing
incumbent Mayor (UDF) was supported by former Prime Minister and
Presidential candidate Raymond Barre (a Lyon *député*), but Noir beat
him in every sector of the city – the first time in this century that an
incumbent Mayor of Lyon has been beaten. A second type of trouble-
maker was the incumbent mayor in trouble with his own party. The one
that attracted the most attention was Robert Vigouroux in Marseille.
The battle for the succession to Gaston Defferre, boss of Marseille for
more than thirty years, started well before his death in 1985 (indeed it
was the cause of his death, according his widow), and continued long
after it. Robert Vigouroux was elected as 'caretaker' Mayor until the
party leadership was sorted out. When Michel Pezet became party leader
in Marseille, he was selected as candidate for Mayor as well. However,
Vigouroux refused to stand down and was supported by Defferre's
widow and discreetly, so it is said, by no less a figure than President
Mitterrand. He beat the official Socialist (Pezet) list in every sector of the
city. Incumbent Communist mayors in trouble with their party
included Robert Jarry, the veteran Mayor of Le Mans, and Gaston
Viens, Mayor of Orly. Both were expelled for deciding to lead Union of
the Left lists instead of official Communist lists in their towns, and both
won.

The Greens did well – a first indication of the success they would have
right across Europe in the European Parliament elections three months
later (see chapter 12). They scored around 15% and won council seats
in many towns (Rennes and St Brieuc for example), and gained their
first Paris city councillor. In most cases where they were eligible to do
so they maintained their lists at the second ballot rather than negotiate a
merged list with one of the major parties, and usually increased their
score except where there was a particularly exciting contest between left
and right (e.g. in Strasbourg). In Lille, they formed an alliance with the
Socialist leader and incumbent Mayor Pierre Mauroy which gave them
five seats. After the 1989 elections there were approximately 1,500
Green councillors in France.

The Front National also in most cases maintained its candidates.

Table 14.2. TOWN AND CITY COUNCIL ELECTIONS – MAYORS OF
CITIES OVER 30,000

	1977	1983	1989 (cities over 20,000*)	
Communists	75	59	68	(– 14)
Socialists and allies	81	67	122	(+ 22)
UDF	37	42	72	(– 10)
RPR	23	41	80	(– 7)
Other right	8	14	26	(+ 1)

* Large cities where no cross-voting is allowed were redefined as over 20,000 in 1989.

Table 14.3. MAYORS OF PRINCIPAL CITIES, 1989

RPR	Paris, Bordeaux, Lyon (gain from UDF), Grenoble, Nice, Dijon
UDF	Toulouse, Nancy, St Etienne, Rouen, Amiens (gain from PC)
Other right	Tours
PS	Strasbourg (gain from UDF), Nantes (gain from RPR), Lille, Rennes, Montpellier, Clermont Ferrand, Limoges, Brest (gain from RPR), Orleans (gain from UDF)
PC	Le Havre, St Denis, Calais
Dissidents	Le Mans (Communist), Marseille (Socialist), Metz (UDF Mayor 'Presidential majority' and Minister in Socialist government)

Unlike in the 1985 cantonal elections, perhaps because the city elections
have a proportional element, their vote at the second ballot held up well.
They did best as usual on the south coast – Perpignan 25% at the first
ballot, 29% at the second, with six councillors; Toulon 20%, 24%, and
seven; Nice 18%, 20%, and seven. The FN in 1989 had about 330
councillors in the large towns and cities of France.

  The other interesting points from these elections were the success
once again of Jacques Chirac in Paris, winner in every sector; the fact
that the Union of the Left was maintained, after months of threatening
press statements from both Socialists and Communists, in most towns
held by the left; a turnout much lower than usual (as in all the elections
of 1988–9 after the Presidential) with over 40% abstaining in the biggest
cities like Paris; and the defeat of some very long-established 'notables'
of whom the most famous was Michel Debré, former Prime Minister
and Mayor of Amboise.

Regional Council elections

One of the Decentralisation reforms of 1982–3 was the introduction of direct elections for the regional councils. There are twenty-two Regions in metropolitan France with wonderful historic names like Aquitaine, Burgundy and Île de France. Before 1982 the councils were composed of the Region's Members of Parliament and a selection of local councillors chosen by their councils. Directly-elected regional councils, with some taxation powers of their own and an important role in economic development, could become a very significant part of the political system. So far, however, this has not happened. There is no very strong identification by the public with their Region, except perhaps in the case of the Bretons, and the elected members still see themselves as delegates going to the regional council to get grants for their local area rather than see themselves as part of a genuinely regional government. Also the first regional elections passed almost unnoticed because they occurred on the same day as the 1986 Parliamentary elections, and operating under the same proportional representation system (for details of the system see chapter 13 – section on the 1986 election). Thus electors voted for *département* lists of their preferred parties in both elections. Corsica had its first regional elections in August 1984 in an attempt to generate some feeling of self-government as an antidote to demands for independence.

The party that did best in the 1986 regional elections was the UDF. This tends to be an organisation of local notables. Negotiations with its Gaullist partners saw a trade-off whereby the UDF had two-thirds of joint list leaderships in the regional council elections while the RPR had two-thirds of joint list leaderships for the Parliamentary elections (see chapter 13). The UDF, after the 1986 elections, held the Presidency of fourteen out of the twenty-two Regions (RPR 6, Socialists 2). The President of Auvergne Regional Council is no less a person than ex-President Giscard d'Estaing.

The Front National did as well in the Regional elections, naturally, as in the Parliamentary elections the same day. As a result it held the balance in a number of regional councils between the mainstream right and the left: Corsica, Languedoc, Aquitaine, Upper Normandy, Picardy and Franche Comté.

In 1989 the Socialist government announced that it would reform the electoral system for regional council elections to make them more like town council elections – with a list for the whole Region instead of one for each *département*, so that the list leader of the winning list would

Table 14.4. REGIONAL COUNCIL ELECTIONS, 1986

	Seats	*Presidencies*
Communists	178	–
Socialists and allies	590	2
Greens	4	–
Regionalists (Corsica)	6	–
RPR/UDF	883	20
(RPR	345	6)
(UDF	399	14)
(Other	139)	
Front National	137	–

have the kind of legitimacy as President that the mayor of a city has, and a combination of the majority principle and the proportional principle so that there would be a clear winner but with some representation for the opposition.

Cantonal elections

The Cantonal elections elect the *conseil général* in each *département*. The term of office of a councillor is six years, but Cantonal elections are held every three years when half of all the seats come up for renewal. In 1985 it was the councillors who had faced the electors in 1979 who faced them again, in 1988 those elected in 1982. These elections are single-member two-ballot elections – like Parliamentary elections. The left's greatest success was in 1976 – the heyday of the Union of the Left – when they won over 52% of the vote, and hastened the departure of Prime Minister Chirac. Most of the left's gains were Socialist – a first warning to the Communist Party that the Union of the Left did not only contain benefits from their point of view. The 1982 Cantonal elections were the first real sign of the diminishing popularity of the Socialist government, and losses were suffered by the left in both 1982 and 1985. Under the Decentralisation Laws the president of a *conseil général* becomes a much more important local figure with greatly increased powers, so the losses and gains of Presidencies really started to matter. After the 1985 elections, only twenty-six out of ninety-five Presidencies in metropolitan France were held by the Left – mainly in the industrial north, on the south coast and in the south-west.

The performance of the Front National attracted considerable attention in the 1985 Cantonals, through both its relative success at the first

ballot and its complete failure at the second. In the first ballot its share of
the national vote was 8.8%–10.4% in the cantons where it presented
candidates (1,460 out of 2,044). In five cantons of the Var *département*
(Provence) and in the cities of Marseille and Perpignan the Front scored
over 25%. However, all but 114 of its 1,460 candidates were eliminated
by the 10% rule (minimum score permitting access to the second ballot).
In the second ballot the Front had to decide whether the 114 or some of
them should withdraw in favour of RPR or UDF candidates better
placed to beat the left. It also hoped that the RPR/UDF would
withdraw in favour of it where it, the Front National, was better placed.
In the event the RPR/UDF made no concessions, and the Front pulled
out in thirty-nine cantons. FN candidates, therefore, contested the
second ballot in eighty-five cantons and won only one seat – in
Marseille, and that mainly because of the unpopularity of the local RPR
leader. Where they were the sole candidates against the left they failed to
attract votes from the moderate right and consequently lost. Where
there were three-cornered contests with the left and the RPR/UDF,
their second-ballot score was lower than their first – sometimes drama-
tically so. It all goes to show that the two-ballot electoral system
punishes extremists and favours alliances. As with regional council elections, there was talk of electoral reform in 1989, but in the case of

Table 14.5.   CANTONAL ELECTIONS, 1979–88
1st Ballot %

	1979	1982	1985	1988	1988 (No. of Conseil Général Presidencies)
Turnout	65.4	68.4	66.7	49.9	
Communists	22.5	15.9	12.5	13.2	2
Socialists and allies	28.9	31.7	26.4	34.2	25
Other left	4.0	2.0	2.4	.1	–
Total left	*55.4*	*49.5*	*41.3*	*47.5*	27
Greens	.5	.8	.4	1.7	–
RPR/UDF	44.6	50.0	49.1	44.7	68
(UDF	21.1	18.8	18.1	*	45)
(RPR	12.3	18.0	16.6	*	22)
(Other	11.2	13.2	14.4	*	1)
Front National	–	–	8.8	5.5	–

* Mainly joint candidatures in 1988.

cantonal elections, this was mainly directed at the elimination of 'rotten boroughs' with very small electorates.

In all the elections in 1988 and 1989 that followed the re-election of President Mitterrand, including the Referendum on New Caledonia (see Chapter 15), the most interesting fact was on each occasion a record low turnout – partly from electoral fatigue (six elections, mainly two-ballot ones, in just over a year) and partly from the feeling of electors that they had made the choice that really mattered in the Presidential election. This was certainly the case with the 1988 Cantonal elections with a turnout below 50%, and led to a debate on methods of grouping elections together. The political points to note were a minor recovery of the Socialists (a less unpopular government party than in 1982 and 1985) and 5% for the Front National – much less than in the Presidential election but still a presence. There was no sign yet of the Greens, who started to do much better in the city council and European Parliament elections the following year.

A note on local by-elections

Parliamentary by-elections hardly ever occur in France. Under the 1986 proportional representation system, vacancies were filled by the next name on the party list. Under the two-ballot system, vacancies are filled by a substitute or running-mate (*suppléant*) whose name is on the ballot at the original election. The main reason for by-elections is when Ministers who lose office wish to regain their Parliamentary seat (see chapter 12). However, local by-elections occur all the time – look in *Le Monde* any Tuesday – and give a valuable indication of the trend of public opinion. They gave the first signs, for example, of a Socialist recovery in 1987. The most frequent are Cantonal by-elections where members of *conseils généraux* die or resign. Sometimes, however, a large part or even all of a town council has to be replaced – either because a group of councillors has resigned, either (as often happens) over a dispute within their own political group, or when the previous election has been annulled by the courts for some breach of the electoral law. Such by-elections can gain national attention.

In recent years most of the local by-elections regarded as significant have involved the Front National. In Dreux, near Chartres, the 1983 election was annulled, and at the by-election the FN obtained its first real success of the 1981-6, period by polling 17% at the first ballot. Furthermore (see chapter 10) they made a local second-ballot pact with the RPR in which they were offered some posts of responsibility on the council. This exposed some divisions in the party's national leadership regarding the appropriate attitude to the FN. In 1987 there was a by-election at Grasse, the perfume town in Provence, after a split in the UDF/RPR majority on the council. Grasse, like other towns in the south, had given strong support to the Front in the 1986 elections. The UDF mayor, seeking re-election, formed a joint list at the first ballot with the FN. The list won. Since the mayor was a member of the Radical Party, he was summoned to the Party's executive committee and expelled. Once again, however, there was a wide divergence of views within the UDF and the RPR on the appropriateness of such an alliance. On the whole, local by-elections have shown that both UDF and RPR are prepared to accept pacts with the FN if the alternative is losing an election – 'to Communism', as they always put it.

NOTE

1. Pierre Gremion in *Les facteurs locaux de la vie politique française*, Bordeaux: Institut d'Etudes Politiques, pp. 94 and 107.

15

THE REFERENDUM

The electorate in the Fifth Republic is not only invited to choose its rulers and its representatives at local and national level; it is also periodically called upon to pronounce on laws and policies. Article 11 of the Constitution reads as follows:

> On the proposal of the Government . . . or on the joint proposal of the two Assemblies . . . the President of the Republic may submit to a referendum any Government Bill dealing with the organisation of the public authorities, approving a Community agreement, or authorising the ratification of a treaty which, though not in conflict with the Constitution, would affect the working of institutions.
>
> If the result of the referendum is favourable to the adoption of the Bill, the President of the Republic promulgates it . . .

Notice that the initiative for a referendum is supposed to come from government or Parliament, and not from the President – a provision more honoured in the breach than the observance so far. De Gaulle and his successors have decided on their own referendum and then asked their Prime Ministers to write a letter suggesting it, beginning: 'In conformity with Article 11 of the Constitution I have the honour to propose. . . .' The Article also says nothing specific about amending the Constitution. Constitutional amendments can be submitted to referendum but only after both houses of Parliament have agreed (Article 89). As we have seen in Chapter 2, this did not prevent de Gaulle from submitting two major constitutional revisions directly to the people.

Direct democracy in the form of a popular referendum always arouses intense debate. In the United States it is considered appropriate for local issues but not for national policy-making. In Britain, despite the mature manner in which the British people participated in the referendum on European Community membership in 1975 and that on Welsh and Scottish devolution in 1979, the conventional wisdom is to regard the referendum as a threat to the sovereignty of Parliament and to the whole notion of representative government, which declares that the job of an electorate is to choose its representatives and not to decide complex policy issues. In France this is the traditional 'Republican' view; the referendum is a threat to democracy, according to the Left in France, principally because it allows authoritarian leaders to obtain plebiscitary votes of confidence for themselves and hence free themselves from the constraints of representative institutions. Memories are long in France. The referendum made an unpromising debut in modern times with the famous question in 1804: 'Napoleon Bonaparte, shall he be consul for life?' His nephew Napoleon III also won plebiscitary approval for his dictatorship at a referendum. Some of de Gaulle's referendums were seen as part of the same tradition of Bonapartist manipulation, notably the controversial one in October 1962 on direct presidential elections. At the height of the turbulent Events of May 1968, de Gaulle proposed a referendum on participation, and the comment of Pierre Mendès-France, one of the left's most distinguished leaders, was 'Plebiscites? You don't discuss them, you fight them.' In other words the referendum was merely a device for de Gaulle, threatening chaos if he were to depart, to renew his mystical communion with the people and obtain a personal vote of confidence at the expense of intermediaries who were trying to represent the discontents of the nation.

So these are the main democratic objections to referendums: that ignorance and prejudice would inevitably carry the day against wisdom and reason, and that referendums would lead to the abuse of power by leaders. It is a view, one is compelled to remark, that expresses little confidence in the perspicacity of the common people. In fact, in reasonably mature democracies people have proved much less malleable than critics of referendums imagined. The British would vote 'No' to Europe because the price of butter had risen and they hate foreigners; but they voted 'Yes'. The Italians would vote 'Yes' to the petition outlawing divorce because they would docilely do what the Church told them to do. They voted 'No'. The Swiss (after a few valiant years of prejudice) voted responsibly on feminine suffrage and on the rights of foreign workers. The French too have supported measures they really wanted to support and which have turned out well – colonial independence, a directly-elected Presidency, the Constitution of the Fifth Republic. They have withheld support from more dubious measures – the Constitution of the Fourth Republic, which they never really liked and which was very narrowly adopted indeed, and the referendums of 1969 and 1972, both of which smacked of abusive attempts to get presidential votes of confidence or bad laws. In both cases the French administered a raspberry to executive power: in the first by voting 'No'

Table 15.1.　REFERENDUMS SINCE 1945

		Abstained %	Yes %	No %
4th Republic				
21 Oct. 1945	(a) New Constitution?	24.2	*96.4*	3.6
	(b) Limited powers for constituent Assembly	24.4	*66.3*	33.7
5 May 1946	Adoption of Constitution	21.3	47.0	*53.0*
13 Oct. 1946	Adoption of Constitution	32.5	*53.5*	46.5
5th Republic				
28 Sept. 1958	Adoption of Constitution	16.2	*79.2*	20.7
8 Jan. 1961	Self-determination for Algeria	25.6	*75.2*	24.7
8 April 1962	Algerian independence	28.4	*90.7*	9.3
28 Oct. 1962	Direct election of President	24.7	*61.7*	38.2
28 April 1969	Reform of Senate and regions	21.6	46.7	*53.2*
23 April 1972	Enlargement of EEC	*39.3**	*67.7*	32.3
6 Nov. 1988	Future of New Caledonia	*63.0**	*80.0*	20.0

* Plus 7% (1972) and 4% (1988) spoilt votes.

and provoking the resignation of de Gaulle, and in the second by abstaining in millions to the chagrin of President Pompidou.

There have been ten referendums so far in France since the Liberation. The three in the Fourth Republic were all related to the adoption of a new constitution. Did the people want one? Yes. Did they like the Constitution eventually proposed? No. Did they, having elected a new Constituent Assembly in June 1946, like the Constitution it eventually proposed. Only just: a third of the nation voted in favour, a third against, and a third abstained. In the Fifth Republic there have been seven (not counting partial referendums like the consultation of Algerian voters on independence in July 1962 or the referendum in September 1987 for inhabitants of the Pacific islands of New Caledonia only – not to be confused with the national referendum of 1988 described below): five under de Gaulle, one under Pompidou, none under Giscard, and one under Mitterrand up to the time of writing. In the Fourth Republic the referendum was used only to establish 'parliamentary sovereignty' with no further recourse to direct democracy. In the Fifth Republic, however, the referendum is always there as a normal device in the constitutional armoury of the President.

28 September 1958: Fifth Republic Constitution

The Constitution of the Fifth Republic swept away the impotent and ever-changing governments of the Fourth Republic which had been at the mercy of their over-mighty Parliaments, conferred real powers on the executive – in particular on the President – and cut Parliament down to size; it was massively adopted in September 1958 by a four-to-one majority. The Constitution had been drawn up in the summer of 1958, very much along the lines of de Gaulle's famous speech at Bayeux in 1946. The powers of the President were somewhat ambiguous in relation to those of the Prime Minister, but in his hands were special powers in an emergency (Article 16), recourse to referendum (Article 11), dissolution of Parliament (Article 12) and appointment of the Prime Minister (Article 8). All kinds of restrictions were put on Parliament's capacity to impede or overthrow the government, and all kinds of powers were given to the government to control Parliament (Articles 25–51).

The new Constitution was presented to the people at a vast rally in the Place de la République by de Gaulle. These were troubled times. It was only four months since the *coup d'état* in Algiers had caused the collapse of the Fourth Republic. Its last President, René Coty, had turned to 'the most illustrious of Frenchmen' to form a government, and Parliament had authorised the new Prime Minister, de Gaulle, to prepare a new constitution. If ever there was a vote of confidence referendum, this was it: the heroic wartime leader called back from the wilderness to save his people again. The whole enterprise – crisis leadership and the type of constitution now presented – was condemned as Bonapartist by the Communists, the CGT, about half the Socialist Party (SFIO) – though not by its leader Guy Mollet, who played a part in drafting the Constitution – and other important figures on the left, notably Pierre Mendès-France and a future President François Mitterrand. Despite their campaign, however, only 5 million voted 'No' – less than the 1956 Communist vote alone. Some 1.5 million Communist voters in fact voted 'Yes' and there were majorities for 'Yes' in even the most solid Communist suburbs of Paris.

In overseas territories the electors were asked a second question: did they want independence or membership of a new organisation called the French Community? Only Guinea in West Africa chose independence – which was immediately and rather ruthlessly granted: all French aid was cut off.

8 January 1961: Algerian 'Self-Determination'

The referendum on the policy of self-determination for Algeria fits into the dramatic story, already briefly recounted in chapter 2, of how General de Gaulle, brought back to power by those who wished to keep Algeria French, was able to lead the nation, and his own supporters in particular, to acceptance of the need for Algerian independence. The January 1961 referendum lies between two Algiers revolts – the 'week of the barricades' in January 1960 (brought on by de Gaulle's announcement that Algeria was to be given the choice of determining its own future) and the 'putsch of the generals' in April 1961, when four French army leaders seized the city. The result of the referendum was a victory for self-determination by a three-to-one majority. The Communist suburbs of Paris voted 'No' and so did some of the economically backward areas of the centre and south which had become rather Poujadist in the 1950s. The Catholic and conservative regions gave overwhelming support to the General and his policy.

8 April 1962: Algerian Independence

The 90% for 'Yes' to Algerian independence was the high point of support for de Gaulle, who had held the country together the previous year when important parts of the army in Algiers had been in revolt against his policy (chapter 2) and emergency powers under Article 16 had been used to deal with insubordination in the army and the civil service. In the April referendum the people were asked to approve the Evian agreement – the independence negotiations completed with the Algerian independence movement (FLN). The referendum was surrounded by some worries about the abuse of power by de Gaulle. The period of emergency powers (April to September 1961) had been very long and had included some arbitrary acts of government. The Evian negotiations had been very secret – even the government had not been privy to them. The referendum text conferred additional powers on the President to implement Evian by regulatory measures. The PSU campaigned for a blank vote as a way of saying 'Yes' to peace and 'No' to the abuse of power. However, it was the desire for peace, an end to the long and costly Algerian conflict, an end to the terrorism of the extremist supporters of *Algérie française* (the OAS), and support for a national leader who had stood firm throughout the crisis that carried the day by a crushing majority.

28 October 1962: Direct election of the President

This was the most far-reaching and controversial of the Fifth Republic referendums (see chapter 2 and, as the issue dominating the 1962 Parliamentary elections, chapter 13). It proposed the direct election of the President by universal suffrage – a constitutional amendment of fundamental importance, giving additional legitimacy to the Presidential leadership already established in practice by de Gaulle.

We looked earlier (chapter 2) at the General's masterly sense of when the right moment had come to put to the people the question of how to maintain the legitimacy of the Presidency when charismatic authority had disappeared. After the settlement of the Algerian conflict with a 90% majority in April, after the drama of the Petit Clamart assassination attempt in August, the time had come for de Gaulle to use his personal authority to shift the regime on to a new basis. He declared that a referendum would be held. This was unconstitutional: Article 89 clearly lays down that changes to the Constitution must be approved by Parliament first. An outraged National Assembly passed a motion of censure on 4 October, and the government resigned. The President dissolved Parliament. All the traditional parties campaigned to defeat the referendum: the conservative Independents, the MRP, the Radicals and the Socialists formed a *Cartel des Non*. Note the plural: it suggests a number of different reasons for proposing 'No', and indeed the different elements of the *Cartel des Non* were united only by a preference for the traditional and discredited Fourth Republic conception of Parliamentary democracy. The Communists also campaigned for 'No'. It was thus a straight confrontation: de Gaulle specifically put the issue in terms of himself or the parties of the 'bad old times'. The threat that he would resign if the vote was unsatisfactory unleashed claims that this was another plebiscitary Bonapartist operation. This, of course, is what it was, but such a view overlooks the important fact that the people had demonstrated, on the evidence of opinion polls since 1945, that they preferred stable executive leadership based on a directly-elected Presidency.

The result was not the triumph of April 1962 – under two-thirds (62%) of those voting, themselves under half (47%) of those entitled to vote, voted 'Yes'. There was a majority for 'No' in fifteen traditional left-wing *départements* in the economically backward Centre and South. However, the strongholds of the left in the more prosperous and modern industrial areas like the Paris region and the north voted 'Yes'. The leaders of the right and centre who had campaigned for 'No' did

disastrously badly against Gaullists in the Parliamentary elections a
month later (chapter 13). The October referendum was the last stand of
the 'third force' of the Fourth Republic – the bloc of centre-right,
centre-left and Socialists who, in various combinations, had governed
France from 1947 till 1958. Attempts to resuscitate the 'third
force' – the abortive attempt by the Socialist Gaston Defferre to put
together a Presidential candidature in 1965, the Poher presidential
campaign in 1969 (chapter 12), even President Mitterrand's attempts at
ouverture in 1988 – have all failed. The people in the autumn of 1962
chose majority government under a strong Presidency which gave a
better chance of effectiveness and stability. In future only an opposition
which looked like a coherent alternative majority would have any chance
of winning.

27 April 1969: Reform of Regions and the Senate

After the Algerian crisis and the reform of the Constitution had been
disposed of in 1962, there followed six years of normal times in which
the Fifth Republic settled down to its 'cruising speed'. When this was
shattered by the Events of May 1968 and the six-week general strike, de
Gaulle decided to call a referendum. People were discontented, he
considered, because the state attended to their every need without ever
giving them a chance to have a say. There would be a referendum on
'participation'. The proposal had no effect on the strike, so in his famous
broadcast of 30 May 1968, in which he said that he would stay and
announced new Parliamentary elections, he said of his referendum 'I
defer its date.' True to his word, almost a year later, he called the
referendum. It proposed, first, a reform of the Senate in which economic
and social interests such as unions, industry, agriculture and parent-
teacher associations would be directly represented alongside the existing
geographical representation. The second proposal was to create regional
councils also containing designated representatives of social and
economic interest groups as well as of local councils.

Like the October 1962 proposal, this was unconstitutional because
amendments to the Constitution have to be approved by Parliament
before being put to the people. It was, in a way, worse because in 1962
one could argue that the measure proposed was one the people wanted
(direct election of the President) and which would have been
systematically frustrated by a Parliament rooted in the discredited traditions of the Fourth Republic. There was no evidence this time of a

popular demand for these constitutional changes. It was also much more like a plebiscite seeking a vote of confidence rather than a referendum seeking approval for important constitutional changes. The actual text on which people were required to vote had sixty-nine detailed and technical articles, and it lumped two separate propositions – reform of the Senate and reform of the regions – into one question to be answered 'Yes' or 'No'. 'To separate the two questions would of course have been possible, but it might have resulted in a mixture of victory and defeat which was incompatible with de Gaulle's intentions. An artificial agglomeration of issues has at all time been the characteristic of a plebiscite.'[1] The General wanted the people 'to give to the state, and, in the first place, to its leader, a mandate for renewal'. In repeated broadcasts the General made it clear that he would resign if the referendum was not carried and, in a final appeal, that his present term of office would in any case be his last. A final objectionable characteristic of the 1969 referendum was the abuse of executive power during the campaign – particularly the way in which the resources of television and radio including audience research, news bulletins and interviews were at the service of the government in securing a victory for 'Yes'. The opposition parties only had one hour, divided between them all, to put the case for 'No' although it was enough for Alain Poher – President of the Senate, round, amiable, fumbling with his notes, and presenting a striking contrast with de Gaulle – to make a sufficiently favourable impression on the public to launch him as a Presidential candidate after de Gaulle's resignation (chapter 12).

In the event, the people voted 'No' by 53% to 47%, and de Gaulle resigned that very night. Some leading political figures like Giscard d'Estaing, who had supported de Gaulle in the past but had become increasingly critical of his 'solitary exercise of power', had withheld their support from 'Yes' this time. Gaullists of the true faith still blame Giscard for the General's defeat and resignation. Some also felt that if Pompidou, widely credited with restoring order during the Events of May 1968, had only declared that he was not willing to be a Presidential candidate, he would have contributed to fears of chaos if de Gaulle went and thus to a vote for him to stay. Only the Catholic and Gaullist bastions of Brittany, Alsace-Lorraine and the Massif Central voted 'Yes' this time. Industrial and modern France voted 'No'.

Many people have asked themselves why de Gaulle staked all on success in this unnecessary and unconvincing referendum. He needed, after the turmoil of 1968, a restatement of public confidence in his leadership or a reason to leave office. For de Gaulle popular confidence was like the 'fire of life' for the poet Walter Savage Landor: 'It sinks and I am ready to depart.'

23 April 1972: Enlargement of the European Community

The referendum of April 1972 is a warning to Presidents not to play with a dangerous constitutional device. President Pompidou thought that the enlargement of the European Community would be a good pretext for a referendum. The French people were therefore asked if they would be good enough to allow Britain, Denmark, Norway and the Irish Republic into the European Economic Community. Norway, without the permission of the French electorate, later declined the invitation.

The referendum seemed an excellent idea. It was constitutional: Article 11 specifically mentions as an occasion for a referendum 'the ratification of treaties . . . which could affect the working of institutions'. It was an opportunity to take an important presidential weapon out of the armoury, dust it down and make sure that it was still in working order. It would democratically involve the people in a decision about the EEC. The result was certain to be satisfactory because very few people were actually opposed to enlargement to include Britain and the others. It would therefore be a vote of confidence in the President and in his European policy, which differed markedly from that of de Gaulle. It would reinforce Pompidou's authority at the Paris summit due in October. Finally, it would divide the opposition parties, which were just then engaged on putting together the Union of the Left: the Socialists had always supported British entry to the EEC, and the Communists had always opposed it.

Things seemed to go well for the President. The Socialists sensibly suggested to the Communists that both parties should campaign for abstention and concentrate not on the issue of British membership of the EEC but on attacking the referendum as a cheap Presidential popularity device. If the Communists abstained, there would be no opposition at all and therefore no victory for the President to enjoy. The PCF nevertheless decided to campaign for 'No'.

Despite this (from the President's point of view) helpful decision, the referendum attracted very little public interest. Some 40% of the electorate abstained and a further 7% spoilt their ballots – the lowest turnout in a national vote since manhood suffrage began in 1848. Only

36% of the electorate (68% of those actually voting) voted 'Yes'. The Communists saw a satisfactory 5 million vote 'No'. The result was regarded as a great success not for the President but for the Socialist Party, which had campaigned for abstention. Indeed this was the beginning of the meteoric advance of the Socialist Party under the leadership of François Mitterrand in the 1970s. The poor result for the President brought on anxieties about the 1973 election (chapter 13). It signalled the end of the more liberal regime in radio and television, and the return of the Ministry of Information.

It proved a great mistake to use the referendum for other than a serious constitutional reform which deeply affects the population.

6 November 1988: Future of New Caledonia

There was no national referendum between 1972 and 1988, but it was always hard to believe that the referendum had completely fallen into disuse. President Mitterrand would surely not let fourteen years in office go by without making some use of so important a constitutional instrument. Properly used it is an extension of democracy. In 1988 Prime Minister Michel Rocard said he would propose a national referendum as part of the settlement of the New Caledonia issue, which had become so inflamed during the period of Chirac's premiership (1986–8).

New Caledonia is a group of islands in the Pacific administered not as a colony but as part of France – that is, as an Overseas *département* which has Mayors in all its towns and sends *députés* to the National Assembly in Paris. The population is around 40% European and 40% Melanesian (Kanak). There has for some years been an established Kanak independence movement, the leading representative of which is the FLNKS. The European population (known as the '*Caldoches*'), who dominate the administration, the nickel-mining industry and agriculture, are vehemently opposed to independence and mainly support the RPCR (Caledonian RPR). After a prolonged period of violent unrest the Socialist government in Paris sent a plenipotentiary, Edgard Pisani, to negotiate and set up a more equitable set of local institutions in which the Kanaks would have more autonomy in the parts of the territory where they were in a majority. The Chirac government (1986–8), in which one of Chirac's closest associates Bernard Pons was Minister for the Overseas Territories, took a much more nationalist line, destroyed the Pisani settlement, and held a referendum in 1987 for the population of the islands, but boycotted by the Kanaks, to say they wanted to stay part of France. Violence started up again, and New Caledonia became a major political issue. President Mitterrand wanted more understanding for Kanak discontent, while Prime Minister Chirac wanted tougher action against terrorism. In the 1988 Presidential election campaign (chapter 12) some French military personnel were ambushed, as the result of which four were killed and others were kept hostage by the FLNKS in Ouvea. The day before the second ballot Pons, with the approval of Chirac and, apparently, the signature of the President as Commander in Chief of the Armed Forces, sent in the army which released the hostages unharmed but killed a considerable number of Kanak French citizens including some who were not carrying weapons.

It was against this violent background that the new Socialist Prime Minister Michel Rocard tried to tackle the New Caledonia problem in June 1988. He was thought to have achieved a major political success when he got Jean-Marie Tjibaou, the leader of the FLNKS (later assassinated by Kanak extremists in 1989), and Jacques Lafleur, the leader of the RCPR together in Paris to reach an agreement on the future of the islands. Three new provinces would be created in the islands (two would have a Kanak majority and one, around the capital Nouméa, a *Caldoche* majority), there would be a New Caledonia Congress composed of the Provincial Councillors, there would a Consultative Council on Custom in order to give Melanesian tradition its proper part in legal and property matters, and last but not least there would be a referendum in 1998 on independence, and only those already resident in the islands in 1988 would be able to vote in it. It was this agreement that Mitterrand decided to put to the whole French nation in a referendum.

The referendum was not a success for the President. The whole point of having it was to give the New Caledonia settlement legitimacy and permanence. This meant that a high vote and a substantial majority for 'Yes' was required. There was a substantial majority for 'Yes' – 80% to 20%. Important parts of the opposition like the UDF supported 'Yes'. Only the Front National campaigned for 'No'. Ominously the *Caldoches* voted 'No', despite the support of their leader Lafleur for the agreement. Unfortunately, however, the most significant fact about the referendum was that the level of abstentions was the highest ever recorded in France – 67% if spoilt votes are included. A further blow to legitimacy and permanence was that the RPR stressed throughout the campaign that it would not consider itself bound by the result.

Why was participation in the referendum so low? One factor was that

the main opposition party, the RPR, was divided between those who
wanted to vote 'Yes' and those who wanted to vote 'No', and
campaigned for abstention, rather as the Socialists had done in 1972,
saying that the referendum was just a trick by Mitterrand to get a vote of
confidence (not a very convincing argument six months after his
triumphant re-election). However, the main reasons for the low turnout
were electoral exhaustion (the French had already been to the polls six
times in 1988, including the two rounds of the Presidential election) and
a feeling that a constitutional settlement for some remote islands in the
Pacific was a difficult technical matter and not a pressing concern.

There was, as we have noted, no national referendum between 1972
and 1988. In the post-de Gaulle era it has come to be an instrument to
be used only on very rare occasions. All Presidents, however, seem to
experience a need for a 'referendum of confirmation' when their
electoral mandate begins to show signs of wear. The 1969 and 1972
referenda were of this type: intended as a renewal of confidence in the
President. Giscard d'Estaing contemplated a mid-term referendum on
the principle of direct elections to the European Parliament. Mitterrand,
three years into his first term, actually proposed one: to extend the
subjects on which referendums could be held to include 'liberties'. Had
it been passed, he would then have had another on the reform of education (which involved 'liberties'). The pretext was the massive show of
opposition to his government's plan in 1984 to reform the private sector
in education: an issue which brought 2 million demonstrators on to the
streets of Paris in the name of liberty. However, no referendum took
place because Mitterrand, unlike de Gaulle in 1962 and 1969, submitted
the proposed constitutional amendment to Parliament first for it to be
passed by both houses. The Senate, which had an anti-Socialist majority,
voted it out, so that was the end of the matter.

One final word: in the Fifth Republic the successful referendums
have been ones in which the people were being asked their opinion on
something they regarded as of vital importance (a new constitution,
Algerian independence, direct election of the President). The 1969 and
1972 referenda were the most glaring instances of 'referenda of
confirmation', primarily seeking votes of confidence rather than popular
approval of fundamental constitutional reform, and the most significant
thing about them is that they both failed. In a democracy people are not
so easily taken in as is commonly supposed.

1. H.W. Ehrmann, *Politics in France*, Boston: Little, Brown and Co. 1972, p. 112.

16

CONCLUSION

This book was completed during a stretch of still water in elections and political leadership. The incredible number of elections in the year 1988–9 (you could have voted twelve times if you had lived in a constituency with a by-election) was given as a principal reason for the record levels of abstention. Barring accidents or dissolutions, however, the next set of national elections takes place in 1993. There is a stillness too in the unchanging set of political leaders. Mitterrand is still President but there is no clear successor to him in the Socialist Party. Marchais is still General Secretary of the Communist Party. Chirac is still leader of the RPR though considerably less visible than in the past. Giscard d'Estaing has, if anything, reappeared as the leading figure of the centre. There is political torpor in the realm of ideas and the only movement is the internal rivalry within the parties. This of course partly explains the continuing sucess of Le Pen and the Front National.

There are numerous contenders to be the next Presidential candidate of the Socialist Party: Michel Rocard and former Prime Minister Laurent Fabius, to name two of them. Marchais orthodoxy is threatened by dissidents – notably Charles Fiterman, a minister under President Mitterrand from 1981 to 1984. Chirac is under attack from younger and more radical Gaullists like Philippe Séguin or the big-city mayors of Lyon and Grenoble (Michel Noir and Alain Carignon respectively) with their important regional centres of power, but he still controls the RPR machine. In the Centre there is no-one who looks like a future national leader. Everyone seems to agree that the right and centre need a single candidate for the next Presidential election, but there is no consensus on how to choose one. An intelligent guess, however, would be that the second ballot of the 1995 Presidential election will be between one of the Socialists and one of the younger Gaullists mentioned in this paragraph.

On the wider question of democracy in France, alternation of power between moderate Presidents and moderate political parties, who respect the broad lines of the national consensus on foreign affairs, defence and even social and economic policy, has become well-established. The task for the next President will be to try to make France a more liberal state. France has had a prolonged period of economic growth and in consequence there has been little genuine discontent – over unemployment, inflation, public services or public investment. Executive power in the Fifth Republic has therefore not been put under much scrutiny or challenge, and the institutions that should provide checks and balances on the exercise of power are remarkably ineffective. Parliament, which is supposed to control the executive, in fact has no real procedure for investigating or debating government failures or abuses of power, and it is in any case not the central arena for the nation's political debate.[1] Informal institutions like television and radio, which are an important part of the way democracies keep an eye on what their leaders are doing and debate it, are, in France, far too respectful to those in power – so the national political debate does not take place there either. In fact there is virtually no issue-centred national political debate in France of the kind so familiar in the Anglo-Saxon democracies. There is plenty of discussion of personalities, rivalries and parties but not much about the health service, or unions, or nuclear defence, or transport policy. The result is that those in power in France during the last thirty years have been able to do more or less what they have wanted – build nuclear power stations, send paratroops to Kolwezi, send the secret service to New Zealand to sink a Greenpeace ship, explode nuclear devices in the atmosphere, nationalise and privatise, change the electoral system and change it back again – without any real public debate at all. The only check on executive power has been agitation in the streets: this is what stopped the two attempts at reform of the education system – by the Socialist government in 1984 and the Chirac government in 1986.

The first challenge for democracy in the Fifth Republic was to show that power could pass peacefully from government to opposition. This was admirably demonstrated in 1981. The second was to show that the system would work when there was '*cohabitation*' between the President and a Parliamentary majority composed of his political opponents. This was achieved in 1986. The next democratic challenge is to make executive power in the Fifth Republic more accountable, more subject to scrutiny, more willing to engage in debate, more accustomed to explain itself, and more ready to involve the people.

October 1990

NOTE

1. See John Frears, 'The French Parliament, loyal workhorse, poor watchdog', *West European Politics*, special number on executive-legislative relations, July 1990.

APPENDIXES

A. PRESIDENTIAL ELECTIONS IN THE FIFTH REPUBLIC
(% of vote) (1 = 1st ballot, 2 = 2nd)

	Gaullist/Centre	1	2	Left	1	2	Green	Ext. right
1965	*de Gaulle*	43.7	54.5	Mitterrand	32.2	45.5		5.3 (Tixier)
	Lecanuet	15.8						
1969	*Pompidou*	44.0	57.6	Duclos (PC)	21.5			
	Poher	23.4	43.4	Defferre (PS)	5.1			
				Rocard (PSU)	3.7			
				Ext. left	1.1			
1974	*Giscard d'Estaing*	32.5	50.7	Mitterrand	43.4	49.3	1.3	0.8 (Le Pen)
	Chaban-Delmas (UDR)	14.6		Ext. left	2.8			
1981	Giscard d'Estaing	28.2	48.2	*Mitterrand*	25.9	51.8	3.9	
	Chirac (RPR)	18.0		Marchais (PC)	15.4			
	Debre (Gaull)	1.7		MRG	2.2			
	Garaud (Gaull)	1.3		PSU	1.1			
				Ext. left	2.3			
1988	Chirac (RPR)	19.9	46.0	*Mitterrand*	34.1	54.0	3.8	14.4 (Le Pen)
	Barre (UDF)	16.5		Lajoinie (PC)	6.8			
				Juquin (PC – diss.)	2.1			
				Ext. left	2.4			

Turnout (%)

	1965	1969	1974	1981	1988
1st ballot	85.0	78.8	84.9	81.1	81.4
2nd ballot	84.5	69.1	87.4	85.9	84.1

B. PARLIAMENTARY ELECTIONS IN THE FOURTH REPUBLIC
(% of vote)

	1945		June 1946		Oct. 1946		1951		1956	
	Seats	*%*	*Seats*	*%*	*Seats*	*%*	*Seats*	*%*	*Seats*	*%*
Turnout	79.9		81.9		78.1		80.2		82.8	
PCF	26.2	161	25.9	153	28.2	183	26.9	101	25.9	150
SFIO	23.4	150	21.1	129	17.8	105	14.6	107	15.2	99
Rad., UDSR, RGR	10.5	57	11.6	53	11.1	70	10.0	95	15.2†	94
MRP	23.9	150	28.2	169	25.9	167	12.6	96	11.1	84
Ind./Con.	15.6	64	12.8	67	12.9	71	14.1	108	15.3	97
Gaullists					3.0		21.6*	120	3.9	22
Others	0.1	4	0.1	15	0.8	22			13.2‡	50

*RPF.
†Radicals split into two factions.
‡Mainly Poujadists.

C. PARLIAMENTARY ELECTIONS IN THE FIFTH REPUBLIC
(% of vote – 1st ballot)

	1958	1962	1967	1968	1973	1978	1981	1986 %	1986 Seats	1988 %	1988 Seats
Turnout %	77.1	68.7	81.1	80.0	81.3	83.4	70.9	78.5		65.8	
Communists	19.2	21.7	22.5	20.0	21.4	20.7	16.1	9.7	35	11.3	27
Socialists and allies	15.7	12.6	19.0	16.5	20.8	25.0	37.8	32.1	216	37.5	277
Radicals	8.3	7.8	*	*	**						
Other left	–	2.4	2.1	4.7	3.6	3.6	1.9	2.2	–	0.4	
Total left	43.2	44.5	43.6	41.2	45.8	49.3	55.7	44.0		49.2	
Greens	–	–	–	–	–	2.1	1.1	1.2		–	
Opposition centre	11.1	9.1	13.4	10.3	13.1	–	–				
Gaullists and allies (1986 and 1988: RPR/UDF)	19.5	37.8	37.7	44.7	36.0	43.9	40.1	43.1	291	40.5	273
(RPR)									(151)		(128)
(UDF)									(130)		(130)
(other)									(10)		(14)
Other right	22.9	8.6	4.9	3.5	5.1	4.7	3.0	1.9	35		
Front National	–	–	–	–	–	–	–	9.8	35	9.9	1

*Radicals allied with Socialists (see chapter 6).
†Radicals split (see chapter 5).

D. PARLIAMENTARY ELECTORAL SYSTEMS
IN FRANCE SINCE 1848

Date of law	Type of constituency	No. of ballots	Method of allocating seats
1848	Multi-member	1	Simple majority of the electors voting.
1849	Multi-member	1	As in 1848.
1852	Single-member	2	*First ballot*: absolute majority of electors voting. *Second ballot*: relative majority of votes cast.
1871	Multi-member	1	As in 1848.
1873	Multi-member	2	As in 1852.
1875	Single-member	2	As in 1852.
1885	Multi-member	2	As in 1852.
1889	Single-member	2	As in 1852.
1919	Multi-member	1	List system. Candidates with the votes of an absolute majority of the electors voting were declared elected, any remaining seats being allocated to the lists by means of a quotient. Any seats still remaining went to the list with the highest average of votes per candidate.
1927	Single-member	2	As in 1852.
1945	*Département* Multi-member	1	List system of proportional representation by quotient and highest average of votes per seat won.
1946	*Département* Multi-member	1	List system of proportional representation by highest average of votes per seat won.

1951	*Département* Multi-member	1	*Paris region*: list system of proportional representation by the greatest remainder. *Provinces*: list system. In any constituency, an isolated list or an alliance of lists winning an absolute majority of the votes cast won all the seats. If an alliance won all the seats, they were distributed among the allies by the system of proportional representation by the highest average. If no isolated list or alliance won an absolute majority, the seats were distributed by the system of proportional representation by the highest average.
1986	*Département* Multi-member		Substantially as in 1945.
1988	Single-member		As 1958–86.

Source: P. Campbell, *Electoral Systems in France since 1789*.

SELECT BIBLIOGRAPHY

Politics, government, political parties – general

W. Andrews and S. Hoffmann (eds), *The Impact of the Fifth Republic*, Albany: State University of New York Press 1981.

F. Borella, *Les partis politiques dans la France d'aujourd'hui*, Paris: Eds du Seuil 1973 (regular new editions).

Jean-Louis Bourlanges, *Droite Année Zéro*, Paris: Flammarion 1988.

Jacques Chapsal: *La vie politique en France depuis 1940*, Paris: Presses Universities de France (PUF) 1966.

——, *La vie politique sous la Ve République*, Paris: PUF (regular new editions).

Maurice Duverger, *Les partis politiques*, Paris: Colin (7th edn) 1969.

H.W. Ehrmann, *Politics in France*, Boston: Little, Brown and Co. 1958 (regular new editions).

J.R. Frears, *France in the Giscard Presidency*, London: George Allen and Unwin 1981.

Charles de Gaulle, *Mémoires de guerre* (3 vols), Paris: Plon 1954, 1956, 1959.

——, *Mémoires d'espoir*, Vol. 1: *Le renouveau, 1958–62*; Vol. 2: *L'effort*, 1962–, Paris: 1970, 1971.

François Goguel, *La politique des partis sous la IIIe République*, Paris: Eds du Seuil 1948.

J.E.S. Hayward, *The One and Indivisible French Republic*, London: Weidenfeld and Nicolson 1973 and subsequent editions.

Jean-Louis Quermonne, *Le gouvernement de la France sous la Ve République*, Paris: Dalloz, regular new editions.

René Rémond, *The Right in France from 1815 to de Gaulle*, Philadelphia: University of Pennsylvania Press (2nd edn) 1966.

Richard Rose, *The Problem of Party Government*, London: Macmillan 1974.

Ezra Suleiman, *Politics, Power, and Bureaucracy in France*, Princeton University Press 1974.

David Thompson, *Democracy in France*, Oxford University Press 1958.

Philip Williams, *Crisis and Compromise: Politics in the Fourth Republic*, London: Longman Green (3rd edn) 1964.

——, *The French Parliament, 1958–67*, London: George Allen and Unwin 1968.

F.L. Wilson, *French Political Parties under the Fifth Republic*, New York 1982.

Vincent Wright, *Politics and Government in France*, London: Methuen (regular new editions).

Political Parties (specific)

Anderson, Malcolm, *Conservative Politics in France*, London: George Allen and Unwin 1973.

D.S. Bell and Byron Criddle, *The French Socialist Party: The Emergence of a Party of Government*, Oxford: Clarendon Press (2nd edn) 1988.

F. Bon *et al.*, *Le communisme en France*, Paris: Fondation Nationale des Sciences Politiques 1969.

David Caute, *Communism and the French Intellectuals*, London: Deutsch 1964.

J. Charlot, *L'UDR: Étude du pouvoir au sein d'un parti politique*, Paris: Cahiers de la Fondation Nationale des Sciences Politiques 1967.

——, *The Gaullist Phenomenon*, London: George Allen and Unwin 1971.

Ariane Chébel d'Appolonia, *L'extrême-droite en France de Maurras à Le Pen*, Paris: Eds Complexe 1988.

Jean-Claude Colliard, *Les Républicains Indépendents: Valéry Giscard d'Estaing*, Paris: PUF 1971.

Anthony Hartley, *Gaullism: the Rise and Fall of a Political Movement*, London: Routledge and Kegan Paul 1972.

S. Hoffmann, *Le mouvement Poujade*, Paris: A. Colin 1956.

Christiane Hurtig, *De la SFIO au nouveau Parti Socialiste*, Paris: A. Colin 1970.

R.E.M. Irving, *Christian Democracy in France*, London: George Allen and Unwin 1973.

R.W. Johnson, *The Long March of the French Left*, London: Macmillan 1981.

Annie Kriegel, *The French Communists*, University of Chicago Press 1972.

Edward Mortimer, *The Rise of the French Communist Party, 1920–1947*, London: Faber and Faber 1984.

Nonna Mayer and Pascal Perrineau (eds), *Le Front National à decouvert*, Paris: Presses de la Fondation Nationale des Sciences Politiques 1989.

Jean-Thomas Nordmann, *Histoire des Radicaux, 1820–1973*, Paris, 1974.

Pouvoirs No. 28, *Le RPR*, Paris: PUF 1984.

N. Nugent and D. Lowe, *The Left in France*, London: Macmillan 1982.

R. Tiersky, *French Communism, 1920–1972*, New York: Columbia University Press 1974.

F. L. Wilson, *The French Democratic Left, 1963–1969*, Stanford University Press 1971.

Elections and electoral behaviour

Association Française des Sciences Politiques series (Paris: Cahiers de la Fondation Nationale des Sciences Politiques):
Les élections du 2 janvier 1956 (1957).
L'établissement de la Ve République: Le référendum de septembre et les élection de novembre 1958 (1960).

Le référendum du 8 janvier 1961 (1962).

Le référendum d'octobre et les élections de novembre 1962 (1965).

L'élection présidentielle des 5 et 12 décembre 1965 (1970).

Les élections législatives de mars 1967 (1971).

Peter Campbell, *French Electoral Systems and Elections since 1789*, London: Faber and Faber 1958.

Jacques Capdevielle *et al.*, *France de gauche vote à droite?*, Paris: Presses de la Fondation Nationale des Sciences Politiques (2nd edn) 1988.

J. Charlot (ed.), *Quand la gauche peut gagner*, Paris: Moreau 1973.

J.R. Frears and Jean-Luc Parodi, *War Will Not Take Place* (on the 1978 election) London: Hurst 1979.

Alain Lancelot, *L'abstentionnisme électorale en France*, Paris: Cahiers de la Fondation Nationale des Sciences Politiques 1970.

Howard Penniman (ed.), *France at the Polls: The Presidential Election of 1974*, Washington, DC: American Enterprise Institute 1975.

——, *France at the Polls, 1981–86*, Washington, DC 1988.

R.G. Schwartzenburg, *La guerre de succession* (on the 1969 Presidential election) Paris: PUF 1969.

Philip Williams, *French Politicians and Elections, 1951–1969*, Cambridge University Press 1970.

C. Ysmal, *Le comportement électoral des français*, Paris: Eds du Seuil 1987.

INDEX